LEXINGTON
in Old Virginia

by Henry Boley

PUBLISHING HISTORY

Garrett & Massey, Richmond, Virginia: 1936
Liberty Hall Press, Lexington, Virginia: 1974
Rockbridge Publishing Company, Natural Bridge Station, Virginia: 1990

Manufactured in Virginia, United States of America.

About the Photographs . . .

All the photos in *Lexington in Old Virginia* are believed to have been taken by
Michael Miley (1841-1918), "General Lee's photographer." Several of the prints
were made directly from Miley's original glass plates; some of the plates, a
century or more old, are in poor condition and show marked imperfections.
Many of the photos are those selected by Boley himself for the book, but in the
years since its original publication (1936) a number of "lost" Miley negatives were
discovered. When these were either more interesting or of superior quality, a
substitution was made. All the photographic work was undertaken for the 1974
Liberty Hall Press edition by Ms. Sally Munger Mann, a professional
photographer who has catalogued and indexed more than 10,000 photographs in
the Miley Collection at Washington and Lee University.

About the Book . . .

Lexington in Old Virginia was originally published in 1936 by Garrett & Massey,
Publishers, Richmond, Virginia. In 1974 an introduction was added, and the book
was published by Liberty Hall Press, Washington and Lee University, Lexington,
Virginia, as a part of the university's program in connection with the American
Bicentennial Celebration. This edition, published in 1990 by Rockbridge
Publishing Company, has been printed on alkaline paper, using the offset
negatives from the 1974 edition.

Library of Congress Cataloging-in-Publication Data
Boley, Henry. 1883-1939.
    Lexington in old Virginia / by Henry Boley.
        p.   cm.
    Reprint. Originally published: Richmond, Va.: Garrett & Massey, 1936.
    Includes index.
    ISBN 0-9623572-2-7 : $16.95
      1. Lexington (Va.)--History. 2. Lexington (Va.)--Biography.
I. Title.
F234.L5B6   1990
975.5'853--dc20

                                      90-8889
                                      CIP

Rockbridge Publishing Company
P.O. Box 70 - Natural Bridge Station, VA 24579
(703) 291-1063

TO THE GALLANT MEN
WHO FOLLOWED
LEE
OF WHOM
MY FATHER WAS ONE

INTRODUCTION

FROM ITS FOUNDATION in 1777 Lexington has beguiled and charmed its residents. Few cities in this country, and certainly few small towns, have inspired so many rhapsodies and have produced so many delightful eccentrics (not to mention notables, native and adoptive) as Lexington. Affection for the town shows itself in many ways and especially in an eagerness to talk and write about its appealing, often diverting, past and present. Henry Boley takes his place among a long line of those who have recorded memorable events and accounts of unique personalities, from Farnum in 1805 to such recent annalists as Edmund Pendleton Tompkins, Mrs. Charles McCulloch, and the scores of contributors to volumes of the Rockbridge Historical Society.

Boley regards Lexington as a community just this side of paradise. He tries to explain the distinction of the town, and to account for the fact that so many Lexingtonians are worthy of being remembered, whether as saints or sinners, as heroes, as wits and savants, as contributors to the gaiety of life as well as to the daily delight of living. Part of its notability, he is sure, must be attributed to its setting in the Valley of Virginia. He is eloquent in his descriptions of House Mountain, Goshen Pass, Natural Bridge, the Brushy Hills, and the glories of the procession of seasons. More fundamental, perhaps, is his certainty that Lexingtonians have been blessed by their Scotch-Irish ancestors: his dozens of paragraphs about these pioneer forefathers are eloquent and always laudatory, even when he is acknowledging their stubbornness and rigid Calvinism. The presence of Washington and Lee University and the Virginia Military Institute, with the stimulation of their faculties and the variety of their constantly changing student bodies, is a third part of his analysis of what has made Lexington "this little Athens of the Old South."

That phrase, like the "Old Virginia" in his title, sets the tone of his book. It is a series of sketches of the past and of "the wealth of memories" that center "about this little village." Boley reveals no interest whatever in growth or progress; and while he accepts paved streets and the automobile and recorded music, technology with its mixed blessings simply does not interest him. He mentions neither telephones nor radios (television, of course, did not exist in the Lexington of 1936). He casually notes the advent of the railway, but he clearly prefers the leisurely days of canal boat, horseback, and carriages. The original edition of his book depicts Confederate flags on the cover, and the dedication is "to the gallant men who followed Lee." His volume, he says, is about "people, places, and events connected with Lexington, past and present"; but even the "present" he records is one of quiet streets and of people who have time to sit and chat with each other, of people who treasure traditional definitions of what constitutes the character of ladies and gentlemen.

Boley's Lexington, past and present, is a stable, orderly world. With his characteristic kindliness of spirit, his genuine friendliness, and his ability to see only the pleasant aspects of life, he pictures a community without violence and crime, without poor people and illness, without social or economic or political problems. He cannot even bring himself to mention one of Lexington's darkest days, the "Black Friday" in 1895, when the impeccably respected cashier of the Bank of Lexington absconded with all the bank's and the town's money, including life-long savings of most of its thrifty citizens. Almost every page unconsciously bespeaks Boley's own personality, although his one personal reference is to his bookstore, a familiar landmark of Lexington in the 1920s and 1930s. _W H B 1889_

William Henry Boley was born in Lexington on January 8, 1883. As a boy of seventeen he became a clerk in the bookstore of W. C. Stuart, and in 1914 he took over the store in partnership with H. Crum _s_ Peck. That store was one of the centers of intellectual life in Lexington, as it had been since it was first founded in the mid-nineteenth century by the benign and sociable John Blair Lyle. Washington and Lee textbooks in Boley's day were sold at his store; the result was that the owner, with his outgoing fondness for people, counted as close friends hundreds of the students. Although he never attended the university, its alumni in 1938 elected him an honorary alumnus of the school. Because he always had time for conversation, his bookstore drew people who like to talk and reminisce. It was perhaps, as it had been in Lyle's and Stuart's day, Lexington's equivalent of the London coffee-house. The stories of older residents, together with incidents from boyhood stored up in his excellent memory, constitute the chief source of Boley's book, rather than documents and written histories.

Boley died on February 28, 1939. The high regard for the town's gracious bookman is attested by the fact that all Lexington stores were closed during his funeral. Moreover, although he was a member of the Presbyterian church and a teacher of a boys' class in its Sunday School, the Episcopal and Methodist ministers shared with Boley's own pastor the funeral service.

Literary organization is not Boley's strong point. True, he begins logically with an historical sketch, but he soon interrupts himself to recount anecdotes. One good story leads to another until the reader often forgets the theme of a chapter. Boley's serious pages about the crisis of the Civil War contain surprising disquisitions on herb gardens and Lexington entertainments. The moving account of Lee's death calmly digresses to comment on two fine faculty members Boley knew and then to a paragraph about a devoted black servant at the college. In a reminiscence about the swallows which appeared by thousands on summer evenings, the author is suddenly reminded of chess games at the old Eagle Hotel, and this in turn brings to his mind the story of a student's attack on a professor who lived at the hotel.

Boley simply cannot resist a good story, no matter what a chapter's announced subject may be; moreover, he frequently succumbs to the temptation that beguiles every author (including students who write term-papers) of including all the notes he has taken, whether relevant or not. The Society of the Cincinnati gave a gift to Washington College, and so we have a chapter on the history of that Society. The Marquis de Chastellux visited the Valley of Virginia in 1782, and consequently Boley reproduces two letters from George Washington to the Marquis, one about a gift of claret, the other about friendship. But why not digressions, indeed? They recall the good talk in Boley's bookstore; and when did charming conversation ever follow an organized plan, with no by-ways and divagations?

Many of Boley's stories are in the repertoire of every authentic Lexingtonian, but others surely need revival. For example, the austere image of Stonewall Jackson is considerably lightened by the story of his reluctant agreement to sit for a photograph: when his attention was called to the fact that a button was missing from his uniform, he called for needle and thread and sewed it on—out of line, as is evident from the photograph. Or again, one relishes the tale of the statue of George Washington on the V.M.I. grounds which, on a bitterly cold night, suddenly "spoke" to the startled sentinel: "Hell, this ain't cold weather. You should have been with me at Valley Forge." One likes the picture of Stuart's bookstore (predecessor of Boley's), where cronies gathered around a huge stove in the rear for interminable talk, and where customers who grew weary of waiting for service simply sought out what they wanted and then either left the cash or a charge slip. On one occasion Stuart and a friend, engrossed in talk, heard the front door open. "There's a customer, Cal," said the friend. "Be real quiet, Frank, and maybe he will go on out," said the proprietor.

Boley occasionally has a droll way of putting things, as when, commenting on style of a former age, he notes that ladies "moved about rather mysteriously on some unseen lower extremity." He remarks of alumni of the two schools that "it has always been true that men think of their days in college as the best in the history of the institution and feel that after their departure a rather rapid decline took place." He often engages in wry irony, as when he quotes the opponents of moving the college from the old Liberty Hall site nearer to Lexington: "By bringing the institution into immediate contact with the miscellaneous population and frequent gatherings and the tempting shops of a country town, they greatly increased the difficulties of academic government and the temptations to idleness and vice among the students." He tells of the mother of a cadet who rejoiced at the "protected life in the barracks," saying that "it was such a comfort, when in her far-off Louisiana home, to know that at ten o'clock every night her boy at Virginia Military Institute was in bed and fast asleep." That mother is matched by the one who, after visiting her Washington and Lee son's fraternity house, said enthusiastically, "These are such wonderful boys; none of them ever drink, do they?" (Was it irony or naiveté that led Boley to remark that Washington and Lee, although non-denominational, "still keeps an evangelical religious spirit"?)

It would be easy to cite Boley's shortcomings as an author. Many of his sentences are awkward, and some are ungrammatical. His statements about Indians, early settlers, "inherent" qualities of the Scotch-Irish, and the meaning of indentures, contain sentences that would make an historian wince. He sometimes goes wrong on names of former citizens, though considering the hundreds of people he mentions his score here is very high. The only tedious sections of his book are those in which, because of his desire not to offend by omission, he makes lists of names. (One such list follows a pleasant chapter on Lexington personalities; at its end Boley simply records the names of 146 other people he "remembers with affection and gratitude.") His only blatant errors are insignificant, as when he refers to Harvard College of 1800 as "Cambridge University in Massachusetts."

The book is liveliest when its author remembers things past, and is least satisfying when he uses the present tense, since the present, for Boley, was the decade before World War II. A reader of our own time gains nothing by being told that an early building was located near some shop present in 1936 but long since demolished. Accounts of the "present" V.M.I. curriculum, of the elderly lady who "was here last summer," of the Old Blue Hotel as "one of the College dormitories," make one vividly aware of the impermanence of even Lexington humanity and its creations. Perhaps the references that most date the book and mark the rapidity of change are Boley's remarks about blacks in Lexington, all kindly, yet all completely patronising. A modern reader is startled by dialect stories, tales of faithful darkies, and generalizations about irresponsibility and childish vanity.

One is reluctant to criticize a book whose delights far outweigh its faults. The amount of information amassed by Henry Boley is remarkable. He notes that his main reliance is upon his own observations and memory, and upon stories gathered from old Lexingtonians; yet he makes excellent use of the limited number of biographies and historical papers he examined. The account of the execution of John Brown is splendid, with its focus upon the part played in that memorable event by Robert E. Lee and by the V.M.I. cadets. Familiar stories about Stonewall Jackson are enriched by a singularly judicious estimate of his classroom teaching at the Institute and by details of his personal foibles and human idiosyncrasies. The longest chapter in his book is one of the most valuable: his twenty-eight pages of biographical sketches of noted Lexingtonians, from early McDowells and Reids to Boley's contemporaries who belong in his private Hall of Fame.

After two centuries Lexington continues to exert its attraction and to make its mark upon the people who know and love it. It does well to preserve, by reprinting his annals of Lexington in Old Virginia, the gracious memory of Henry Boley.

James G. Leyburn

Dr. James Graham Leyburn is Dean Emeritus of Washington and Lee University and Professor Emeritus of Sociology. He is the author of The Scotch-Irish, The Haitian People, and a large number of other books, articles, essays and reviews. Dr. Leyburn was graduated from Trinity (now Duke) and Yale Universities, and holds honorary degrees from Duke (1962) and Washington and Lee (1974).

PREFACE

THESE sketches of people, places and events connected with Lexington, past and present, are historical, and are based upon fact, though the book does not purport to be a history. From many sources they have been gathered; some from written and authentic records, others picked up at random, through conversation, while others are from memory.

One Sunday afternoon, last spring, while sitting all alone in the sun-room, listening to the immortal Ninth Symphony of Beethoven, as the sun was setting in all its majesty behind Brushy Hills, the thought came to me; fortunate is he whose lot is so pleasantly cast: music, magnificent scenery, fine fellowships, abiding friendships and, in fact, everything that makes life worth the living. All of these, and more, one has in Lexington. With this appreciation came the desire to put in writing some of the "interesting bits" about the old town, which have given, and still give, that something which sets it apart.

One cannot study local history, without a feeling of very humble gratitude for the wonderful men and women who made Lexington. They loved and labored for this community, and one of the aims of this book is to add a word of praise and thanksgiving for these good men and women of other days. Particularly indebted am I to the Presbyterian Committee of Publication for permission to quote from Chester's *Autobiography;* to Paul M. Penick and E. S. Mattingly for access to the historical papers of Washington and Lee University; to Miss Lucy Withrow for access to her interesting old Scrap Book on Lexington; to Harrington Waddell for access to Foote's *Sketches;* to Mrs. Elizabeth Valentine Huntley for information regarding the work of Valentine on the recumbent statue of Lee; to John Preston for access to the *Life of Archibald Alexander;* to Morton's *History of Rockbridge County;* to Allen's *Life and Letters of Margaret Junkin Preston;* to Vinson's *Life of Morrison;* to Dabney's *Stonewall Jackson;* to Jones' *Robert E. Lee;* to McElhenney's *Recollections; to Moore's Memories of a Long Life in Virginia;* and to a few friends who spurred me on when I was ready to quit.

In writing these sketches, I have had constantly in mind countless friends among the alumni of Washington and Lee University and the Virginia Military Institute, scattered, as they are, throughout the whole world.

HENRY BOLEY.

Lexington, June, 1935

CONTENTS

House Mountain, Lexington's Fujiyama

CHAPTER I: LEXINGTON

LEXINGTON, VIRGINIA! What a wealth of memories centers about this little village! Washington and Lee University, the Virginia Military Institute, the home and tomb of Robert E. Lee, the home and tomb of Stonewall Jackson, the Natural Bridge, and Goshen Pass, are some of its claims to preëminence and a place unique.

Richmond, the Capital of the Confederacy, has its stately Battle Abbey, its White House of the Confederacy, and its handsome monuments to illustrious Southerners; St. Augustine has its Old World flavor and its sumptuous hotels; Charleston has its world-famed Magnolia and Azalea gardens and its lovely wrought-iron balconies and gateways; New Orleans has its French Quarter and its foreign atmosphere; San Antonio has its Alamo; Fredericksburg guards the ashes of "Mary, the mother of Washington"; Williamsburg, Savannah, Mobile, Vicksburg, Montgomery, Chattanooga and many other Southern towns and cities have their charm and interest, and rich and sacred associations, but none excel in sentimental appeal this little Athens of the Old South.

Seen from Reservoir Hill on a summer afternoon, nestling among the trees like a jewel in a perfect setting of green fields and wooded country, with the everlasting hills forming a great amphitheater, Lexington suggests Elysium. A visitor of long ago claimed that the scenery was unsurpassed and lovely beyond description.

When, in 1805, Professor Farnum viewed the country from the top of the college building he exclaimed: "If this scene were set down in the middle of Europe, the whole continent would flock to see it."

The sapphire Blue Ridge to the south and east, and to the north, Hog Back and Jump Mountains, guarding The Pass and to the west, grand old House Mountain, Lexington's Fujiyama, standing like a sentinel overlooking the town and dominating the landscape, it seems to extend a cordial welcome to the returning traveler. All of these mountains belong to the great Appalachian system and are from ten to fifteen miles distant, close enough to be intimate and interesting, and yet not close enough to cause that smothering sensation experienced by people from the great open spaces when too close to mountains.

The countryside is rolling, well cultivated and interspersed by large tracts of forests, with streams and rivers fed by multitudinous and unfailing mountain springs, all adding beauty and charm to the rides and drives about old Rockbridge. With an altitude of eleven hundred feet and with very pronounced seasons, Lexington enjoys a varied and delightful climate which may account for the presence of so many octogenarians among its thirty-seven hundred. Visitors have compared the countryside to rural England, to southern France, to Switzerland and to other God-favored places.

[1]

A superabundance of soft, free-stone water, which analyzes practically as Poland, supplies the town. It is piped many miles from a lake in Short Hills, where the town owns thousands of acres of virgin timber land, which is rigidly protected for the safety and purity of the water.

The Athenians loved sunshine and Helios, the Sun God, was generous. Virginians, too, love sunshine and Helios is still generous, giving, as he did to Athens, more sunny than cloudy days.

Residents who have lived in many parts of the world declare Lexington unsurpassed as a year-round climate. Because of this, together with the intelligence of its society, graced by the faculties of its two great schools, it has always been a popular and congenial home for retired Army and Navy people, and because of its fine religious atmosphere it has become the home of many outstanding retired missionaries.

When one tires of summer, autumn days have arrived, and if one season is more delightful than another in the Valley of Virginia, it is autumn.

The Valley of Virginia! A magic name to add to "Tidewater Virginia, the chateaux of France, the castles on the Rhine, the Bay of Naples, the canals of Venice, the lakes of Killarney and the Spanish Main." The Valley of Virginia is not only an expectation and promise, but a realization and a fulfillment. At any season of the year it is a place of beauty, whether its hills, vales and mountains are seen under a blanket of snow or in the very early springtime, clad in apple blossoms, dogwood, azaleas, redbud, and many other blossoming trees and shrubs, bounded on all sides by the bluest of blue mountains; or later in the summer, when the grains and grasses in great variety are being harvested and stacked, it never fails to present a happy and satisfying sight. The very name, the Valley of Virginia, means home and loved ones to countless thousands throughout the world, who trace their ancestry, if not their very own childhood days, to this favored spot.

A Virginian, living in beautiful California, confides in a friend: "Like all Virginians, I long to get back to Old Virginia. I dream of her glorious springtime, her mid-summer charm, her heavenly Indian summer, and her snow covered hills and mountains and, above all, her people—my people. All is only appreciated by a Virginian who has to live elsewhere."

One is lifted nearer the Creator of all beauty as he drives the highways and byways around Brushy Hills, to Lover's Leap, the Sunnyside Road, the Collierstown Way, through The Pass, over the Jordan Trail, the Amherst route, along the Big Spring bypath, and recalls stirring and historic days of a glorious past. Everywhere one finds the perfect maples, oaks, elms, chestnuts, beeches and sassafras, touched by the early frosts, interlaced among the greens of the hemlocks, pines and cedars, giving to nature her glorious, multi-colored autumn attire.

The Virginia red clay banks add color to the roadside and, at a safe distance, are lovely, but not to be indulged in when wet. Few situations are worse than to have one's automobile stuck fast in red clay; under such conditions, called "mud."

There is a legend that many years ago a knight bidding his sweetheart goodbye tried to get an audible assurance of her love. She gave him a piece of honeysuckle with the command that he throw it over his shoulder and that if it grew he would know that she loved him. It did grow like the bay tree and ever since that far-off day has literally covered the red clay banks on either side of the Natural Bridge Road for a long distance.

Another feature that attracts the lover of roadside beauty is the picturesque rail fence, sometime called the snake fence, reminiscent of pioneer days, before the coming of the neat, straight wire fence, a decided improvement for keeping cattle within bounds, but, for interest and beauty, the old, crooked rail fence, with its ins and outs, furnished a perfect harbor for scores of lovely things in which the roadside should and does abound. Clumps of blackberry and dewberry, beautiful in the springtime, when covered with millions of white blossoms and more beautiful later, when laden with luscious berries! What a safe home these briar patches are for brer rabbit and his family! Impenetrable as they generally are, he is secure from man and dog. There is virtue even in briar patches! In the "ins and outs" of the old rail fences are patches of wild strawberries, iris, hepatica, phlox subulata, bloodroot, butterfly weed, "good-bye-to-summer," goldenrod, fall asters and innumerable other botanical gems that would delight the heart of Wherry.

Autumn, too, is a time when one turns to books and the open fire, about which he has known little during the past months, when gallery, lawn and motor have occupied his evenings or, by chance, he has had a boat, a guitar, and a friend and has spent his evenings idling in the moonlight on old North River. While enjoying autumn days and nights it is soon evident that winter is just around the corner. This, too, is a season of delight in Lexington, with Hallowe'en, Thanksgiving, Christmas and Saint Valentine's Day festivities, all made merry by the school dances and parties. Nothing adds more charm to the community life than the college activities.

"O wind, if winter comes, can spring be far behind?" And so the winter passes and signs of spring are unmistakable in the swelling buds of jasmine, japonica, forsythia, and redbud showing color and the brave little heralders of new life, the crocus and the snowdrops, appearing on the lawns. But the surest and most welcome of all harbingers of spring, the lordly robin, with his return from his far Southern retreat, brings the final assurance and receives a welcome such as is given only to royalty.

Added to the natural beauty of the countryside is that of lawn and garden, for Lexington excels in its homes and gardens, as evidenced by the oldest and best in architecture and by the spaciousness of the grounds. Outstanding among these is Col Alto, built by the celebrated McDowell family, in 1810. Here Governor and Mrs. McDowell and their charming daughters dispensed rare hospitality and from this home went forth gracious influences to bless mankind. This was the Manor House of Lexington of long ago. The traditions of this famous estate have been maintained by the honored and beloved Henry St. G. Tucker, whose home it was until his recent death; Dr. Reid White's home, with its wealth of century-old boxwood and its quaint stone kitchen, noted in Hale's *We Discover the Old Dominion* and in Nutting's *Virginia Beautiful;* the Lee Mansion on the college campus, built for the great General and in which he lived and died; the Letcher home, also on the college campus and of which a later resident wrote: "Once the home of Virginia's War Governor, now, by process of residential degeneration, the home of just a college professor"; The Rectory, the Pines, the Barclay's, the Manse, Stono, Sunnyside, Morningside, Thorn Hill, Mulberry Hill, Clifton, Spring Meadows, Silverwood, and others, attesting to the excellent taste of the early builders. Each of these houses has its own history and tales of romance.

The old Withrow House on Main Street, built in 1788, by William Alexander, was recently proclaimed by a visiting artist, the most interesting structure in the town and equal in beauty to anything that he had seen in Williamsburg. He was especially interested in the diamond arrangements of the bricks. Lexington's first bank, the Lexington Savings Institute, was located in this building and, during his residence here, Stonewall Jackson was a director in this bank. Prior to the grading of Main Street, before the Civil War, the present second story was on the street level, as was the Dold Building, across the street. By noting the present level of the courthouse yard, the original steep grade of old Main Street can be appreciated. Both McCoy's Store and Dold's were, in the early days, underground basements.

William Alexander, a pioneer merchant of Lexington, acquired much real estate in the town. He owned the lot on which the Lee Memorial Church stands and he built and owned the house, which in 1858, was sold to Major Thomas J. Jackson and which is now the Jackson Memorial Hospital.

Another artist considered the old Jordan house a thing of rare architectural beauty and good taste, with its hand-carved cornice and fine chimneys.

Many quaint brick, stone and plastered cottages, homes of the humble, are objects for study to artists and visitors.

CHAPTER II: IN THE BEGINNING

IN 1777 the county of Rockbridge was formed and Lexington, its county seat, was chartered and named for the Revolutionary Battle of Lexington (Massachusetts) where was fired, three years before, the shot heard round the world. It is not known who was responsible for the naming of the town. Gilbert Campbell owned the land on which it was built and in 1750 he left his "hoose and personalty" to his son, who owned it at the time of the Revolution. It contained about twenty acres and was a rectangle, nine hundred by twelve hundred feet and was laid off with three streets running longways, named Randolph, Main and Jefferson, and three running crossways, named Henry, Washington and Nelson. With one exception, they bear the names of Virginia statesmen of Revolutionary times.

When the Port of Boston was closed by the British, the people of this section sent 137 barrels of flour, raised, ground and barreled locally, to the people of Boston. This was hauled by wagons to Fredericksburg and thence by water to Boston. The two oldest Commonwealths, Virginia and Massachusetts, have always had strong and affectionate ties. They have much in common.

Lexington's first courthouse was built in 1778 and was destroyed in the big fire of April 11, 1796. Like London, Rome, and Chicago, Lexington was once laid low by fire. The buildings were mostly of logs and, as there was no fire company, it was impossible to conquer the flames, and practically everything was destroyed. This stimulated the people to be better prepared in the future and, immediately, fifty of the leading citizens organized themselves into the Lexington Fire Company. This fine organization has continued through one hundred and forty nine years, giving unselfish service day and night. Immediately after the fire, the "town fathers" raised $25,000 by lottery, for the purpose of rebuilding the town. After the fire a better class of houses was built, and Isaac Burr of New York, traveling through the Valley in 1804, wrote in his journal: "Lexington is a handsome village, with good buildings." He complained, however, that the only pies he could find were peach and apple and that they were scarce. Not until Governor Spotswood and his Knights of the Golden Horseshoe came to the top of the Blue Ridge in 1716, in their effort to find a route to the Great Lakes, did these early adventurers in Tidewater Virginia have any idea of the beauty that lay beyond the Blue Ridge—a country that they had only thought of as vague and unimportant and inhabited by wild savages. Tidewater was satisfied with its tobacco. It was their everything, even their money, and supplied all the ease and comfort desired. The Arcadian life amid green fields and rich herds beyond the Blue Ridge had no charm for them.

[5]

Many years before Spotswood's view of the Valley, a German traveler visited it and left this record: "We traveled through the Sawanae amongst vast herds of red and fallow deer, which stood gazing at us as we came to the promontories or spurs of the Appelataean Mountains. The luxurious grass grew so high that a man passing through on horseback could tie it across his saddle-bow." Tichnor, the well-known Georgia poet, penned these lines, on the theme of Spotswood's Knights of the Golden Horseshoe:

THE VIRGINIANS OF THE VALLEY

The knightliest of the knightly race
    That since the days of old
Have kept the lamp of chivalry
    Alight in hearts of gold;
The kindliest of the kindly band
    That, rarely hating ease,
Yet rode with Spotswood round the land
    And Raleigh round the seas.

Who climbed the blue Virginian hills
    Against embattled foes,
And planted there in valleys fair
    The lily and the rose;
Whose fragrance lives in many lands,
    Whose beauty stars the earth
And lights the hearths of happy homes
    With loveliness and worth.

We thought they slept, the sons who kept
    The names of noble sires,
And slumbered while the darkness crept
    Around their vigil fires;
But aye, the Golden Horseshoe Knights
    Their old Dominion keep,
Whose foes have found enchanted ground
    But not a knight asleep!

After taking possession of the Valley in the name of George I, Spotswood returned to the colonial capital and speedily sent the good news to his Royal master. The choleric old King, in recognition of this exploit and in consideration of the vast territory thus added to the Crown, bestowed the order of knighthood upon his representatives across the sea and sent as further token of his approbation a miniature golden horseshoe with this commemorative legend: *Sic jurat transcendere montes.* These trophies must have met the ambition and extinguished the enterprise of the governor, for tho he had glimpsed the fertile lands and the lovely streams and rivers beyond the Blue Ridge, there was no effort on his part to explore further. His successor, Gooch, however, sought eagerly to occupy and develop the new territory and in 1730 offered abundant inducements to newcomers; the most noted grants of the time being the Beverly Manor and the Borden Tract.

Spotswood was willing that the future development of the Valley be left to a people entirely different in every way. Later, some of the immigrants were from the eastern part of the Colonies, but the early settlers were mostly Irish-Scots, known in their new land as Scotch-Irish, who had come from the Province of Ulster, where the Presbyterian Scots had settled in the time of Cromwell's invasion of Ireland and the Covenanting wars of Scotland. They came in a tide of immigration and settled first in Pennsylvania, where they were not well received. They were considered a pugnacious people and in 1724 the secretary of the Province of Pennsylvania wrote: "It looks to me as if Ireland is to send its inhabitants hither, for last week not less than six ships arrived. The common fear is that if they thus continue to come they will make themselves proprietors of the Province. It is strange that they thus crowd where they are not wanted." They later moved on down the Valley into Virginia, where they found their forest primeval. The hard treatment they had received in the old country under William and Mary, Queen Anne and the Georges, because of their religion, seemed to spur them on in their determination to conquer and, here in this Valley, they found their dwelling place, free from interference, which had been denied them in Penn's land of brotherly love.

No sooner had they found their homes in the new land than they built schools and churches, cleared fields and planted orchards and, in general, cultivated the arts of civilized life. These people believed in the firm and just execution of law, as the only safeguard in maintaining this civilization. An old scrapbook reports that "in the latter years of the eighteenth century, in the good old breezy days of Lexington, the bench of gentlemen justices adjudged that a malefactor should hang by the neck till dead. Another requirement was that his head be severed from his body and exposed on a pole at the crossroads, at the head of the town, as a solemn warning to transgressors of the law. This gruesome sight was made convenient many times for the citizens of old Lexington, by the mandate of the court, before this relic of the Middle Ages gave place to purer manners and nobler laws."

It is easy to believe that these early times were not altogether pleasant times in Lexington, nor was this an altogether pleasant generation with which to live.

They were of upright lives, high standards, and fearless in the pursuit of religious and intellectual freedom, unafraid of hard work, which they considered a sacred and honorable means to an end. Characteristic of this spirit is the Latin inscription, *Laborere est ovare,* on the old Red Mill, at Stone Castle, near the Natural Bridge, put there many decades ago. The ravages of time have dimmed the lettering and, it is feared, something of the significance of this lofty ideal. They willingly paid the price, and a great price it was for their freedom, but great was their reward.

Their distinguishing peculiarities were very pronounced, and some are noticeable in their descendants today. "They remain a praying people, often Covenanters, with courage, sturdiness, industry and faith, and so afraid of God that they hold in their hearts no fear of man." When once their mind was made up on a certain course, they must act accordingly. A typical prayer was: "Dear God, set our feet in the right way, for if we start in the wrong way, there can be nae changing." They admitted that they were open to conviction but added, "where is that mon who can convince us?"

They were decidedly Presbyterian, very decidedly. A story is told of one of them, who, strange to relate, had married a wife of the Episcopal faith. She would not willingly go to the Presbyterian church. "Very well," said the husband, "you go to your meeting-house and I will go to the House of God."

God-fearing and God-loving, keeping holy the Sabbath and with a reverence for the sanctuary, they had an appreciation for the real values of life and their influence was, and is, far reaching.

Dinner parties, dances, cards, horse-racing and the like, common in Tidewater Virginia, were either despised as vanities or loathed as abominations in this primitive society. There were few roistering blades, broken-down gentlemen, gamblers, spendthrifts or, indeed any of the seed of the Cavaliers. Such would have been out of place among the seed of the Covenanters. Yet, after the Revolution, "some of these" became idle and dissipated.

To some of that day and to most all of today, they seemed straight-laced and narrow. They hated Popery and disliked Episcopacy, and this was natural, since they remembered the oppression of Claverhouse. It was said that as late as the middle of the nineteenth century, negro nurses, who had never seen Scotland, were often known to frighten Scotch children into obedience with "Claverse ketch you," meaning an evil spirit of Claverhouse.

Heraldry had taken little notice of most of these people and yet they had a real pride in the fact that they had come of that fine and unquestioned lineage of the Covenanters of old Scotland. Persecuted for the cause of Christ, despite the curses of the Stuarts and the Claymores, they had remained strong in the faith.

Many of them were descendants of those who fell at Bothwell Bridge and the siege of Londonderry. They were dissenters from the established church and only partial freedom was granted them under the Toleration Act of 1688. This was one of the many reasons for their coming to America after the Rebellion of the Irish Earls of Tyrconnel and Tyrone. Prior to this, they had fled from the Heaths of Scotland to the bogs of Ireland to escape Claverhouse, and others had been sent to Ulster by King James.

They were not aristocrats or gentlefolk like the Tidewater English, but farmers, mechanics, laborers—well fitted to develop the fertile fields and to conquer the wilderness. They were readier with the ax and the plow than with the pen. Later, there came some aristocratic blood and breeding from Tidewater and since then much has been heard of ancestry. Thrift and economy were characteristic of the early settlers. This is told as a true story which happened in old Lexington: Mrs. Blank, a widow of a short while, was ill and knowing that her end was near, called to her daughter to get out her black satin dress and to cut out the back of the very full skirt and that she could have a dress made for herself, as the front was all she would need to be laid away in. The daughter was horrified! "Why ma," she said, "what would you look like going up the Golden Stairs with no back in your dress?" "Don't worry, my child, won't nobody be looking at me, they'll all be looking at your pa; I buried him without his pants."

CHAPTER III: INDIAN ENCOUNTERS

HISTORY has no sufficient record of frontier Indian troubles; so far away in the uninhabited forests, the ear of history could scarcely catch the sound of the battles and no earthly eye was witness, save that of the wheeling vulture and the hungry wolf. The very term Indian, so euphonious in itself, became a synonym for savagery. The untutored Indian, in this rude forest life, devoid of all motives to soften or conceal his passions, displayed but the common weakness of man's nature, in colors the more vivid, only because on simpler ground.

Savage life had its vices a-plenty, but it also had its virtues, and many touching instances of magnanimity are known, from the romantic tenderness of Pocahontas, down to the homelier tales of kindness toward the early settlers in the Valley.

The settlers were intruders and must fight, if they were to hold this land of beautiful prospects and sylvan scenes, transparent streams and majestic woods, this veritable Virginia Arcady. On the Tidewater rivers, a race of planters, called Tuckahoes, lived on large plantations, dressed richly, rode in fine coaches and attended the Church of England. Then, there were, nearer the mountains, the Cochees, clearing land and building homes and churches and, still further toward the frontier, the sturdy Scotch-Irish Presbyterians. Between these types of settlers, there was little resemblance. While the planter of the seaboard was asleep in his curtained bed, the frontiersman was in the mountain looking for food. While the one was riding in his fine carriage to lovely entertainments, the other had his ear a-tune for the Indian war whoop. Thus the Lowlanders and the Tramontese differed greatly.

For many years the Indians were friendly to the newcomers in the Valley, but, gradually, they began to resent being elbowed out of their happy hunting ground. This had been their happy home, no one knows how long. It is claimed that the Quakers never had trouble with the Indians, because they were fair and square in all their dealings with them, never taking anything without giving a fair and satisfactory exchange.

The first real clash, in this section, occurred near the mouth of North River, a few miles from Lexington, on December 18, 1742, when thirty odd of the Iroquois came into the Borden Tract, on their way to fight the Catawbas and gave the settlers some trouble. Captain McDowell entertained them for a day and then they went down South River, where they stayed several days, fishing, hunting, and taking what they wanted. They finally became so disorderly that the militia was ordered out to conduct them beyond the settled area. Trouble ensued and the fight was on. The Indians at length took to the Blue Ridge and on to the Potomac. Many Indians and whites were killed.

Doubtless the most disastrous massacre in the Valley occurred at Kerr's Creek in July, 1763, when the Shawnees, who had completely annihilated the Greenbriar settlement, before coming over North Mountain, came upon the Kerr's Creek settlement. An incident is recorded that at this bloody massacre, an Indian, while scalping Thomas Gilmore, was knocked down by Mrs. Gilmore, with an iron kettle. Another Indian ran, with uplifted tomahawk to kill her and was stopped by the one who lay bleeding from the blow she had given him, calling, "don't kill her, she's a good warrior."

The great Emperor Pontiac, chief of the Ottawas, was the first to appear against the Valley settlers. Cornstalk, in youth a follower of Pontiac and Chief of the Shawnees, was distinguished for beauty of person and for agility and strength of frame. In manners, he was graceful and easy and, in movement, majestic and princely. He commanded the Indian forces, composed of over a thousand picked men, at the battle of Point Pleasant, the most noted pitched battle ever fought with the Indians on this continent. He was considered a great orator and it was claimed by those who heard him, that he was unsurpassed by Patrick Henry, Richard Henry Lee, or any others of his time.

Volumes could be written about the Red Terror in the Valley. At times it seemed that they would completely depopulate the white settlements and a tremendous price was paid in subduing them. The tragedy of the Moore family—a tale of horror—is doubtless the most thrilling story of Indian outrage that has come down to us. The following appeared in print some years ago and is worthy of repetition here, for it is one of the most stirring and romantic legends in the annals of this country:

"Eight miles this side of Staunton, on the right of the road, my attention was arrested by the venerable appearance of a large stone church, densely surrounded by forest trees, on whose sere and yellow leaves the setting sun shed his most glorious rays. The Presbyterian congregation that first worshipped here was organized in 1740 and the original house was of logs. The present edifice was begun in 1747 and, at that time, there was not a wheel-carriage in the settlement. The stone was hawled on sledges, the sand was transported from the distant river on horseback, mostly by the women and the glass and the nails were brought from Williamsburg.

"At the time of Braddock's defeat, this part of the Valley was in a state of universal alarm. Some of the people wanted to fly beyond the Blue Ridge, but the pastor, the Reverend Mr. Craig, vehemently opposed it and, at his suggestion, a stockade was built around the church, the lines of which are still visible. Here, on each Sabbath, they worshipped, the preacher taking his rifle into the pulpit and every male hearer being armed in like manner. They acted on Cromwell's advice, 'Trust in God and keep your powder dry.'

"Among those who served this congregation, was Conrad Speece, a man of extraordinary learning and eloquence, who, had he flourished during the Reformation, would have been among the ablest coadjutors of the illustrious Luther.

"The minister who now serves this congregation is a son of the Reverend Samuel Brown and Mary, his wife, a lady known alike to fame for her unparalleled sufferings in early life and her ardent piety during her pilgrimage on earth. She was a daughter of James and Mary Moore, who resided in Botetourt County until they removed to Abb's Valley on Bluestone Creek in Tazewell County:

"'A wild and lonely region, where retired from little scenes of art, great nature dwelt in awful solitude.'

"Here, retired from all the world, he built his cabin and worshipped the God of his fathers, with his household, contented and happy. In 1781 he was summoned from his secluded spot to the American camp and fought in the well contested field of Guilford. Who remained to protect his family, while he was absent in the army is not known. It is certain, however, that at that time and for many years prior and subsequent to this period, numerous hostile tribes of Indians, extending from the Northern Lakes to the Western rivers, down to the Valley of Virginia, were committing frequent and wanton murders on the helpless inhabitants and carrying terror to every bosom. Still he remained in his perilous location. On the 7th of September, 1784, his second son was captured by the Indians and carried away to the forests of the west. How many anxious days and nights the distressed parents spent on account of a lost son no one can tell. Notwithstanding this premonitory event Mr. Moore remained in this dreary, unfrequented region until July 14, 1786. Now the awful scene of blood began. Thirty armed Indians, with heart-rending yells, rushed on this unoffending family. Mr. Moore was first slain in the yard. Three of his children soon fell, next the house was broken open, plundered and burnt. Mrs. Moore and her four surviving children of whom Mary, then in her eighth year, was one, together with Martha Ivins, a domestic, were bound fast and hurried off to the Shawnee town on the margin of the Scioto.

"Thus, in one short hour, the peaceful home is destroyed and the dead bodies of its inmates are exposed to the burning sun. Silence and desolation reigned instead of peace and contentment. The captives must have cast a longing, lingering look behind as they bade adieu to the lifeless forms of their dear ones. They were being taken, they knew not where nor to what, doomed to toil, privation and exposure in traversing mountains, wading streams and crossing rivers, destitute of the necessities of life, lying down at night with no hope of a mitigation of their sorrows, and rising from the hard earth with no refreshment from sleep. On their march two of the children were killed by the savages and now, on the spot where the city of Chillicothe stands, in a council held by the chief, it is determined that Mrs. Moore and her daughter Jane shall be burned at the stake. Martha Ivins and little Mary were the only whites to witness the awful scene. The shrieks and cries of the child must have reëchoed through the surrounding woods, mingling with the savage yells of their tormentors. Not so with the mother. She was calm and serene, conversed with Mary and the faithful Martha and earnestly prayed in the midst of the surrounding flames for the moment when her spirit should take its flight to those blessed mansions in Heaven, 'where not a wave of trouble would roll across her peaceful breast.' Her death was more terrible than that of John Rogers at Smithfield. He was a martyr for his religion and his last hour was therefore one of triumph. The surviving prisoners are still in bondage. The next intelligence is that Mary is sold to a man named Stogwell, residing on the western end of Lake Erie, distant more than five hundred miles from the late residence of her father. How it was possible for a child of her age to endure the fatigue of such a journey I am at a loss to conjecture. So it is, however, that her new master treated her cruelly. Here she remained until October, 1789, when she was restored to liberty by her brother, who had been captured two years prior to the capture of the family and sent, it would seem, by kind Heaven in advance to the neighborhood of Detroit, whence he traveled in pursuit of his sister."

The first interview of Esau and Jacob, after their long separation and estrangement, could not have been more thrilling than when these two orphans fell into each others' arms. They, together with Martha Ivins, returned in the autumn to Augusta County, where Mary, some years later married the Reverend Samuel Brown, pastor of New Providence. She became the mother of five ministers of the Presbyterian Church.

This famous heroine sleeps in the lovely church yard at New Providence, eighteen miles from Lexington.

This lovely old church and this fine neighborhood is also famous for the annual Chrysanthemum Exhibition, to which great crowds come from all over the Commonwealth and the "turkey dinner of the day" is long remembered. This exhibition has been held annually since 1900.

It would be difficult to determine whether the women of this neighborhood, excel in the culinary art or in horticulture. Both have been highly developed.

CHAPTER IV: POWER OF THE ESTABLISHED CHURCH

WHEN Rockbridge was still a part of Augusta County, court was generally held in Staunton, the county seat, but at other times it was held in its far-off corner at Fort Duquesne, near the present city of Pittsburgh. Before the building of courthouses and meeting houses, no records were kept with any degree of accuracy. Until 1745, all official records were kept at Orange Court House and anyone in the Valley, who had any court business, had to journey there on horseback, a considerable distance, by trails through or over the Blue Ridge. The established Church which was a very large part of the colonial government, had no minister in the Valley, so it was necessary for couples who wanted to be married, to cross the Blue Ridge to Orange Court House, where they would find a minister empowered with Royal authority to perform the ceremony. Years later, the established Church had a minister in the Valley.

Cooke tells us that in Virginia, as elsewhere, toward the middle of the eighteenth century, religion and piety had grown to be conventional, the gangrene of society was living for the life that now is and depending on religious observances as a sufficient performance of religious duty. This state was not peculiar to the "Church of England-Virginia." It was seen, also, in Calvinistic New England. Men were earnestly attached to their church and their religion: they would fight and die for it; but living in accord with its precepts was a different thing. Undoubtedly, there were many who detected the flaw in this agreeable philosophy. Unfortunately, some of the clergy were no better than their fellowmen. Some of them played cards and hunted the fox and indulged in drink. And, what was worse, they had very little love for their neighbors, the Dissenters. Likewise, the Dissenters cordially returned this dislike. The Church of England clergymen denounced the New Light preacher as a disturber, and the New Light preacher denounced the clergymen as a disgrace to the cloth. On one occasion a clergyman became very unclerical and quarrelled with his vestry and made an attack upon one of his high dignitaries, pulled off his wig and preached on the following Sunday from the text: "And I contended with them and cursed them and smote certain of them and plucked off their hair."

Cooke tells us further that the Virginia church had not fulfilled the promise of its earlier years. It had once been a church of vital piety and had founded churches at Jamestown, Williamsburg and other places. These churches became very much of a "Drowsyland" and a trumpet blast was needed to arouse the sleepers. He, who in 1740, sounded the summons to a more evangelistic faith and a purer life, was a young man from England, George Whitefield. At Oxford, Whitefield and John Wesley became great friends and, moved by strong feelings, they formed an association for religious work, which their fellow students jeeringly called the "Methodist Association." Methodism was thus launched and was the protest of evangelical against formal Christianity. In doctrine, they differed little from the English church, of which they were offshoots. The two sacraments were baptism by sprinkling and the Lord's Supper by kneeling. Infants were eligible to the first, and penitent seekers after salvation to the last.

Whitefield came twice to America to visit his friend, John Wesley, in Georgia, who was working for the conversion of the Indians.

It was claimed that these New Light preachers and the Presbyterians would lay the foundations of religious freedom.

This case occurred in Old Lexington: A couple (Presbyterian), applied to the local minister of the parish. All went well until the minister read the words: "With my body I thee worship." At this the groom said: "I'll nae say that, it's idolatry." The minister repeated the clause and the enraged man said: "I towld ye I wudn't say that." The minister continued with the ceremony, but the groom did not promise idolatry.

Wedding fees were customary then as now, and one minister had this experience: A couple presented themselves to be married and after the ceremony the groom pulled from his pocket a very thin purse and with difficulty succeeded in producing two silver coins (eighteen pence) and handing it to the minister asked if that would do. Being assured that it would he said: "Well, you made that easier than I did. I made it splitting rails."

In McElhenney's *Recollections* is recorded this instance: An old Irishman had a daughter who was to be married. No priest could be obtained, so a young Methodist preacher was asked to perform the ceremony. For some reason he failed to appear at the appointed time. The wedding party waited long, but waited in vain for the recreant preacher (The truth was, he had forgotten his engagement). "I towld yes ye oucht t'ove sent for Micklehinney," burst out the irate father. "He'd a bin and had it over long ago and gone home agin by this."

The minister's life in those days was not a bed of roses. He traveled hundreds of miles on horseback to visit the sick, to marry the living, and to bury the dead. The funeral sermon was the order of the day and it was considered a mark of disrespect if one lasted less than an hour. There are those still living who remember funeral services in the Lexington church lasting two and three hours. One such was when Dr. Mullaly preached nearly three hours over the remains of a prominent citizen. Most of the homes had the New York *Observer,* the Philadelphia *Presbyterian* and the Central *Presbyterian.* The secular news was confined to a single column of the religious journal and with these scanty gleanings from the great Babylon beyond, readers had to be content. Such items as the Massacre of

Cawnpore, the Slaughter of Allahabad, the Relief of Lucknow, the Sepoy Rebellion and the tragic stories of the British and American missionaries in India held intense interest for them.

Until recent years a Lexington Sunday was a veritable Scotland Sabbath. Amusements, common elsewhere, were not indulged in, but, gradually, changes have come and today Sunday newspapers, Sunday golf and tennis and Sunday everything else that would be shocking to the Sabbath observers of other days. They considered everything wrong. Today, nothing is considered wrong—from one extreme to the other.

A saintly old Scotch lady, visiting Lexington for the first time, was horrified to hear a lad whistling on the Sabbath. "They nae hae done that in Edinburgh on the Holy Sabbath Day," she said.

Early Lexingtonians believed in the literal and strict obedience to the Scriptures as "they" interpreted them. One good lady would not consent to have her picture made because "it would be making a graven image and the Bible forbids it." They knew their Bibles. There was a custom among them of reading it through once a year, following the old fashioned method of five chapters each day and seven on Sabbath.

A minister who drank hot coffee on Sabbath morning was accused of Sabbath breaking. He cornered his critics and they confessed that they heated their mush on Sabbath morning. "All right," said the minister, "when you eat cold mush, I'll drink cold coffee."

About 1816 the town physician was Samuel Campbell, an eccentric gentlemen of fine sense, kind heart, good culture, and liberal views; a man eminently useful and much loved. Few callings have given to man such wide scope for usefulness as the old time country, or small town, general practitioner, who was the counsellor, friend, and healer of the community.

Riotous stories were told of the members of the local bar—Chapman Johnson, Daniel Sheffey, Howe Peyton, and Briscoe Baldwin.

Washington and Lee University in the snow, circa 1900

Entrance to Virginia Military Institute

Goshen Pass

Timber Ridge Church

Valentine's recumbent statue of General Lee

Main Street, looking north from the Lexington Presbyterian Church

CHAPTER V: TAVERNS AND LIQUORS

FROM the earliest days Lexington has been on the thoroughfare from eastern Virginia to the west, by way of the Old Plank Road, over which rolled and rumbled the wagons, carrying beeswax, tallow and feathers, and the stagecoach, the popular mode of travel from Baltimore to far-off Tennessee. These coaches brought many visitors to Lexington in these early days. From frontier days, by Indian trail and, later, by ox-cart and the covered wagon, followed by the stagecoach, many travelers came this way, especially those from the Old World. The rumble of the wagons and coaches could be heard many miles on the Plank Road, for it was built of planks, laid crossways, as the only means of keeping above the mud. The ample accommodations of the stagecoach were nine passengers inside, nine on top, and two by the driver, which were considered choice seats.

For the comfort and care of these travelers many taverns, inns, and ordinaries existed along the way. Some of them were very famous. One such was the Old Blue, formerly known as Clice's Place, and widely known for its comfortable and generous hospitality. On the grounds of this tavern the menageries, which traveled through the country, by wagon train, often exhibited, much to the delight of the populace. The Washington Tavern, which stood on the corner now occupied by the Rockbridge Motor Company, and the Eagle Hotel, which stood on the site now occupied by the McCrum Drug Company, were also famous stopping places. After a fine service as a tavern the Old Blue passed into the possession of the college and many generations have known it as one of the College dormitories. It still serves this purpose as well as a popular tourist resort during the summer months. Strong sentiment is held for this old landmark.

The Fancy Hill Mansion, south of Lexington, was another famous tavern, where the hospitality of Benjamin Welch was known far and wide just a century ago.

The following tavern rates about the close of the eighteenth century are recorded:

Hot diett with small beer, 3 shillings.
Cold diett with no beer, 2 shillings.
Stabblage and hay or fodder (24 hours), 2 shillings.
Good pasture (24 hours, per horse), 1 shilling 8 pence.
Good pasture (24 hours, per cow), 1 shilling 3 pence.
Lodging with feather bed and clean sheet, 1 shilling.
Lodging with chaff bed and clean sheet, 6 pence.
Corn, per gallon, 1 shilling 3 pence.
Oats, per gallon, 1 shilling.

For this travel the old double covered bridge at East Lexington was built in 1810 by Colonel John Jordan and Mr. Moorehead. This was a toll bridge, with the following charges: Man on horse, 6¼ cents; sheep or hog ½ cent; cart or turmoil 25 cents; riding carriage 6¼ cents per wheel. The bridge was burned in 1864 by the Confederate forces in their effort to keep the Federals back. Some years later it was rebuilt as before.

In 1825 the Duke of Saxe-Weimar-Eisenbach made a visit to this country and reported that he passed from Staunton to Lexington in a miserable stagecoach and over very bad roads. The wooden bridge over the river was used only in times of high water. (This was doubtless to avoid the toll.) He said that the only decent places he saw were Fairfield and Lexington, though he noted many handsome country places along the way. At one of these places he saw eight eagles sitting on the fence, which were cared for by the owner, and seeing snipe flying in the tavern yard in Fairfield, he concluded that the people were not fond of shooting. Game was plentiful and a whole deer could be had for $1.50. He was surprised to find that all the coachmen were white.

Being a German, the Duke was of much interest to the few Germans he met along the way. From all accounts, the Duke enjoyed the quadroon balls of New Orleans more than anything that Lexington had to offer. It is possible that the French influence of Louisiana was more conducive to the Duke's type of entertainment than was the Scotch-Irish influence of Lexington!

Another visitor of that early day, an Englishman, thought that Lexington had many attractions and reported that it was situated in a pleasant valley flowing with milk and honey and that flowers and gardens were more prized than in most places.

Howe's *Sketches* tells us that about the middle of the nineteenth century Lexington had four churches, two printing houses, and twelve hundred people, and that it was a very pleasant place.

Another visitor of that time claimed that Lexington was a very indifferent place with small, muddy streets. Florence McCartney, the Baptist minister, reported that the town looked as though it had been built many years before and that a new house was quite an event.

Many things tended to neighborliness in the early days of Lexington, such as borrowing a bucket of water or a coal of fire. It was a familiar sight to see a person carrying a burning plank or a live coal from house to house. Matches had not come into use and when they did, they sold for 37½ cents per dozen. They were little blocks, fastened together at the butt ends. One was split off at a time. They were made of sulphur and had to be held far away when lighted. Homes were lighted by candles, made in the homes. A little later, lard-oil lamps came into use and were much brighter than the candle-light.

Between 1790 and 1810 the increase in the consumption of liquor was greater than the increase in population and an Englishman wrote that intemperance was the chief characteristic of Americans.

Bad as the situation was before the Revolution, it was far worse after. Arch Alexander claimed that a Continental bought a house in Lexington, where he collected all the vagrants, ex-convicts and ex-soldiers about him and that drinking bouts lasted for weeks at a time. It was also claimed that most of the elders had their own private stills.

The drinking habit was very conspicuous in the town and there were many unlicensed drinking places reported. Just before the War between the States there were eight groggeries and court day was no time for a self-respecting woman to be seen on the streets.

The *Gazette* of December 26, 1873, reported that Christmas Day was celebrated by an unusual amount of noise and profuse liquoring; that Main Street was blocked by crowds of boisterous negroes and that no lady ventured out. It stated further that if excessive use of liquor be abolished and carrying of pistols be stopped, three-fourths of the crime of Rockbridge would be eliminated. Reminiscent of the popular stills, is the ornament on the steeple of the Presbyterian Church. It is hard to understand how this piece of lowly handiwork was ever so highly exalted. For many years the Baptist Church stood just behind the Presbyterian Church and on its steeple was a "worm" pointing Heavenward. A Baptist deacon was asked why they had a cork-screw on their church. "To pull the stoppers out of the Presbyterian bottles," was the quick reply.

From 1777 to 1850, Lexington was governed by a board of trustees. In February, 1850, James G. Paxton was elected the first mayor of the town and he has been succeded by the following:

Jacob M. Ruff: 1851.
William Jordan: 1852.
John H. Myers: 1852.
William Jordan: 1853.
J. C. Middleton: 1855.
Geo. W. Adams: 1863.
Wm. White: 1866 (elected but refused to qualify).
J. K. Edmondson: 1866.
Jacob M. Ruff: 1867.
H. H. Henderson: 1868.
Calvin Dold: 1874.
William T. Jewell: 1877.
Calvin Dold: 1879.
G. P. Chalkley: 1883.

J. W. Houghawout: 1885.
T. E. McCorkle: 1897.
Frank T. Glasgow: 1899.
James D. Anderson: 1899.
P. M. Penick: 1901.
W. F. Pierson: 1901.
Sam'l B. Walker: 1903.
W. R. Kennedy: 1907.
Sam'l B. Walker: 1909.
E. S. Shields: 1911.
O. C. Jackson: 1913.
G. A. Rhodes: 1920.
H. Crim Peck: 1929.
G. A. Rhodes: 1931.

CHAPTER VI: THE PRESBYTERIANS ASSEMBLE

INTERESTED especially in religion, education and home life, the founders of Lexington have many enduring monuments in schools, churches and homes. The stately old Presbyterian Church on Main Street, with its pilasters and columns of Grecian design, showing a slight English influence, its spacious interior seating 1,300, and its perfect acoustics, is always of interest to visitors. Here, too, Stonewall Jackson served as deacon and conducted his famous Bible School for the slaves of the community.

In 1922 Thomas Nelson Page, being the guest of honor on General Lee's birthday, spoke to the college students assembled in the Presbyterian Church, this being the largest auditorium in the town. He dealt mostly in reminiscences of his own college days under General Lee's regime. He said that when he was a student, he attended this church and that he often marvelled at its vastness and wondered if anywhere in the world there could be another building as large! Years later, when visiting in England, he discovered that Westminster Abbey was as large!

In 1780, Lexington consisted of a half dozen houses and no church at all. To these people such a condition could not long continue. That year a Presbyterian congregation assembled at Timber Ridge and another at Hall's Meeting House (now Monmouth), which had been served since 1775 by the Reverend William Graham, the first rector of Liberty Hall Academy. Mr. Graham preached occasionally in the village, but not statedly until 1788, and that year one-fourth of his time was engaged for Lexington. A subscription of twenty pounds was raised for him and the following call extended:

"We, of the congregation of Lexington, being desirous of having the ordinances of the Gospel administered unto us and hoping that you, Sir, may be induced to take the pastoral care of us, until Providence shall call you to remove elsewhere and being persuaded from past experiences that your labors will be profitable unto us, do earnestly call and invite you to take the pastoral care of this congregation, promising you all obedience and encouragement in the Lord.

"We do hereby promise and oblige ourselves to pay you twenty pounds, lawful money of Virginia, annually, so long as you remain among us a regular minister of the Gospel. If the sum shall not amount to twenty pounds, a proportionate amount of your labours shall be deducted."

Success crowned this connection and the next year the Lexington congregation was able to double its contribution and secure one-half of Mr. Graham's time. In 1790, the church had its first revival and many were added to its roll. Many of the converts were over-demonstrative in their great fervor and were overtaken by the "jerks."

[20]

Through the succeeding years, stormy and balmy, this church has been a fine influence in this community and to the utmost parts of the earth. Few congregations in America have been so intimately associated with the missionary enterprise, both on the home and the foreign field. Its long list of gifted men and women, who have served it through the years, constitute its Honor Roll.

In his report to the General Assembly, April 29, 1793, Graham gave some rather severe counsel:

"1st: That all Presbyterians banish the spirit of the world from their dress, manners and conversations and adopt the plainness, simplicity, self-denial and holiness of life, so remarkably exemplified in the first and most successful ministers of the Gospel.

"2nd: That dry, formal and unaffecting harangues, be banished from our pulpits and that the simple truths of the Gospel be addressed to every man's conscience in the sight of God, with that fervour and solemnity which the dignity and interesting importance require.

"3rd: That our private preparations for the pulpit consist chiefly of prayer, self-examination and a practical study of the Bible.

"4th: That we endeavor always to enter on our public ministrations with a deep sense of the presence of God and the awful importance of eternal judgement, in which we and our hearers must shortly share; that we have no other object in view, but to recommend the Gospel as the only means of escape for condemned perishing sinners. That an active, persevering zeal in preaching and exhorting in season and out, be a leading trait in the character of a Presbyterian clergyman. In fine, let us endeavor to know nothing, in our official character, but Christ and Him crucified."

Simple food and simple clothing was the common lot in the early days and only domestic clothes were worn to preaching. It was reported: "To-day, one in every hundred is wearing foreign clothes and if their son can get a fine horse, a pretty saddle and bridle and a broadcloth coat, and their daughter can get a new bonnet and dress to show off at preaching on Sabbath (which is probably attended with no better consequences), it is the height of their ambition. If their wives can succeed in converting their butter, eggs, cheese and feathers into as much coffee, tea, sugar and other flippery as will serve them through the year, the men are well content."

The village church was the pride of the community and the center of interest, and was surrounded by the Kirk Yard with its lichened stones. Both villages and churches were few and far between. Some families had to travel far; nevertheless, they went, male and female, old and young, generally on horseback, but often on foot, walking ten miles or more. Many carried their shoes and stockings until they reached the last water before arriving at the church. Here, they would "bathe and clothe their feet."

Some of the churches built by the first generation are yet standing, substantial monuments to these great people. The minister of that day had strong Calvinistic principles, deeply rooted. The sum and substance of his preaching was the fall of man, the depravity of human nature, and salvation alone through Christ. False doctrines did not bother him, for he led too busy a life to be involved in metaphysical fogs. Births, marriages, and deaths among his people cemented the most sacred ties of friendship and confidence, which served to compensate for his very arduous life. He considered the comforting of God's people second only to the salvation of souls. His motto, "speak to sad hearts, you will find them everywhere."

Night services were rare. The custom was two services on the Sabbath, one in the forenoon and one in the afternoon, separated by a short interval of half hour, during which the people were refreshed in body and mind. These services were very prolonged, but were always well attended. Those from a distance brought their entire household, including their dinner baskets.

Social intercourse was mostly religious. When the Lord's Supper was administered, the services began on Friday and lasted for four days. A plurality of ministers was present and people flocked in from everywhere. The Sacrament of the Lord's Supper was served on long tables and each communicant was expected to present a "token," which admitted him to the table. An old minister, who recalled this custom said: "Although the present mode of administering the Lord's Supper is not without its advantages, yet when I look back at the course pursued by the Presbyterian Church from its beginning and connect with this the many delightful hours I have spent distributing the elements of the supper to God's people, when seated around the table, properly called the Table of the Lord, I cannot but feel some regret that this custom has been changed and nothing has come in its place to make the same solemn impression."

The ministers of the early church in the Valley of Virginia were the real trail-blazers: men of courage, men of piety, men of intellect. Their contribution to the development of this great country has never been fully appreciated. But for their leadership, how slow would have been the conquest of the wilderness! In the tide of immigration to the New World, were many of the most gifted Scotch clergy, who were attracted to America, not because of ease and comfort, but because it offered freedom to worship God according to the dictates of their own conscience and unlimited opportunities to serve their fellowmen.

Typical of the Scotch clergy of the early day was the Reverend James Waddell, born in Ulster, Ireland, in 1739. Like most of the clergy, he was both minister and educator, being skilled in Latin, Greek, and Hebrew, and in the literature of those tongues. "It is to the immortal honor of the Scotch-Irish that, cumbered as they were by the embarrassments of a new settlement in a wilderness distant from the sea and exposed to its imminent dangers, they would not place the hands of their Presbytery on the heads that would not learn and could not teach, but guarded their pulpits with zealous care and exacted a high order of attainments from every candidate for the ministry. It would form a characteristic picture of that era to present on canvas a committee of a Scotch-Irish Presbytery convened in a log house, rudely constructed, examining hour after hour a candidate for the ministry in the peculiarities of Latin, Greek and Hebrew, in the metaphysical refinements of theology and in the knowledge of general literature, before he was permitted to enter a career that involved personal danger, untiring and self-denying labors and limited comforts, if not positive poverty, to the very gates of the tomb. Excellent men! We now enjoy the results of their far-sighted wisdom. They thought not of present gain, but of the temporal and eternal welfare of those whom Providence had committed to their charge. They only thought of pure morals, of skill in interpreting the oracles of God, of the diffusion of sound instruction and a pure religious faith among men."

After a long service in the Valley, James Waddell removed to Orange County, where he built a crude structure in which he preached for the remainder of his life. He was known as the "Blind Preacher." It was here that William Wirt heard him preach his great sermon described in the *British Spy,* which gave him fame. Wirt says:

"It was on Sunday, as I traveled through Orange County, that my eye was caught by a cluster of horses tied near a ruinous old wooden house in the forest, not far from the roadside. Having frequently before seen such objects in traveling through these states, I had no difficulty in understanding that it was a place of religious worship. Devotion alone should have stopped me to join in the duties of the congregation. I must confess that curiosity to hear the preacher of such a wilderness was not the least of my motives. I was struck by his preternatural appearance. He was a tall and very spare old man. His head was covered with a white linen cap. His shriveled hands and his voice were shaking under the influence of a palsy and a few moments ascertained to me that he was blind.

"The first emotions which touched my breast were those of mingled pity and veneration. But, ah, sacred God! how soon were all my feelings changed! The lips of Plato were never more worthy of a prognostic swarm of bees than were the lips of this Holy man! It was a day of the administration of the Sacrament and his subject was the Passion of our Saviour. I had heard the subject handled a thousand times and had thought it exhausted long ago. Little did I suppose that in the wild woods of America I was to meet with a man whose eloquence was to give to this topic a new and more sublime pathos than I had ever before witnessed.

"As he descended from the pulpit to distribute the mystic symbols, there was a peculiar, a more than human solemnity in his air and manner, which made my blood run cold and my whole frame shiver. He then drew a picture of the sufferings of our Saviour; His trial before Pilate; His ascent up Calvary; His crucifixion and death. I knew the whole story, but never till then had I heard the circumstances so selected, so arranged, so colored. It was all new and I seemed to hear it for the first time in my life. His enunciation was so deliberate that his voice trembled on every syllable and every heart in the assembly trembled in unison. His peculiar phrases had that force of description that the original scene appeared to be, at that moment, acting before our eyes. We saw the very faces of the Jews; the staring frightful distortions of malice and rage. We saw the buffet; my soul kindled with a flame of indignation and my hands were involuntarily and convulsively clenched.

"But when he came to touch on the patience and the forgiving meekness of the Saviour; when he drew, to the life, his blessed eyes streaming to Heaven, his voice breathing to God a soft and gentle prayer of pardon on His enemies, 'Father, forgive them for they know not what they do,' the voice of the preacher, which had all along faltered, grew fainter and fainter, until, his utterance being entirely obstructed by the force of his feelings, he raised his handkerchief to his eyes and burst into a loud and irrepressible flood of grief. The effect was inconceivable. The whole house resounded with the mingled groans and shrieks of the congregation.

"It was some time before the tumult had subsided so far as to permit him to proceed. Indeed, judging by the usual, but fallacious, standards of my own weakness, I began to be very uneasy for the situation of the preacher. For I could not conceive how he would be able to let his audience down from the height to which he had wound them without impairing the solemnity and dignity of his subject or, perhaps shocking them by the abruptness of the fall—but no, the descent was as beautiful and sublime as the elevation had been rapid and enthusiastic.

"The first sentence with which he broke the awful silence was a quotation from Rousseau: 'Socrates died like a philosopher, but Jesus Christ died like a God.' I despare of giving you any idea of the effect produced by this short sentence, unless you could perfectly conceive the whole peculiar crisis of the discourse. Never before did I completely understand what Demosthenes meant by laying such stress on delivery. You are to bring before you the venerable figure of the preacher, his blindness constantly recalling to your recollection old Homer, Milton, and Ossian, and associating with his performance the melancholy grandeur of their geniuses. You are to imagine that you hear his slow, solemn enunciation and his voice of affecting, trembling melody—you are to remember the pitch of passion and enthusiasm to which the congregation was raised and, then, the few minutes of portentous, death-like silence which reigned through the house—the preacher removing the white handkerchief from his face and slowly stretching forth his palsied hand, begins the sentence: 'Socrates died like a philosopher,' then pausing, raising his other hand and pouring his soul into his tremulous voice—'but Jesus Christ—like a God.' If he indeed had been an angel of light the effect could have scarcely been more divine."

Waddell swayed his audience simultaneously and irresistibly like trees in the woods, shaken by a tempest. When he rose in scornful argument, it was like a sweeping torrent, which carried everything before it. Patrick Henry called the "Blind Preacher" the greatest orator he ever heard. During the Revolution, the "Blind Preacher" spoke to Tate's Company at Midway, near Lexington, just before they marched away. This great divine was a trustee of Washington College.

Religion was a matter of paramount importance in early Lexington and Rockbridge and meetings were numerous. In 1802, seventy young people from Rockbridge went by horseback to Bedford to hear the eminent Conrad Speece. In the midst of his sermon he stopped short and appealed to the thoughtless crowd: "O, you young people from Rockbridge, I want you to become religious, I want you all to get religion." Prior to this revival, there was in 1789 a meeting in Prince Edward County, when thirty young people from Rockbridge were converted by the preaching of Turner, who was known as "Nature's orator." The meeting was known as the Great Awakening in Virginia.

Foote says of Turner: "Dr. Baxter, conversing with a friend in the year 1831, respecting the prayerfulness and spiritual-mindedness of Turner, said that on one occasion, when the Synod of Virginia met in Lexington in 1805, during recess, Mr. Turner, walking down the street to a friend's house, became absorbed about the things of eternity and apparently unconscious of the place or company, took off his hat and began to pray aloud for a blessing on the place and the people and, said the doctor, after a pause of deep emotion, "there are souls rejoicing in Heaven over the results of that meeting."

Lacy, Allen, Legrand, Hill, Alexander, Lyle and Houston were among the great preachers of the day.

This sketch of a Presbyterian pastor's wife is from an old minister's reminiscences: "She was not destitute of humor; she often told, with a twinkle in her faded eye, that the Methodists said she was not a Christian because she wore rings and ruffles. As time rolled on she laid away these frivolities and her Methodist sisters forgave these vanities in the young bride of twenty, who had been reared in the college town of Lexington. Very soon after she entered upon her thirties, the smooth brown hair was folded away under a stiff cap and a little shoulder cape and a Swiss embroidered collar replaced the rings and ruffles of her earlier years. She had a long cloak of blue broadcloth, fashioned after the Conemara. For gala days she reserved a black satin and a silk shawl, presented to her by the ladies of the congregation on the occasion of her wedding anniversary. These she called her 'grave clothes' in which she wished to be laid away."

The pastor's garb was of black broadcloth, with a cutaway or pigeon-tail coat and of these he had two, the best one for Sabbath and the second best for every day use. He wore a high stock, a blue silk cravat about his throat, his chin being always clean shaven. A tall hat of drab beaver completed his clerical attire. This was encircled with a broad band of black cloth. The Sunday beaver was kept carefully in a bandbox under the head of the bed, where for six days of the week, it reposed free from dust and flies.

It was the universal custom for the clergy, when they traveled to wear some kind of badge of their profession. It preserved them from unpleasant encounters and caused them to remember their sacred office, for "when a clergyman thinks that he is not recognized as such, he is very apt to yield to unsuitable compliances and often when he seeks to be incognito, he is known to all the company—this, in defense of the 'band and the cocked hat.' "

Favorite commentaries of the early ministers were Scott and Henry. For history, they read Flavius Josephus, Rawlings, and Robertson, the sermons of Saurin and Newton, the Institutes of Calvin and Knox. Doddridge's and Baxter's *Discourses* were among the much used volumes and Blair's *Lectures* and Bunyan's *Allegories* stood side by side with Chambers and Hall. In their reading, as in their life, they preferred the solid ore of nature to the sparkle of polished society.

CHAPTER VII: LEXINGTON CHURCHES

O N Washington's birthday, 1796, the sum of $2,500.00 was subscribed for the purpose of building a Presbyterian Church in Lexington, but the big fire interrupting, the building was not completed until 1802. It stood in the cemetery and seated 800. It had a spacious gallery for the slaves. In 1819 the trustees of the college "bought" three pews for the use of students, as an inducement for church attendance. This, however, did not work any more than the free pew which had been set aside for the community's poor. After a few years the trustees despaired and sold the pews. The rent of pews varied in price, depending upon location, those nearest the door being the most expensive. When it is known that sermons often lasted for hours, such as one preached by the Reverend Craig, which had fifty-five divisions and subdivisions, certainly seats near the door were advantageous to a getaway!

Prior to the building of this church, the congregation worshipped, in the summer, under a tent in Taylor's Grove and, in the winter, in the courthouse. The present church was built in 1840 and the ministers who have served through the years have been:

William Graham: From the establishing until 1819.

George A. Baxter: 1819-1832.   D. C. Irwin: 1882-1883.
J. W. Douglas: 1832-1834.   Thos. L. Preston: 1883-1895.
W. W. Cunningham: 1834-1840.   James A. Quarles: 1895-1896.
George S. Skinner: 1840-1847.   Thornton Whaling: 1896-1905.
W. S. White: 1848-1867.   T. B. Southall: 1905-1907.
J. L. Kirkpatrick: 1867-1868.   A. T. Graham: 1907-1917.
J. W. Pratt: 1868-1874.   Thos. Kay Young: 1918-1924.
J. A. Waddell: 1874-1877.   James J. Murray: 1925—
E. P. Mullaly: 1877-1882.

Probably of this line of gifted and consecrated men, the one who left his mark most indelibly upon his church and community was Dr. Alfred T. Graham, a gentle, even tempered man and the most understanding of friends. He left no unkind remembrances of hard words or bitter speech or un-Christian thoughts. "The spoken word, the sped arrow, the lost opportunity," three things that can never be recalled, caused him no regret, for in his words and acts he was cautious and in seizing his opportunities he was diligent. His work was a benediction upon all whose life he touched. Seldom is so well-rounded a character found in the ministry or out. He was eminently useful in his day and generation and eternity alone will reveal his accomplishments. In godliness and consecration he was unsurpassed by any of his time.

The Presbyterian Sunday School first assembled in 1831, in the old church in the cemetery. It was organized by Mr. Garland, a professor in

Washington College and a man of "no ordinary metal." He later became president of Vanderbilt University.

In connection with the establishing of the Presbyterian Church in Lexington, Colonel Preston, in his semi-centennial address before the Franklin Society in 1873, gives this picture of the community in 1816:

"The town was in about the same limits decreed in 1777. Main Street was not compactly built up. The finest structure was the Ann Smith Academy and beyond it were corn fields. On each side of the college were two brick halls, two stories high. Water was from the pump and from the back spring and hawling water by sleds was quite an institution. Ice houses were unknown. The Presbyterian was the only church, with two services on Sabbath, separated by an 'intervale' of one-half hour and both were well attended.

"A large oak grove extended from the church gate to Wood's Creek and this was a rambling ground during the intermission."

These Scotch-Irish, unlike the German settlers in the Lower Valley, who were Lutherans, Mennonites, and Calvinists, with a few Dunkers, or Dippers, who believed in immersion, as the only baptism, were Presbyterians 100%. They also differed from the Germans and the "Irish Presbyterians" in that they did not countenance dancing and other worldly amusements, being exceedingly serious minded, their principal entertainment was "attendance upon religious services." The finest recommendation that a young man could have was that he had been a regular and orderly attendant of the Sabbath School.

Along with the winter services of the church held in the courthouse were those of the singing school and the literary society.

The Presbyterian was followed by the Methodist Church and William Cravens, a stonemason and local preacher, was the first Methodist in Lexington. He came to build Liberty Hall Academy at Mulberry Hill. He was followed in 1823 by John Burgess and his very large family, and in whose home the first Methodist preaching was done. The first church building was a small frame structure on Randolph Street and this was later replaced by a brick building on Jefferson Street. (This later became the Town Hall or Opera House, and years later was destroyed by fire. Many of the good people claimed that this was inevitable, when the Lord's House was so desecrated.) This church was celebrated for its congregational singing, especially that of the Senseney brothers, who came from Woodstock, before the War Between the States and set up their forge on Jefferson Street, near the church.

The Randolph Street site became the property of the colored members of the congregation and remains so today. In the rear of this property are rather indistinct remnants of the old white Methodist cemetery, long since abandoned.

In 1894 a new church was built on Main Street and in 1926 this was replaced by the present edifice. The following ministers have served through the years:

George T. Williams: 1854-1855.   J. R. Waggoner: 1857-1859.
C. B. Riddick: 1855-1856.   H. V. Mitchell: 1859-1860.
Paul Whitehead: 1856-1857.   E. M. Peterson, J. S. Rees, 1861-1862.

(The Lexington Station of the Baltimore Conference was without a minister from 1862 to 1866, except for the service of the Reverend J. S. Martin, who served when the opportunity permitted from his duties as Presiding Elder of the Rockingham District.)

P. H. Whistler: 1866-1867   J. T. Wightman: 1896-1898.
Samuel Rogers: 1868-1869.   H. P. Hammil: 1899-1900.
I. R. Finley: 1869-1871.   J. H. Light: 1901-1903.
W. G. Cross: 1871-1872.   J. O. Knott: 1904-1906.
J. L. Clark: 1873-1874.   W. S. Hammond: 1907-1910.
W. K. Boyle: 1875-1876.   M. D. Mitchell: 1911-1912.
I. W. Canter: 1877-1878.   W. F. Locke: 1912-1915.
W. H. Seat: 1879-1880.   E. L. Woolf: 1916-1918.
L. C. Miller: 1880-1883.   G. G. Martin: 1919-1922.
Wm. A. Wade: 1884-1885.   J. J. Rives: 1923-1924.
J. W. Waugh: 1886-1887.   T. M. Swann: 1925-1927.
A. M. Kackley: 1887-1890.   J. H. Smith: 1927-1930.
F. J. Prettyman: 1891-1894.   James A. Johnson: 1931——
J. S. Gardner: 1895-1896.

Dr. Ruffner in writing of the churches of Lexington said that he would not attempt to recall the names of the ministers of the Methodist Church because they changed so often.

Older residents of Lexington recall with great admiration and affection that sturdy saint of the church, James M. Senseney, who, for more than a half century, was known far and wide as the Gospel singer of this church. His favorite hymn, *Palms of Victory,* which he sang on all occasions, was also a favorite of his friends, who were legion. Mr. Senseney belonged to a family famed for longevity, most of his brothers and sisters becoming octogenarians. He, too, reached this pinnacle of years. One sister, Mrs. Ann Elizabeth Kirkpatrick, still hale and hearty and living in the same house on Main Street to which she came as a bride in 1855, recently celebrated her ninety-seventh birthday. At the age of ninety-five she underwent an operation for appendicitis and on the second day after the operation she said that she felt fine and asked for some boiled cabbage. She still tends her old-fashioned garden and it is truly old fashioned, for she here cultivates the flowers reminiscent of her childhood. From this old garden, "a friendly path leads through a friendly gate" into another interesting old garden, that of Mrs. Pitzer's. Here, in a charming and careless fashion, columbine, bluebells, candytuft, hollyhocks, larkspur and many other old favorites push and vie with each other for first place.

Mrs. Kirk's cakes and pies are unsurpassed, as is her salt-rising bread. Nowhere South of the Mason-Dixon line can their equal be found. She is a delight to her hosts of friends and can easily be termed ninety-seven years young. Her sister, Mrs. F. P. Rhodes, recently passed away, having exceeded her four-score milestone, retaining to the end her charm of manner and person; a rare and interesting personality and a walking encyclopaedia of Lexington history. When a small child, she witnessed the shelling of the town by the Federal forces, and picked up the first shell which fell. This shell is in the Virginia Military Institute museum. After the war, the citizens were not allowed to carry any side-arms, so many carried loaded canes. Mr. Rhodes was one of these and his cane is now in the possession of Captain Greenlee Letcher.

The Lexington Baptist Church was constituted May 9, 1841, with sixteen members. The founders were Colonel and Mrs. John Jordan, Reverend Cornelious Tyree, Mrs. Joseph Tolley, and others. The following ministers have served through the years:

Cornelious Tyree: 1841-1845.	Thomas A. Johnson: 1896-1898.
A. J. Huntington: 1850-1851.	T. A. Hall: 1899-1902.
Gilbert Mason: 1854-1856.	Charles Manly: 1903-1914.
Florence McCartney: 1859-1861.	William O. Beasley: 1915-1918.
Samuel Huff: 1861-1862.	J. M. Hester: 1919-1920.
John William Jones: 1865-1871.	J. B. Hill: 1920-1922.
A. C. Barron: 1872-1875.	Henry W. Tiffany: 1922——.
George B. Eager: 1876-1878.	E. B. Jackson: 1922-1928.
J. L. Carroll: 1879-1882.	E. H. Potts: 1928-1934.
James B. Taylor: 1884-1891.	Carleton S. Prickett: 1935——.
B. H. Dement: 1892-1896.	

Dr. Charles Manly, a great soul and a great mind, was one of the most beloved men ever to have lived in Lexington. He was known as Lexington's pastor, going in and out among all classes and conditions of men, knowing no denominational, social, or racial lines, but loved and was loved by everyone. With boundless sympathy and understanding and with words of comfort he healed many a broken heart and restored many a shattered life to respectability and usefulness. By precept and example he led many to his Master, whom he reflected to the world.

In 1867, the negro members of the church, at their own request, were dismissed, that they might organize their own church, the white membership pledging their support in the undertaking.

The first Episcopal service in Lexington was in 1840, and was held in the Presbyterian Church. It was conducted by an English minister, the

Reverend Mr. Tyne. Soon thereafter, a church was built on the present site of the Lee Memorial Church and was called Grace Episcopal. Many Presbyterians were helpful in contributions and interest.

The Reverend Mr. Bryant, the first rector, has been succeeded by Robert Nelson, Lewis Clover, William Nelson Pendleton, George Norton, R. J. McBryde, W. Cosby Bell, O. DeW. Randolph, Churchill Gibson, Vincent C. Franks, and Thomas H. Wright.

Because of the feeling against the established church during the colonial period, it was claimed that there were those who did not relish the coming of the Episcopal faith into this community, and it was also claimed that the "Presbyterians had the lid on so tight, that the Episcopalians could not get a lot on which to build their church and had to buy through an intermediary." The original communicants, ten in number, were General and Mrs. Francis H. Smith, Mr. and Mrs. Henry Nargrove, Mrs. Ruff, Mrs. Bradshaw, Mrs. Echolls, Mrs. Bryant, and Colonel and Mrs. Williamson. Other additions soon followed, including Judge and Mrs. Brockenbrough, Mrs. John Letcher, Major Dorman, Mr. and Mrs. Stevens, Mrs. John Bowyer and her daughters. Colonel Bowyer did not belong to any church and when all his family united with the Episcopal Church, he said: "I'll be damned if I am not a Presbyterian still." Like the Presbyterians, they worshiped in the courthouse until they had a house of their own.

One of the richest connections that this church has had in its long history was that of General Robert E. Lee, who was a vestryman. After his death it became the Lee Memorial Church.

One who boasted of aristocratic English lineage and who was connected with the Episcopal church, asked a man who had left this fold and married into the Presbyterian church: "Well, sir, how do you like being in the church with the tradespeople?"

An old-fashioned Methodist woman upon learning that her grandson had embraced the Episcopal faith said: "Well, I have always observed that after young people join the Episcopals or the Masons, they seldom join 'any' church."

The Catholic Church was never large in Lexington, but it has always been well represented. John Sheridan, its outstanding member for many years, was one of, if not the most charitable citizens who ever lived in Lexington. Thousands of good deeds to the poor and needy graced his long and useful life.

The Associated Reformed Presbyterian Church, though very old in Rockbridge, is young in Lexington. Under the Reverend Mr. Lauderdale, the father and founder of the local church, a fine work is being done in this community. We read from an old scrapbook that this denomination has had a very influential part in Rockbridge history. The Old Providence Church was organized in 1762 and the land on which it was built was given by Patrick Hall, the grandfather of Cyrus Hall McCormick, inventor of the reaper. The early members of this faith were Covenanters and Seceders and fought for our country in the Revolution of 1776. William Baldridge, one of the earliest ministers of this church, was twice offered the presidency of Washington College, but declined because of the scarcity of ministers and his love for the pastorate.

The Presbyterians of the Valley had continued the custom of singing in public worship only Rouse's version of the Psalms, until the religious revivals of 1789, when the smoother versification and evangelical diction of Watts was more acceptable to many, especially to the younger people. The Providence Church did not consent to accept the new style in singing. The Reverend John Brown, a good, easy man, invited the Reverend William Graham to assist in the Sacrament of the Lord's Supper. Mr. Graham, warm with the recent revival of religion, determined on this occasion, to introduce Watts' hymns. He indiscreetly did this without giving notice at the beginning of the service. Many of the elder members immediately left the church and many more were offended. The consequences were agitation and ill feeling during the communion, a schism among the members, terminating in a secession of the most discontented and a formation of a church by the seceders, called Old Providence.

What made the offended party irreconcilable was the sarcastic remark of the Reverend Graham, when he heard that some talked of seceding: "Let them go," he said, "let them go without the walls, they are but the dung of the sacrifice." This caustic and unpardonable allusion to the removal of the offal of the Jewish sacrifices, without the walls of the temple, was spoken under a sudden impulse of feeling, but was characteristic of the man—bold and resolute in pursuing what he believed to be right, though often devoid of tact.

The two colored congregations, Methodist and Baptist, are comfortably churched, with creditable organizations.

In connection with the spiritual life of the time, it is rather surprising that lottery was not looked upon as a form of gambling. In 1832, Lexington authorized the raising of $12,000.00 by this means for the purpose of paving the streets and bringing water into town.

The history of Lexington's water supply is interesting. Nothing is more important to a village or a city than abundant water. The early settlers saw to it that they should locate their homes within easy access of this important feature. A fair sized river, several streams and unfailing springs must have been a deciding element in the establishing of Lexington. This location is remarkable for its numerous sources of water supply and also for its fine natural drainage. The spring most used in the early days of the town and the college was at the corner of Jefferson and Washington Streets. (The spot is now covered by the pool room.) It was several feet below the level of the street and was enclosed in a stone box. A tall wooden pump, with a long iron handle, was the means by which the water was lifted to street level for accommodation of the multitudi.ous buckets, which hourly came to be filled. The affluent had their water brought to them on sleds or cartwheels.

In the early 1830's water, brought from Brushy Hills through pipes, was connected with the college campus and a hydrant was put in front of the center college building and the pure, sparkling semi-freestone water gushed forth in abundance. From that time the old town pump was all but deserted, except in very hot weather when "ice-cold" drinking water was wanted. Like all town pumps, this one had a history. Many scenes occurred there between the students and the townspeople.

A summer night's amusement was bathing at the pump. Unhappily, the sport would sometimes begin too early in the evening. At such times, Mr. Gold would rush forth like a roaring lion and immediately would occur either a fight or a foot race, perhaps a succession of fights, followed by arrests and examinations by the magistrates and the board of trustees. From such beginnings set in a state of war, known as the "war between the students and the mechanics." The armed sentinels patrolled the college grounds, while squads of the enemy, armed with knives, river jacks, and sticks, hung around the outskirts.

The old Back Spring, Letcher's Spring, and Plunkett's, all played their part in the early days of Lexington.

The first day that water came into town through pipes was a gala day. A huge crowd assembled in front of the Washington Inn (now the Rock-bridge Motor Company), kept by Robert McDowell, to see water gush from the pipe. Hydrants were placed along the streets. Each householder possessed a key to the hydrant, as a protection against waste by the careless.

Many residents had rather primitive bathrooms, generally disconnected from the house. A trough from the hydrant supplied cold water, and hot water was carried in kettles from the kitchen. Tubs large enough to lie down in were considered quite a luxury and "gentlemen" would often lie down in their "abundant" water to read. The less fortunate had foot tubs and Sitz baths. The Sitz bath was a very large, flat tub, with a wide brim, like a hat, upon which one could "sit and bathe."

CHAPTER VIII: THE BEGINNING OF WASHINGTON AND LEE UNIVERSITY

PART I

FOREMOST among the educational triumphs of the early settlers in the Valley of Virginia are Washington and Lee University and the Virginia Military Institute. Both have exerted a fine influence upon Southern education and thereby upon the world.

Augusta Academy, the very germ of Washington and Lee University was founded in 1749 by Robert Alexander, a Master of Arts of Trinity College, Dublin. This was the first mathematical and classical school in the Valley and was located near Staunton. Alexander was succeeded by the Reverend John Brown, who moved the school to Old Providence and then to New Providence. Shortly before the Revolution, it was again moved to Mount Pleasant, about one mile west of Fairfield, the highest point of the Ridge. The short time of its sojourn here was amid the heavings and tossings of the all-absorbing Revolution.

"Before dwelling upon the origin of this great institution, take a rapid glance at the people who reared it and who made so great a contribution to the development of the Colony, to the Commonwealth, and to America. They were Scotch-Irish and professors of the Presbyterian faith. But who were the Scotch-Irish? They were the people who, wherever they were borne on the tumultuous tide of a various and constant emigration that rolled through the channels of centuries, carried with them a stout and stalwart body, a clear head, a physical courage that feared not mortal enemy, a moral courage superior to disaster, indomitable industry, a scorn of ease, a love of letters, a thirst for freedom, and who inscribed on their banners the name of the Lord God of Hosts. Confined to the region of recorded history, we traverse a space of two thousand years and read in the thrilling narrative of Caesar, his conflicts with the native Britons and take our seat in the trireme of Agricola as he courses for the first time around the island of Britain and gather from the pages of Tacitus the lineaments of that picture which the Roman general presented to his son-in-law and which now thrills with the intensity of its colors. From the Roman Invasion to the Norman Conquest in 1066, a period of a thousand years, both North and South Britain were subdued and overrun by hordes of the Scandinavian family and as the Scottish rivers were as easily accessible by the ships of the piratical Northmen as the British, the Forth and the Tay were invaded simultaneously with the Humber and the Thames.

"After the Norman Conquest, Scotland received a large accession of Anglo-Saxon from the South. While the Southern part of the island was becoming modified, in the course of generations, by the blood, language, and habits of the Normans, the simple tongue and taste of the Anglo-Saxon prevailed in Scotland. Hence the purity of the Scotch language in its Anglo-Saxon aspect above the English tongue, which had become mixed with the Latin race. These facts are mentioned to set aside the common error of regarding the Scotch as wholly Celtic or ancient British, instead of being in the main a component part of the Anglo-Saxon family.

"The history of Scotland from the first landing of the Anglo-Saxons to the reign of Mary, Queen of Scots, an interval of more than fifteen hundred years, presents the saddest picture of ignorance, blood, rapine, and violence, variegated indeed at times with intervals of extraordinary splendor, which the historic muse ever drew for the warning and instruction of mankind. It was a time of perpetual wars, within and without. After the Conquest its chiefs were Normans—Randolph, Bruce, Wallace, Campbell, Maxwell, and the Stuarts, and they assumed a kingly jurisdiction.

"The question arises how, from such a people, whose hands were stained by the gore of two thousand years, could spring that type which we call Scotch-Irish? People who built in the same enclosure the fortress, the church and the school: who held the sword in one hand and the Bible in the other: whose valor subdued the foe in the field and in the recesses of the forest, and whose piety filled their humble temples and homesteads with prayer and praises.

"The Reformation in Scotland and the master spirit of John Knox wrought the great change in these people. The Catholic Church exerted a beneficial influence for many years upon the Scotch people. It preserved the records of the past and fostered a taste for letters and, during the dreary millennium of the Middle Ages, it was the one channel through which the blessings of Christianity were conveyed to the people. It presented the one and only curb to the despotism of the feudal system and softened its atrocities. The Catholic Church was kind to the peasant. In the valleys of Scotland it raised those wonderful cathedrals, whose ruins excite the modern traveler. In the distant Hebrides it reared its magnificent structures on whose altars were kindled the flame that shone far and wide over those stormy seas.

"It was during the conflict with this church that the Scotch character was developed.

"Intelligence being the soul of Protestantism, the great Scotch reformers taught their flock and ruled them with rigor. Knox knew that generations must pass away and that Protestantism too, must pass, unless the young were well instructed in the rudiments of knowledge and in the doctrines of the faith. The Presbyterian form of government was the purest republican form of government. Upon ascending the throne, James tried to remodel the Presbyterian Church, thus adding to the already intolerable situation. Soon followed the bloody persecutions of the Restoration and especially during the viceroyalty of the Duke of York, when thousands of men, women, and children were put to death, in a time of profound peace, on account of religious non-conformity. From the Reformation to the departure for the New World, a period of a century and a half, the Scot clung to the Bible as the sheet-anchor of his faith.

"In the early part of the eighteenth century came a pleasant vision over the mind of the Scotch-Irish. The Revolution they termed glorious, as it placed William and Mary on the British throne. For the House of Hanover they cherished affection.

"They were fascinated by reports from the New World, its fertile valleys and mighty streams and, above all, where men might worship God without interference. It was vain to talk to them about the wild savages, for two thousand years they had hardly been without a weapon in their hands. They did not fear the dangers of the New World, so long as they could develop rural life and enjoy political and religious liberty. They plunged into the depths of the forest, cleared farms, built homes, churches and schools. To teach the rudiments of the mother tongue, the reading of the Bible, the longer and shorter catechism of the Westminister Confession, those consummate achievements of human intellect, to worship God in sincerity and truth and to mingle the music of Virgil and Horace, of Livy and Tacitus, of Homer and Sophocles, of Herodotus and Thucydides, of Demosthenes and Aeschines, with the clangor of the ax, with the crack of the rifle and the yell of the Indian, all contributed to the establishing of Augusta Academy."

From Dr. Henry Ruffner's papers is this description of Mount Pleasant:

"The neighborhood was well settled for a new country. The air was remarkably salubrious and living was cheap. The rustic schoolhouse stood in a grove of forest oaks, which shed a shade over it in summer and supplied it with abundant fuel in winter. A spring of pure water gushed from the rocks nearby. From underneath the spreading tree-tops the students had a view of the surrounding country and the Blue Ridge in the distance. In short, all the features of the place made it a fit habitation of the woodland muse and merited the name, Mount Pleasant.

"Hither about thirty youths of the great Valley repaired to taste of the Pierian Spring, thirty six years after the first settlement on the Borden Tract. Of reading, writing and ciphering the boys had acquired some knowledge, but with few exceptions, Latin, Greek, Algebra, Geometry and other scholastic mysteries were things of which some of them had heard and knew, perhaps, to be covered up in the learned heads of their pastors, but of the nature and use of which, they had no conception whatsoever.

"The establishing of such a school in the Valley was of great importance. When we consider the results, we need not blush for the humble beginning of the Academy. It was a one-room log house. The students brought their dinners and stayed all day. They conned their lessons either in the school-room or under the trees, where breezes whispered, and birds caroled. Their clothes were homespun and their amusements were simple, even for that day. They consisted of running, leaping and pitching quoits. Cards, back-gammon, flutes, fiddles and marbles were hardly known to those sober boys of the forest. Firing pistols and shotguns to kill little birds for sport, they would have considered an unworthy occupation and a waste of time. As for frequenting "tippling shops," this was impossible, as no such catch-penny lures for students existed and would not have been tolerated. Had any huckster of liquors, nicknacks and explosive crackers opened his "con-fectionery" in those days, the old Puritan morality was yet strong enough to abate the nuisance."

In this rustic seminary, born of the habitual esteem for learning among the Scotch-Irish, with a genial nurture in the classic taste and training of their pastors, hereditary examplars for their people, not more in piety than in political virtue, many young men began their liberal education and became distinguished in ecclesiastic and civil affairs.

The Presbyterians determined the Scotch flavor of the Valley. Out of their ingrained devotion to religion and education came the little academy, the very beginning of our great school at Lexington, which, though it keeps an evangelical religious spirit, nevertheless, long since divorced itself from denominational cleavage.

It was here, under the beautiful forest oaks of Mount Pleasant, that James Priestly spouted the orations of Demosthenes, in the original Greek with all the fire of the Grecian orator himself, and Mr. Willson, the rector's brilliant assistant, recited hundreds of lines from Homer. About this time, Mr. Graham, the rector, gave some instruction in the science of govern-ment and was accused of meddling in politics.

Dr. Campbell, of Lexington, visited the infant seminary in 1775 and left this pleasant picture:

"I happened at Mount Pleasant Academy during the superintendence of Mr. Graham. It was the hour of recreation. Here was seen a large as-semblage of youths, apparently, ten to twenty years of age. They were mostly engaged in feats of strength, speed and agility, each emulous to surpass his fellows in those exercises, for which youth of their age generally possess a strong predilection. Presently the sound of a horn summoned them to the business of the afternoon. The sports were dropped as if by magic—now you see them conning their afternoon lessons. The dignity of the Preceptor gave him respectability and he was respected.

"The industry, proficiency and decorous demeanor of the boys gave éclat to the young institution. This quondam of the muses was truly sacred ground. A few obscure clergymen, without political power, without pe-cuniary resources, Indians before and the British behind—they trusted

God, labored, persevered and succeeded. They have long slept with their fathers, but their good work goes on."

On the 6th of May, 1776, Hanover Presbytery, under whose direction Augusta Academy had been established, decided to move it from Mount Pleasant to Timber Ridge, where Captain Alexander Stuart and Samuel Houston offered a site of several acres, upon which the neighbors agreed to build a hewd-log house, twenty four by twenty-eight feet, one story and a half high, besides their subscriptions and assurance of firewood for twenty years, gratis. At the same time the academy was going up on Timber Ridge, the village (later Lexington) acquired its first school. It stood near the present site of the railroad station and was conducted by John Reardon, a classically educated young Irishman, who had been transported for crime and sold in Baltimore to pay for his passage, and bought by William Alexander of Lexington.

The Presbytery of Hanover was for a long time the only Presbytery in Virginia. In its early existence it was strengthened by the accession of the descendants of the French Huguenots, who had been driven from their own country by the revocation of the Edict of Nantes and had settled on the James River. They were Calvinistic Protestants and therefore good Presbyterians.

At this time the Reverend William Graham was appointed rector and James Montgomery, assistant, with a board of trustees, among whom were some of the most eminent men of the age in which they lived. They won battles, decided the fate of the great political questions which preceded the Revolution of 1776, and aided in the measures necessary to achieve the blessings of the event. Through the succeeding years the men who have served on this board have typified the great men who founded the institution.

Incited by the patriotic spirit of the time, at the first meeting after the Battle of Lexington, the trustees changed the name of the Academy to Liberty Hall. This name first appeared May 13, 1776, and in those tumultuous times only by careful and tender nursing could the infant academy have survived. The enlightened policy and pious zeal of the Presbyterian clergy, the contributions of the Presbyterians of the Valley, the energy and talents of the rector and the attention given its affairs by the trustees, together with gratuitous aid in land, labor and materials of the local citizens, contributed much to the continuance of the Academy.

It was a bold act of defiance, two months before the Declaration of Independence, with the British flag still floating over Virginia, to adopt the name, Liberty Hall Academy. It was the first outburst of the Rockbridge spirit, which the next year named the county seat for the Battle of Lexington. In 1785 the academy was again moved to Mulberry Hill near Lexington. The cost of the new plant, exclusive of labor, material and land was two hundred pounds. The trustees claimed that here the school "enjoyed an undisturbed retirement for study."

Upon the completion of the Academy this salutation was given: "And now our vessel is safely under way, with sails filled, streamers floating, gliding gallantly over the broad ocean with a strong western breeze —may all on board, fore and aft, from the Captain to the cabin-boy, have good health, good cheer and a prosperous voyage."

The Presbytery now ceased its official supervision and since that time the school has been presided over by its self-perpetuating board of trustees, as its sole guardians, with legal right to manage its interests and to bestow literary degrees. At the first formal commencement on the second Wednesday in September, 1785, twelve A.B. degrees were given.

By 1795 the academy had acquired properties of considerable proportions and this is better appreciated when it is remembered that it was contributed by people with rather scanty funds who, in their own generation, had fled from persecution, which had impoverished them before they left their homes across the ocean. They had settled in a new and uncultivated wilderness, engaged in a relentless struggle with the savages about them. The effects of the Revolution were still present and most of them were without the comforts of daily life.

The Revolution brought a great change over the youth of the land and caused Graham to lose much of his zeal for the liberal education of young men. They were no longer the moral, unsophisticated boys of the ante-Revolutionary period in the Valley, where the fashionable vices of the world were hardly known. Many had been taken to camps and towns, where depraved manners grew familiar to their eyes and corrupted their hearts. On their return they communicated these vices to others and now, as they gathered in school, the good manners and rural simplicity of Mount Pleasant Academy were gone and a generation of profane swearers, card-players, idlers and tippling rioters appeared.

It is of interest to note the quality and price of the diet of the students about this time—1794. "For breakfast, coffee, tea or chocolate with bread and butter. For dinner, bread and meat, with sauce of vegetables. For supper, bread, butter and milk." Excellent fare for young men. High living in a literary institution was considered highly undesirable; it was costly, it injured the health, it obfuscated the intellect and induced habits of sensual indulgence. This diet cost the students $23.75 for the session of five months. The student's room rent was fixed at one half dollar for the session, unless five boys stayed in one room and then they paid two dollars among them.

In the course of time the question arose as to the wisdom of keeping the boys domiciled in the academy building. The result was that they were permitted to live in the homes of the village, where they would be less rude—yet, good manners did not prevail when they ate apart from the families with whom they lived. The worst consequences of this private boarding was that the fare became entirely too luxurious and the homes that gave the most luxurious fare got the most patronage. By 1817 the price of board in these homes rose from eight to eleven dollars per month and then the students, like Dives, fared sumptuously every day. This pleased them more than it did their parents, who had to pay for their delicate living. This was particularly hard on the poor boys, generally the best students, who cared more for their heads than their stomachs.

It was considered good, however, for the boys to be in the homes, rather than congregated in one place, where freedom of speech and action often terminated in rudeness. In private families the presence of females imposed a wholesome influence.

The student body was composed of boys from different parts of the State, from Tennessee, Kentucky, and the Carolinas. Local and social prejudices were strong and despite the fact that the authorities had a ruling against the boys calling each other nicknames, they did it. Such awful ones as Tuckahoe and Kohee. They also played tricks and hurled jibes.

The students must have had lots of fun breaking rules, for they lived under a network of them. There was a rule that all meetings must be opened and closed with prayer. Still another that students must rise and make a proper bow when the rector, tutor, or other gentlemen came in or went out. Readings of the students included Livy, Horace, Xenophon's Anabasis, and many others with which students of a later day would be unfamiliar. Such reading supplied that fine cultural background typical of the time.

Much has been said of the serious attitude of some of the searchers after truth in those early days. However, love and romance played a part then as always. Many of these boys, during their busy days in old Lexington found time for other things! This is a typical case: "To return to our young divinity student, whom we left standing at the door of old Washington College, being prevented from entering Yale College, because of the prevalence of yellow fever, which had caused a suspension of its exercises, he turned aside into the parts of Lexington and completed his education at old Liberty Hall, but recently endowed by George Washington and the name changed in honor of its patron. He matriculated in 1802 and was graduated in 1804, appeared as a candidate in 1806, and was licensed to preach in 1808. He studied the languages under Daniel Blain and read theology with Dr. Baxter, but these occupations did not absorb all of his time. Our theological student, during his six years in the classic village of Lexington attended to other matters; for, two months before his licensure by the Presbytery, he led to the altar, Rebecca Walkup, the pretty and sprightly daughter of a prosperous merchant of the town."

A divinity student had to give proof of his acquirements. One read a Latin exegesis on "Christus Sit Deus," a homily on the Nature of Faith and, after this, he read a lecture on Lazarus and Dives. This done, he was pronounced sound in the faith and in intellect. He was considered to be of unblemished character and strong hopes were entertained that he would become a respectable minister of the gospel.

While many of the students of Liberty Hall did not have extra strong literary ambitions, yet there was always a nucleus of first-class ones, who became sound and thorough scholars and, whatever criticism may be made of the academy in this, one of its most critical periods, it turned out then as it has in every decade of its history, many creditable men who were an honor to their Alma Mater and to their country. Of some of the boys it was said that instead of knowing their books, they knew where the orchards were and the bee-gum and the wild strawberries. They could shoot well and often engaged in 'possum hunts. They could handle stones like a Benjamite, shoot arrows and play marbles and often engaged in a fisticuff.

A certain intolerably idle and mischievous boy was dismissed from school and, as he was saying good-bye to "Professor" John Henry, the janitor, who was a Nestor among the boys, the janitor said: "Mr. ......
I'm mighty 'fraid the next time I hear from you, it will be from the penitentiary." "No, 'Fes,' the next time you hear from me it will be from the theological seminary." And sure enough it was. He became one of the great preachers of his day.

The institution has been successively known as Augusta Academy, 1749-1782; Liberty Hall Academy, 1782-1789; Washington Academy, 1789-1813; Washington College, 1813-1871, and since that time, Washington and Lee University, thus honoring the two greatest Virginians, Washington, who gave it financial assistance and the right to use his name and Lee, who gave it himself.

Its hallowed associations give it a place that is unique among all other American universities.

Those who have guided its destiny from the beginning to the present time have been among the most able men of the day in which they lived. Wise and fearless leaders, marked by high scholarship, they left their impress upon the world and their influence goes on to the end of time.

Robert Alexander, the founder, was succeeded by the following:

John Buchanan
J. Edmondson: 1760
John Brown: 1762
Ebeneza Smith: 1770
Archibald Alexander: 1774
William Graham: 1774
John Montgomery: 1776

Rev. William Graham: 1782
Samuel L. Campbell: 1796
George A. Baxter: 1799
Lewis Marshall (Brother of Chief Justice John Marshall): 1830
Henry Vethake (Native of British Guiana): 1834
Henry Ruffner: 1836
George Junkin: 1848
Robert E. Lee: 1865
G. W. Custis Lee: 1870
William L. Wilson: 1897
Henry St. George Tucker (Acting): 1900
George H. Denny: 1901
John L. and Harry D. Campbell (Acting): 1911
Henry Louis Smith: 1912
Robert H. Tucker (Acting): 1929
Francis Pendleton Gaines: 1930.

Dr. Gaines is a man of youth, vision, mature judgment, of personality extraordinary and a winner in every contact. He is a worthy successor of this long line of gifted men. He accomplishes the almost impossible, that of handling, harmoniously, the student body, the faculty, the trustees and the alumni. His home is the Manor House for the student life, where he and his charming wife entertain so graciously the boys, their parents and other guests of the University.

Though many schools bear Washington's name, this is the only one that he directly sponsored and knowingly endowed with his name. Lee's name was a posthumous honor, not a gift.

"The academy's course of study in 1804 was practically the same that was followed at Princeton and was adhered to for many years. It was a meagre and ill-arranged curriculum. Students continued in the grammar school until they could pass an examination in Virgil and the Greek Testament. Then they gave their entire freshman year to Latin and Greek, without an admixture of other studies. In the first term they read in Horace and Cicero's Orations, and in the second term they read Lucian, Xenophon and Homer. Latin and Greek antiquities ceased to be attended to after the first year. The second year they spent wholly in the study of mathematics. The third year was spent in geography, natural philosophy, and astronomy, and the fourth year was devoted to Blair's Lectures and Logic and Burlemaque's Natural Law, and Locke, Reid and Stewart on the mind."

It was claimed that so great was the academy's influence during its years —1749 to 1796—when it received the endowment from Washington that, had it ceased to exist at that time, had the plough passed over its foundations, had its charter been given to the winds, it had already accomplished an amount of good difficult to estimate. It directed the attention of a rising community, under the most unpropitious circumstances, to a large and liberal moral and intellectual culture. It sent forth hundreds of educated men, who taught schools, filled professorships, brought the aid of science to the Revolution, diffused in the domestic circles the blessings of learning and religion, filled pulpits, shone at the bar, in the halls of legislature and at foreign courts, and whose influence on the mind and heart of man is still felt.

Regarding William Graham, Grigsby gives this brief but clear sketch: "The facts of his life are few. He sprang from a family which for a thousand years had been conspicuous in the annals of Scotland, from the hovel to the palace, in arts, in arms, in eloquence and in song. It was a daring man by the name of Graham who first broke through the walls of Agricula, which the Roman general had built between the firths of Clyde and Forth, to keep off the incursions of the Northern Britons and the ruins of which, still visible, are called to this day, the ruins of Graham's Dyke. They were borderers, as distinguished from Highlanders and, on one occasion, three hundred of the family were banished to Ireland. It is not improbable that the blood of the fiery moss-trooper flowed in the veins of our founder. One of the fairest personifications of the race may be seen from the pen of Sir Walter Scott in his Legend of Montrose. Michael Graham, the father of our William, emigrated from Ireland between 1720 and 1730 and, on the 19th of December 1746, in Paxton Township, five miles from the present site of the Capitol of Pennsylvania, William Graham was born.

"His parents were poor and lived on the outskirts of civilization, and young Graham had none of the advantages which are so efficient in developing the faculties of the mind. He attended the common school, when such existed, and until his twenty-second year, worked in the fields with his father.

"Two things are told of him, which have no relation to each other, but which showed their effect upon his subsequent career. He was fond of dancing and he probably engaged in the Highland Fling, cut the pigeon-wing or danced the horn-pipe as readily as any of his ancestors, who were famed for dancing, ever did before him and with as much ease and grace as he afterwards displayed in solving the most abstruse problems of metaphysics or in explaining a dark allusion in Juvenal or in a doubtful passage in Tacitus. The other was that as his frontier home was ever liable to the inroads of the savages, he learned the use of the rifle and was as familiar with it as he afterwards became with those other instruments of Science, which Hanover Presbytery and the people of Augusta had procured in the midst of war and in the sacrifices of a mountain life to promote the cause of a generous education. On one occasion, the dogs about his father's

frontier cabin began to bark, and one of his sisters detected movements of
Indians and the family determined to make for the fort. Young William,
with musket loaded, headed the sally and conducted the family in safety
to the fort.

"In this stern school of courage he acquired that wonderful faculty, so
often exhibited throughout his life, of stripping a subject of its present and
temporary difficulties and of looking to distant results, which marked his
course in the greatest political crisis in the age in which he lived.

"At one and twenty, that religious change, which at a later date came
over the gigantic mind of Chalmers and which led the Scotch divine to
lay all the wealth of the stars and the greenest garlands of philosophy at
the foot of the Cross, came over the mind of Graham. He determined to
study theology and with only his own exertions to support him and the
light of his mother's love as a lamp to his pathway, he began the study of
Latin. When he had mastered the elementary studies, he entered Princeton College, which was then radiant with its distinguished President,
Witherspoon, who was to sign the Declaration of Independence and the
Articles of Confederation. Witherspoon looked upon the descendants of
his own ancestral land with kindly feelings and he had that rare faculty of
inspiring his students to a love of study.

"In 1773, William Graham was graduated with his class and he held the
same high rank among them which afterward distinguished him in every
sphere in which he moved. He defrayed his expenses at Princeton with
his own efforts. In 1775, he was received as a minister of the Presbyterian
Church and on May 6, 1776, the headship of Liberty Hall Academy de-
volved upon him, with the duties of rector.

"The system of studies followed by him was well calculated to develop
the faculties of the mind and to prepare young men to engage in the active
duties of life. He insisted upon the importance of classical literature as a
proper foundation of a liberal education, with a thorough training in mathematics and the sciences and a knowledge dependent upon the two departments. Moral and Intellectual Philosophy, and introduction to theology,
he also taught, as the gates called Beautiful, leading to that glorious temple
not built with human hands and whose foundations were laid in the Divine
Will.

"While he recognized other authorities, he worked out his own system
of theology, which the eminent Archibald Alexander declared to be the
clearest and fullest of any that had been published on the subject.

"When we reflect that Graham had only a few imperfectly educated
students from the neighboring hills and homesteads around him and, in
the absence of all emulation, put forth his powers so grandly, we can readily
imagine what he would have done if, like Dugald Stewart, Thomas Brown
and Chalmers, he had been surrounded by classes of hundreds of highly

trained young men and a daily auditory of eminent men to quicken his powers and to give him full scope for the excursions of his genius. While we concede that just supremacy to the skill of Graham, which he so justly deserved, it is proper to say that he was assisted by some competent tutors, among them, James Priestly, a poor Rockbridge boy, whose genius was detected by Graham, who instructed him. Priestly devoted his talents to Latin and Greek. He inspired his students to a fondness for literature and Archibald Alexander ascribed his fondness to study to the instruction of Priestly.

"The chair of the professor was the throne from which Graham wielded his greatest influence upon the mind of his generation. The main business of his life was to teach. He considered the object of academic education was to discipline the powers and not to fill the mind with a multiplicity of acquirements, to form the mind and let it work out its own victories. He saw the force of language as an element in the affairs of men and the advantage of a thorough mastery over his native tongue by every student. He saw that the Greeks, who had left us the purest specimens in writing, studied no other language than their own, it was the most perfect that existed and rested on a Pelasgian foundation, it was homogeneous and had attained perfection. But, in looking at the teachings of the Romans, he saw that the policy of teaching a single tongue did not apply and that the Roman student studied, with all diligence, the Greek language. He saw the reason for this. The Latin was a compound language and rested on an Etruscan base, but it borrowed from all literatures and especially from the Greek, nor did it possess those elements of eloquence, history and poetry in which the Greek abounded. He saw that the best orators, historians and poets were those who were most intimate with Greek literature. He then looked into the elements of his own tongue. He recognized in it not only the youngest in the family of languages, but that it was made up of more languages than any other and demanded a more critical study than had been devoted by either Rome or Greece to any foreign tongue.

"Looking to the example of England, he observed that the system of education which had produced her Newtons, her Bacons and her Lockes embraced a thorough knowledge of Greek literature. Hence he taught the Latin and the Greek languages and, as far as possible, the languages that lean upon them and also mathematics and the sciences that lean upon them. He believed that a youth that had been well drilled in these two departments had a good foundation on which to raise any superstructure of active or of studious life that might be desired.

"Such was William Graham, cradled in the forests of extreme frontier civilization, exposed to the incursions of the savages. He resolved to preach the gospel and without means, sustained himself and won the applause of

Witherspoon and the affection of his classmates. He was one of the great powers of his generation.

"While performing the great business of his life, in the double capacity of a servant of his Heavenly Master and as a professor in various departments of science and impressing upon the minds of thousands the cardinal doctrines of the Christian faith and the elements of a large and generous education and building up an institution, which should continue the good work for untold generations to come, this good and great man closed his career and as if the lesson of so pure and so august a life should be purified from the dross of selfishness, he died poor. The talents which would have wreathed his brow with the laurels of the forum and the senate and filled his coffers with the glittering rewards of successful industry, were spent in a private sphere and devoted to his country and his God.

"Posterity bends with reverence at his grave and looks with interest at the mouldering ruins of his infant seminary and traces the careers of thousands, whose genius was kindled by his instruction, who cast the benignant light of letters and love around many a domestic hearth, whose sword flamed on the field of battle, whose eloquence was heard from the pulpit, the bar and on the floors of assemblies, which decided the questions of the age and whose patriotism, waked into vigor by his voice and example, has been the pride and bulwark of their country."

Future generations will delight to ascend the hill, on which rests his Liberty Hall Academy ruins amid fallen trees of a primeval forest and will always remember, among the priceless traditions of Washington and Lee, the memory of William Graham.

After sleeping for more than a hundred years in old St. John's churchyard in Richmond, he was removed to Lexington, to the campus of Washington and Lee. On the marble slab over his last resting place is this epitaph:

Sacred

to the memory

of the

Rev. William Graham

Founder and for twenty years Rector

of

Washington College

in

Rockbridge County

Virginia

Who was born in the State of Pennsylvania,

December 19, 1746
And died in the City of Richmond
June 17, 1799
He was distinguished for the strength and
Originality of his genius;
and the successful tenor of his exertions
in behalf of solid literature and
evangelical piety.

It is not an insignificant coincidence in the mutations of human affairs that William Graham, the pillar and stay of Washington College in its early days, had as his classmate and intimate friend at Princeton in 1773, Henry Lee, the protege of Washington and the father of Robert E. Lee, who, at a low ebb in the history of Washington College, rescued it and so auspiciously advanced the work of Graham, Washington, and the patriots of the past.

In 1773, Henry Lee presented Graham with a copy of Belshaw's *Lectures on Natural Philosophy*, which is still preserved by Graham's descendants.

In the graduating class at Princeton, of which Graham was a member, fourteen became ministers, four became college presidents and three became governors of states.

Reverend Graham left six children, two boys and four girls. One boy became a minister and the other a physician.

Foote reports that "the great error of his life was when he withdrew from Liberty Hall at the time he did, and to those who scan carefully the cause of things as they passed along, looking at the consequences, as well as the causes, by the light of after events, it now seems plain enough that Mr. Graham made a great mistake in the removal.

"The influence of William Graham did not die with his body, nor was it overwhelmed with his temporal losses. It has been spreading like the western waters he so admired. The current grows broader and deeper as it rolls on to the great ocean. We will not say that the large number of eminent men introduced to public life through the instrumentality of education at Liberty Hall, would not have been in public life, or as eminent, had Mr. Graham not been connected with Liberty Hall; but he was the efficient instrument chosen of God for the purpose of introducing these lawyers and political men and ministers into their sphere of life. Without him, Liberty Hall was but a name; by him, Liberty Hall will live forever, for who can forget her sons? Washington College, with her stately and spacious edifices, has succeeded Liberty Hall, with her small frame and stone building for fifty students. The endowment of the Father of His

Country has changed the name of the institution, but posterity will read on these buildings, a thousand fold multiplied, the bright everbeaming letters, WILLIAM GRAHAM."

Typical scenery about Lexington

The Main Portico, Washington and Lee University, a promenade
where thousands have walked to fame.

The Old Blue Hotel

Old mill, Rockbridge County (Note man against wall)

R. E. Lee Memorial Church

Dedication of memorial statue to Stonewall Jackson in Lexington Presbyterian Cemetery, July 21, 1891

CHAPTER IX: WASHINGTON AND LEE UNIVERSITY
PART II

L IBERTY HALL'S primal dowry was a tribute from the Father of His Country to patriotism and valor, so long illustrated under his own eye, from the fatal day of Braddock's defeat till freedom's crowning conflict on the plains of Yorktown. This endowment from George Washington came at a critical time in the academy's history, when it faced bankruptcy. In its distressed condition the trustees knew not whither to turn for aid. The creditors were pressing them and there seemed no way to save the school. An appeal had been made to the State Legislature, all in vain.

When considering what disposition he should make of the James River Canal stock, which the Legislature had given him in recognition of his great service in attaining the independence of America, Washington had Staunton, Lexington, and Fincastle in mind. He selected Lexington because a seminary had already been started there and nothing had been done in the other places. He said that he preferred to aid those who had already aided themselves. Liberty Hall, after a precarious and struggling existence, at length acquired the assurance of means with which to meet its debts and to increase its usefulness as a seminary of learning.

When the trustees obtained official notice of the donation, they addressed the following to the illustrious patron of the Academy:

"Sir:

"It was not earlier than September, 1797, that we were officially informed of your liberal donation to Liberty Hall Academy.

"Permit us, as its immediate guardians, to perform the pleasing duty of expressing those sentiments of gratitude which so generous an act naturally inspires. We have long been sensible of the disadvantages to which a literary institution is necessarily subjected whilst dependent on precarious funds for support. Reflecting particularly on the many difficulties through which this seminary has been conducted since the first moments of its existence, we cannot but be greatly affected by an event which secures to it a permanent and independent establishment. Convinced, as we are, that public prosperity and security are intimately connected with the diffusion of knowledge, we look around with the highest satisfaction on its rapid advances in these United States; unfeignedly rejoicing that the citizen who has long been distinguished as the asserter of the liberties of his country, adds to this illustrious character the no less illustrious one of Patron of the Arts and Literature. And we trust that no effort will be wanting on our part to encourage whatever branches of knowledge may be of general utility.

"That you may long enjoy, besides the uninterrupted blessings of health and repose, the superior happiness which none but those who deserve it can enjoy and which arises from the reflection of having virtuously and eminently promoted the best interests of mankind, is the fervent prayer of the Trustees of Washington Academy, late Liberty Hall.

By order of the Board,

His Excellency
George Washington,

SAMUEL HOUSTON, Clerk.

Late President of the United States."

To this General Washington returned the following reply:

"Mount Vernon, 17th June 1798

"Gentlemen:

"Unaccountable as it may seem, it is nevertheless true, that the address with which you were pleased to honor me, dated April 12th. never came to my hand till the 14th. inst.

"To promote literature in this rising empire and to encourage the Arts have ever been amongst the warmest wishes of my heart. If the donation, which the generosity of the Legislature of the Commonwealth of Virginia has enabled me to bestow upon Liberty Hall, now, by your politeness called Washington Academy, is likely to prove a means to accomplish these ends, it will contribute to the gratification of my desires.

"Sentiments like those which have flowed from your pen excite my gratitude, whilst I offer my best vows for the prosperity of the Academy and for the honor and happiness of those under whose auspices it is conducted.

GEO. WASHINGTON."

By solemn compact on the part of the Legislature of Virginia, in consideration of retiring the stock of the old James River Company, the treasurer of the Commonwealth of Virginia is to pay to Washington College six per cent interest on the sum of fifty thousand dollars, annually, forever.

Every student who attends Washington and Lee is a beneficiary of this great gift.

The academy's student body about this time numbered forty and the tuition was thirty dollars a year. Besides the rector there were two other instructors, Daniel Blain and Edward Graham, teaching the following subjects: mental philosophy, chemistry, astronomy, Latin, Greek, French, English, Hebrew and geography. Most of the boys came on horseback, carrying their possessions in saddlebags.

The two instructors were men of very high scholarship and the rector could not have found more competent assistants. Edward Graham was a brother of the rector and taught for awhile at New London Academy and was instrumental in starting Conrad Speece on his brilliant career.

Daniel Blain, a man of unusual talents, was best known for his lovely spirit. He was witty and fond of jokes, but there was no sting in his mirth. His goodness was without dogmatism and was redolent of that sweetness which made even the wicked love him. Such a man could not be otherwise than popular in college and community. The fine qualities of these two instructors lives on in many valued descendants.

Miss Mary Blain, a granddaughter of Daniel Blain, living in Louisville, Kentucky, is an annual visitor to Lexington and, while here last summer, celebrated her ninety-fourth birthday. With none of the infirmities which such years would suggest, she is a charming personality and tells interesting and intimate memories of Stonewall Jackson, as a young Drill Major at Virginia Military Institute in the early fifties, and of Claude Crozet and his engineering feat of tunnelling the Blue Ridge and building the Chesapeake and Ohio Railroad, in Albemarle County, which she, as a girl, witnessed.

Not all of the semi-local boys in those early days were sent to Lexington. Some went to England, some to Yale College in Connecticut, some to Cambridge University in Massachusetts and others to Nassau Hall in New Jersey.

On Christmas Eve, 1802, the old stone academy was destroyed by fire, losing its entire apparatus, library and furniture. Men, women and children ran the two miles to witness the "conflagration and extinguishment of this focus of elegant learning." A new building was soon seen springing up nearer Lexington, thanks to the generosity of the citizens of the adjacent towns and counties.

Lexington, with its one hundred families, now succeeded, after many attempts, in drawing the academy from its retirement on Mulberry Hill. Many thought to leave Mulberry Hill, with its fine landscape, its ridges and ravines, rocks and cedars, caves and cliffs, wild flowers and bold springs, its umbrageous river, on whose banks the fiery Priestly taught his Greek classes, was highly injudicious. To take boys from such an environment to the association of a village was to defeat the very aim of a college.

Dr. Ruffner says that "we should not censure the people of Lexington because they wanted to make the academy their very own and to have it within the town. They could more conveniently educate their own sons and more copiously extract money from the sons of others. Whether they considered it for the best interests of the academy or not, they were only human and could hardly have preferred the abstract consideration of the interests of learning and virtue to the concrete consideration of the stomach, the back, and the pocket!

"Some considered this change of location the most injudicious measure ever adopted by the trustees. By bringing the institution into immediate contact with the miscellaneous population and frequent gatherings and the tempting shops of a country town, they greatly increased the difficulties of academic government and the temptations to idleness and vice among the students. Henceforth, the students became a part of the town and spent much of their time on the streets. Every sound and every movement of the town communicated itself to them. Every shop and every tavern became familiar to their eyes and ears. Every meeting of every sort, every show, every party, every concert, every riot, every horn, every bell, everything that excites the attention of excitable, imprudent boys, all were henceforth continually attracting the students from their books and from the ways of innocence. These evils would have existed, to some extent, had the academy remained on its Mulberry Hill site, but so considerable a distance between the place of study and the place of temptation would have enabled the faculty, with comparative ease, to guard the youth under their care. Were the town purified of its evil elements, its presence would be an advantage to the school, but in the early days drunkenness and rioting were common. Street fights, even among gentlemen, were also common, and on court days fights among the country people constituted a prominent feature. The college boys often took part in these affairs." However, for good or otherwise, the academy was now in and of the town.

Of the town of Lexington, as the new site for the academy, Dr. Ruffner claimed that it was situated in the center of the largest state in the Union, equally removed from the intense and long-continued cold of the northern winters and from the tedious, sultry and enfeebling summers of the south; elevated above the region where dull and lazy streams, creeping over a dull and lazy surface, produce marshes and stagnant pools, emitting those deleterious vapors which generate agues with their direful train of asthenic diseases, it possesses a climate mild and salubrious. Here mountain streams and mountain breezes, with mountain exercise, insure vigorous health, a keen appetite and easy digestion. All these contribute to the seasonable expansion of the different parts and powers of the youthful constitution. But it seems there must be a supply of food. This is at hand—good solid, roast and boiled, with an accompaniment of esculent vegetables. Also, bread of many varieties, of sound materials, prepared *secundem artem,* with cheese and butter shall not be wanting. And is this not *quantum sufficit?* We think these viands might satisfy an epicure, but, perhaps some fastidious stomach, vitiated by the tyrant custom, not pleased with these alpine productions, will demand foreign articles. These demands shall be met, other climes shall be explored, the stores of the Indies shall be laid under contribution, articles of foreign growth, leaving the place of their nativity and traveling all the way by water, shall arrive at the very verge of Lexington without setting foot on land.

All the country around the academy abounds in all the most necessary articles of living. All the most useful domestic animals, grains, grasses and vegetables, the materials for breadstuff are so plentiful that, after supplying the home market, a large surplus is left for exportation. The buyer here pays nothing more than the prime cost, no profit to dealers, no expense of carriage. Foote reported that the new site enjoyed an extensive prospect of the circumjacent country and a view of the town of Lexington and had, agreeably to its great design, an undisturbed retirement for study. That the situation of the neighborhood, for health, as well as pleasantness, yielded to no land in the Valley. The academy enclosure was primitive and the building unadorned. January 2, 1813, by act of the General Assembly, the name was changed from academy to college and the title of rector to president.

The college museum was established in 1817.

The early treasurers of the college were without salary, but were supposed to use the funds bank fashion in their business. In 1803, Captain William Wilson, a Lexington merchant, was elected treasurer and held the office thirty-seven years. Such was the integrity and responsibility of the men who handled the institution's money that no loss ever occurred.

Captain Wilson built and lived in the stately brick house, on Main Street, with the wide double-decked, pillared portico. The front door of this erstwhile mansion has often been noted the handsomest in the town. (This is now the market place of Harry Walker.)

In 1809 the Graham Literary Society was organized by nine students. This later became the Graham-Lee Society. Secession and slavery were among the first questions debated. Some years later the Washington Society was organized and there was keen rivalry between the two. This rivalry continued until recent years and was entered into by the best brains of the student body. Among the big, outstanding attractions of Final Week, the "Final Celebration of the Literary Societies" was one of paramount interest and importance. Brains and oratory had its place in the appreciation of the public. Mighty factors, these two literary organizations have been in the training of young men who have gone forth as leaders among men.

In 1817 began the controversy regarding the establishing of the University of Virginia. This was a matter of deep concern and discouragement to Washington College, Hampden-Sydney, and William and Mary. Besides the opposition which came from these schools and their friends, were many others who considered such an institution unnecessary. Only the strenuous exertions of the promoters could have carried through the project. When the Legislature voted to establish the institution, the next important feature was its location. At this point the trustees of Washington College determined to enter the contest. They not only offered their property and pointed to the preference of General Washington and the Society of the Cincinnati, but they had a strong financial backing, namely the John Robinson estate and $18,000.00 subscribed by the people of Lexington. This was the best offer made and, doubtless, but for the influence of Thomas Jefferson, would have prevailed. The effect of the creation of a State University at Charlottesville had a depressing effect upon the existing schools. As time went on, however, the old institutions held their own. This gave the State three distinct types of schools, the State, the denominational and the undenominational.

A college which receives no aid from church or State, but is thrown upon its own and makes good has, in many ways, the advantage over the others. Such is Washington and Lee University and its high position and great influence may be partly accounted for because of this. Early in the second decade of the nineteenth century, public exhibitions began to be held at the conclusion of the spring term. This included the exercises of the graduating class with its salutatory, partly in Latin, and a sentimental valedictory, with a speech by each graduate, often humorous and sometimes spoken in costume. The music was by an extempore corps of violins and flutes, but a little later the Lexington Brass Band gave its services, gratis.

About this time a wheelbarrow was added to the working equipment of the college and was so entered in the records of the board.

In 1823, General Sam Houston and General Andrew Jackson visited Washington College.

The Washington Building, with its majestic figure of George Washington crowning the cupola, was built in 1824 by Colonel Jordan and Samuel Darst, with bricks made on the ground. This building remains the loveliest of all the classic halls on the campus. For many decades it was known as "Paradise" and another one story building to the north was known as "Purgatory." These were popular resorts in the early days.

For the laying of the corner stone of this building, a great celebration was planned, for it marked the greatest forward step in building that the institution had known. John Robinson, often called "Jocky Robinson," from his early vocation, had sent from his Hart's Bottom place, a barrel of his fifteen year old whiskey. Robinson was the only man who would have been indulged in a Bacchanalian libation to Pallas, nor would even he have been permitted, had it been foreseen that the offering would be converted into a Circean potation. The barrel contained forty gallons of the finest whiskey that the old Rockbridge sun ever shone upon. This was set up on the campus and, though the authorities looked on with some disfavor, Robinson was too good a friend of the college to be treated with discourtesy. Some of the trustees and faculty members did not partake, but among the spectators was a large contingent of the "tight brigade." Mr. Robinson inaugurated the ceremony of leading officials of the college to the barrel. For a time, some courtesy, in the order of approach, was observed, but the thirsty multitude soon broke through all restraint and, armed with pitchers, dippers, buckets, gourds and basins, some of them more handy than nice, rushed for the barrel and soon gave a glorious exhibition of what free whiskey can do. The agonies of thirst impelled them to the onset, which was irresistible. Before they could complete the process, the barrel was upset and the wreckage about the place, human and inanimate, suggested a battlefield.

Robinson was much embarrassed, for he had intended the gift for the élite and not for the rabble. His estimate of the capacity of the élite was most generous.

About this time the college grounds were fenced and the village pigs and cows moaned the loss of the fine blue grass on College Hill.

At a meeting of the board, October 21, 1829, many rules were passed. One of them was that all students should rise at 5:00 a.m. and assemble for prayer. The hour of prayer was announced by "Professor" John Henry, the negro janitor, by the blowing of a tin horn. The chapel was as cheerless as a barn and as cold in winter as an icehouse. When Professor Calhoun offered prayer, he kept his hands in his pockets to keep them from getting numb. In winter the service was by candle light.

The cardinal hours for retiring were from nine to ten and, though taps was not sounded, lights were out. Early morning prayers ushered in a full day, lasting till about 4:00 p.m., during which time the students were not permitted to leave the grounds. After four they would have their sports, consisting of marbles, cat-ball, chermany, leapfrog, bandy, running and jumping, sometimes excursions to the river for a swim or to the cliffs to pick wild flowers. On Saturday forenoon were the literary society meetings, with Saturday afternoons free. Sunday mornings were lectures by the president on "Natural Theology and the Evidences of Christianity," after which many of the students would attend the Presbyterian Church, principally because the Ann Smith Academy girls went there. Many of the students did not go to church at all and this did not seem to concern anyone.

Sunday afternoons, there were two Bible classes, one in Greek Testament and the other in the English Bible. The rest of the day was free and at night there were many meetings and a great efflorescence of beaux and belles. Nightly at nine, the professors would call at each room to see if the boys were in.

Despite everything, the boys would often slip out and go to the town in squads as late as ten o'clock and visit taverns and barricade the streets with goods boxes, signs, and back-gates, and make night hideous with yells and callithumps.

Instructors did not bother about getting acquainted with the students and had very little to do with them. John Henry was added to the college force in the early part of the nineteenth century. He was a free negro, of gingerbread color, living in Lexington. He was a Methodist, of solid character, polite manners, and infallible tact. He was dignified, without being self-important, active without being fussy. He was popular with the students and was respected by them. They titled him "Fess" (short for Professor). The tin horn which he used was a straight one, five feet long. He was a fine performer and could produce a wonderful variety of melodious sounds. The old stage drivers were expert trumpeters and, as they drove up slowly, in the mud from the river to the town at a quiet hour of the night, their music was sweet and inspiring, especially to citizens who had been long waiting for the tri-weekly mail from the outside world. But none of these drivers could equal the wild, yet tender blasts and the warbling, playful staccatos of John Henry.

Any horn would have sounded good to the boys at twelve and at four and there were always some of them standing near "Fess" as they watched impatiently the slow creeping shadow of the columns of the portico as it approached the twelve o'clock mark on the sandstone curbing. But, strange as it might appear, that horn had a brightening effect upon the sleepy and fretful boys as they gathered in the chapel at five o'clock on a dark winter morning.

John Henry, alas, became one of the victims of the migration to Liberia. In 1826, the African Colonization Society had a flourishing branch in Lexington. All the best citizens seemed to be in favor of the cause, which had attracted attention of the public several years before. Virginia became a leader in the scheme and Rockbridge among the most zealous of the counties. For thirty years liberal contributions were made to the cause by the people of the town and the county and many negroes, both free and slaves freed for the purpose, went from here to Liberia. The majority of those who went died before they became acclimated. They continued to go as late as 1850. John Henry and Diego Evans, two of the most worthy and useful free negroes who ever lived in Lexington, went among the latter parties and they both died shortly after reaching Liberia.

Prior to the Revolution, most of the hired help consisted of redemptioners, or indentured servants. Many were immigrants from Ireland, who had been convicted in England for small offenses and condemned to penal service in America. After a specified service they received their freedom. Others were debtors, sent over by creditors, or poor relations and ne'er-do-wells that they wanted to get rid of. Average time of service was five years. These servants rather liked America and after receiving their freedom, seldom returned to Europe. They were better fed and more humanely treated than in the old country.

After the Revolution this system ceased and negro slave labor grew in favor until the War Between the States.

CHAPTER X: WASHINGTON AND LEE UNIVERSITY

PART III

WASHINGTON'S birthday, 1837, saw inducted into office one of the great presidents of Washington College, Dr. Henry Ruffner, to whose recorded memories is largely due the connected and intensely interesting history we have of the early days of the college.

In his inaugural address, Dr. Ruffner uttered some sentiments rather in advance of his time. Of the barrack life of the students he said: "Students in the higher schools of learning are separated, in a large measure, from the common mass of society and associate chiefly with each other. This seclusion is favorable to their progress in learning, but it generates some moral evils which the faculty find difficult and very often impracticable wholly to correct. It is a common observation that soldiers, seamen and artisans congregated in large manufactories and, in general, wherever men live apart from mixed society, are prone to adopt the vices and neglect the decencies of life. Even the religious communities of monks and nuns, however pure originally, in Europe became most scandalously dissolute. It is only by the intermixture of ages and sexes and the influence of family relations, so wisely ordained by Providence, that human society can be purified and refined."

Regarding the religious attitude of the College, Dr. Ruffner said: "In whatever situation I may be placed, I shall deem it my indispensable duty to teach the Christian religion to all who may be committed to my care. Here, however, to be distinctly understood, by the Christian religion I do not mean the peculiar dogma of any sect or school of theology. In the religious exercises of the college we use no sectarian creed, catechism or formulary. We offer up our prayers to the Divine Father of our race, in terms common to all Christian worshippers. We teach our students to read and to understand for themselves the sacred records to which all Protestants resort for instruction and in our expositions of the sacred text we avoid the discussion of those theological questions which unhappily divide our religious community. Discussions of this sort would be entirely out of place here. The college is designed for the education of youth of all Christian denominations who may choose to resort to us for instruction. We offer to all youth of good, moral character the same benefits and privileges. We enquire not into the articles of their creed; we teach them nothing that is peculiar to our own. We explain to them the grounds and reasons of the Christian faith; we help them to peruse the sacred page and there, at the fountain head, to imbibe the pure and benevolent Spirit of Christ—here we stop. If they are to be indoctrinated with a system of scholastic theology or if they are to be drenched with the bitter waters of sectarian bigotry, they must go elsewhere, we eschew the task."

Except in the emphasis with which they are expressed, these views, in respect to the Christian and yet unsectarian character of Washington and Lee, describe the principles on which the institution has been conducted throughout its history.

Dr. Ruffner's address gave great satisfaction to the trustees and to the friends of education. The papers of the entire country commented upon it.

This same year the college uniform reached Lexington. On petition from the students, the board passed this order: "Resolved—that each student who shall hereafter enter college shall provide himself with a coat made of deep blue cloth, the price of which shall not exceed seven dollars per yard. The coat shall be cut with a straight collar, to be fastened before with hooks and eyes and be trimmed with black braid and buttons, with a black silk star worked on each side of the collar and on each skirt. Every student shall be required to wear his uniform at all times out of college bounds." The coat was double-breasted and swallow-tailed. Dark gray was later substituted for blue.

The ordinance went into effect the next session, but it was never fully carried out. Many of the students did not care for it. Generally the coat was left unbuttoned with the collar turned back on the shoulders and inasmuch as pantaloons were *ad libitum,* the general effect of the uniform was grotesque. At the next meeting of the board the students petitioned that the uniform be abolished. The matter was referred to the faculty and allowed the "conceit to die a natural death."

Commencements were held in the Presbyterian Church and were largely attended by the county people. During the years from 1839 to about 1847, Washington and Lee and Virginia Military Institute held joint commencements in the Presbyterian Church. This was the big event of the year for Lexington people.

Jacob Fuller, a famous pedagogue, was one of the early teachers in the grammar school. He was a man who by his will and emotional vim was able to compel the young Arabs to swallow the rules and to grub out the roots. His long and useful career began in 1838, as a classical teacher in the Franklin Hall.

Though the faculty members were men of unusual ability and brilliance and were free thinkers, yet they dwelt together in unity of spirit and the bonds of peace. Each professor strove to do his whole duty and to avoid all cause of offense, and above all else to confer the greatest possible benefit upon the boys under their care. Their labors were eminently successful. Though idleness and badness were never lacking, there was a preponderance of study and good behavior. In spite of the occasional restlessness under the regulations steadily enforced, there was good feeling between the students and the faculty.

About this time the students, for no special reason, presented the president with a handsome study armchair, and they frequently serenaded the professors' families in a quiet way. This was intended as an acknowledgment of the hospitalities extended them by the president and the faculty members.

This anecdote is related of Dr. Ruffner who, upon entering his classroom one morning, found that the students had tied a calf in his armchair, which greeted him "ba-a." "Young men," said the president, "I see you have an instructor quite competent of caring for you. I bid you good morning." Soon the calf was nibbling grass on the campus and the president was apologized to.

Dr. Ruffner, about this time, struck a very pessimistic note: "Our free mountain air has become tainted, the labor in our fields is done in most part by fettered hands, our manners have become more refined than our morals, and instead of the sturdy, but intelligent simplicity that once reigned through all the land, a half savage ignorance has grown up in its nooks and dells, while in the open country a mixed population shows much that is excellent, but upon the whole, a failing spirit of energetic industry and enterprise."

1847 and 1848 were eventful years in Lexington. Besides the dissolution between the college and the institute, was the notable debate in the Franklin Society on the division of the State of Virginia; the western part contending for a white basis and the eastern part holding pertinaciously to a mixed basis of white and black. Dr. Ruffner, though a slaveholder until his death, considered slavery bad, economically, socially, and politically, and in this view most of the men of Rockbridge agreed. Dr. Ruffner delivered two speeches on Gradual Emancipation. He was out of sympathy, however, with the abolitionists who were filling the country with their incendiary speeches. His argument was that slavery was an evil and that the only way this part of the State could rid itself of it was by separating from Eastern Virginia. This caused quite a lot of bitter opposition throughout the State, which caused a lull in the ranks of the movers in Lexington. The acrid effect of his position was uncomfortable for the doctor and his supporters, but this was mild as compared with the nitric acid which was ejected over all who took part in the prosecution of Dr. Skinner. This unhappy affair drew into its vortex the college president and members of the faculty and some of the trustees.

Dr. John Skinner was a Scotch divine of the dissenting church of Scotland who, in the prime of life came to America and was almost immediately recommended to the Lexington church. At first, he was greatly admired, being quite an impressive looking man, portly in figure, courtly in manner, and gorgeous in his style of dressing. He was also a man of ability, quick of apprehension, a fluent speaker and capable of a great amount of work. His sermons were polished productions, delivered with grace and style.

He was a fine pastor, sympathetic and punctilious. He had a system of visiting his flock, which he termed Parochial Statistical Visitation. He would announce from his pulpit on Sunday morning that he would begin at a certain house at a certain hour on Monday and, after spending a few minutes, during which time he would see all the family who wished to be seen, would refresh the children's minds in the catechism and hunt up all the ages in the family Bible. Before leaving he made a complete record of all that he did and learned during the visit. Then he would proceed to other homes. He was devoted to his work and to his people. He was cordial in manner, entertaining in his conversation, happy in an anecdote, fond of a smoke, and manly in his way of honoring the old Scotch custom of taking a "little speerit" on occasion. While all could not approve of everything he did, he had an attractive side for everyone and hence a popularity for all classes of people.

In spite of all these virtues, his hold upon his people gradually waned. His rhetoric seemed to lose its charm, and after seven years the majority of his people wished he would go. This sentiment terminated in a private letter to the pastor, intimating to him that his usefulness had ceased and suggesting that he seek another field.

Imagine a lot of sportsmen shooting a tiger with squirrel shot and some idea may be formed of the scene which followed. After a variety of scenes, the Presbytery of Lexington, in the summer of 1847 dissolved the relationship between the pastor and the Lexington Church. Dr. Skinner appealed to the Synod of Virginia, and then to the General Assembly in session in Baltimore, in May, 1848.

Shortly thereafter, Dr. Skinner published a pamphlet assailing most of the people of the congregation, to which many of the leading men of the community replied, through the columns of the local newspaper. Dr. Skinner rejoined through the same channel. He was much given to sarcasm and ridicule and on one occasion he read out in church that Mr. So-and-So had given "sax and a quarter cents to convort the world." At another meeting, Dr. McFarland, who had a very large nose, and Dr. Brown, who had protruding eyes, were present and Dr. Skinner announced that the "eyes and the nose" were against him and that he could not hope for justice.

For the object of handling the situation, the Presbytery met in Lexington, to study the charges against Skinner. During the recess, Skinner decided to overhaul the personal and family history of everyone who had opposed him. With great industry he gathered a huge mass of gossip and scandal and called many witnesses to testify in his behalf. When Presbytery reconvened, there was a scene which far surpassed any contest ever witnessed in Congress. After weeks of continuous trial, Skinner withdrew, declaring that he had no hope of receiving justice, and appealed to the

General Assembly. It is hard to appreciate the intense excitement which prevailed during the case; in the Presbyterian Church, in the Presbytery, in the College, in the county of Rockbridge and throughout the United States.

An effort was made before the grand jury to obtain an indictment against the gentlemen who wrote the letter asking for the pastor's resignation. These eight men who wrote the letter were among the most peaceable and orderly Christian gentlemen in the community, yet they were charged with a libelous attack upon Dr. Skinner and a conspiracy against the peace and dignity of the Commonwealth.

Political, business, and social animosity was caused by this long-drawn-out, bitter affair and, as may be imagined, the social life of the community was anything but pleasant, contrasting with the peaceful tenor of the preceding history of Lexington.

CHAPTER XI: THE SOCIETY OF THE CINCINNATI

THE SOCIETY OF THE CINCINNATI, composed of the surviving officers of the Revolutionary Army, organized to perpetuate kindly acquaintance among themselves and to provide a fund for the relief of needy families of officers, decided, in the early years of the first decade of the nineteenth century, to dissolve the association and to distribute its funds to some worthy purpose. Through Providential guidance, Washington College became this worthy purpose.

The following extracts from the Papers of Dr. William Henry Ruffner are illuminating:

"In the spring of 1783, after peace had been proclaimed, but before the patriot army had been disbanded, a feeling of sadness existed among the soldiers, mingled with joy as they remained together, inactive, awaiting the hour of separation. Our soldiers, who lately served for four years together, felt themselves to be united by very strong ties; but had the time been doubled in which they toiled, fought and suffered, the strength of these ties would have been more than doubled. No one can fail to appreciate the fraternal feeling which would lead the old Revolutionary soldiers to consider whether there might not be some means by which their personal and social ties might be preserved and by which they might still help each other and keep watch over the liberties of their country. At the encampment on the Hudson River, General Knox proposed the formation of a general society, with a branch in each State, to be composed of the officers of the American Army. The suggestion was favorably received by all and evoked the hearty approval of General Washington. On the 13th of May, 1783, an organization was effected in the old Verplanck House, then the headquarters of Baron Steuben, near Fishkill.

"It is not stated who proposed the name, but its appropriateness is obvious. The typical character to be represented was the patriotic farmer. The American Army from Washington down was made up almost exclusively of men who had been called from their farms to join in the defense of their country and, now that the dangerous crisis had been successfully passed, they were as anxious as Cincinnatus, after the expulsion of the Aequi, to return to the plough. The parallel goes further. Much as they loved their homes and their rural pursuits, their first duty in the future, as in the past, was to their country. All this is implied in the name. It meant, in a word, self-abnegation, love of home and supreme patriotism. The objects set forth in their constitution were not only harmless, but were noble and patriotic in the highest degree.

"The society badge was to be a bald eagle in gold, suspended by a blue ribbon, edged with white, emblematic of the union between France and America. On the breast of the eagle, Cincinnatus is represented as receiving the military ensigns from three Senators—the implements of husbandry are seen in the background and around the whole is inscribed *Omnia reliquit servare rem publicam*. On the reverse, Fame is crowning Cincinnatus with a wreath having the legend *Virtutis praemium* and encircling the whole, *Societas Cincinnatorum instita A. D. 1783*. A provision was incorporated which made membership in the society hereditary along the male lines of the members. In default of male heirs in the direct line, the nearest collateral male line should inherit. Provision was also made for the election of honorary members for life; distinguished American patriots and French officers who had served the American cause.

"Washington was unanimously chosen president of the society and presided at the first general meeting in 1784. But alas! This monument to friendship and patriotism at once excited the fears of a host of outside patriots: men equally patriotic, but men who had served their country in other spheres of action and, no doubt, in some cases as private soldiers who could not become members. The hereditary feature was promptly attacked by Dr. Franklin, who contended that it would create and perpetuate an aristocratic class, which would be out of harmony with the Republic. Many others took the same view. It attracted attention in Europe also, where unfavorable comments were made and motives and designs were ascribed to the founders of which they were wholly innocent.

"The Legislatures of Massachusetts and Connecticut warned the country against the new order and the alarm spread from state to state. The Father of His Country was so disturbed by the unpopularity of the society and possibly somewhat moved by the arguments against it that, by the time for the annual meeting, he was ready to urge the abandonment of the whole scheme . . . but, owing to opposition among members and complications arising from foreign membership, the Society was continued and certain changes made.

"In 1794, Mr. Jefferson wrote to Mr. Madison attacking the society, which some believed was intended to injure General Washington, in revenge for his open opposition to the Democratic societies, which he believed to be formed in sympathy with the Jacobins of France, but which Jefferson favored.

"As Mr. Jefferson states in his forceful way the objection to the Society, it is proper to quote this passage: 'It is wonderful that the President should have permitted himself to be an organ of such an attack upon the freedom of discussion; it must be a matter of rare curiosity, to see what line their ingenuity would draw between democratical societies whose avowed object is the nourishment of the republican principles of our constitution and the Society of the Cincinnati, *a self created one,* carving out for itself hereditary distinctions, lowering over our constitution eternally, meeting together in all parts of the Union, with closed doors, accumulating a capital in their separate treasury, corresponding secretly and regularly and of which Society the very persons denouncing the democrats are themselves the fathers, founders and high officers.'

"This skillfully worded indictment is followed by a denunciation of the excise law against which the whiskey men of Western Pennsylvania rebelled and, by ridicule of the President's efforts to suppress the Rebellion as he did by the hand of General Henry Lee. This was probably provoked by Washington's declaration that the Whiskey Insurrection was a first fruit of the democratic societies. The immediate dissolution of the democratic societies on the fall of Robespierre, considered in connection with the influence which the revolutionary French minister, Genet, had exerted in promoting their organization, revealed their true Jacobin character and showed that Washington read their designs correctly from the beginning. In regard to Mr. Jefferson's attack on the Cincinnati Society, the best answer to it is the history of the society, which Mr. Jefferson prepared for a French encyclopedia in 1786. It is a perfect vindication of Washington and the Society of the Cincinnati against the charges which Mr. Jefferson subsequently made in his letter to Mr. Madison."

For this reason and because it is a good historical sketch of the Society, it is quoted:

Thomas Jefferson's account of the Cincinnati Society: "When on the close of that war which established the independence of America, its army was about to be disbanded, the officers, who during the course of it had gone through the most trying scenes together, by mutual aids and good offices, had become dear to each other felt, with great apprehension of mind, the approach of that moment which was to separate them, never perhaps to meet again. They were from distant states and from distant parts of the same state. Hazard alone could give them but rare and partial occasions of seeing each other. Why not come together on purpose at stated times? Would not the trouble of such a journey be greatly overpaid by the pleasure of seeing each other again, by the sweetest of all consolations, the talking over the scenes of difficulty and endearment they had gone through? This, too, would enable them to know who of them should succeed in the world, who should be successful and to open the purses to every laboring brother. This idea was too soothing not to be cherished in conversation. It was improved into a regular association, with an organized administration, with periodical meetings, general and particular, fixed contributions for those who should be in distress and a badge by which not only those who had not had occasion to become personally known, should be able to recognize each other, but, which should be worn by their descendants, to perpetuate among them the friendship which had bound their ancestors together. General Washington was at that moment oppressed with the operation of disbanding an army which had not been paid and the difficulty of this operation was increased by some two or three states having expressed sentiments which did not indicate a sufficient attention to their payments. He was sometime present when his officers were fashioning in their conversations their newly proposed society. He saw the innocence of its origin and foresaw no effects less innocent. He was at the time writing his valedictory letter to the States, which has been so deservedly applauded by the world. Far from thinking it a moment to multiply causes of irritation by thwarting a proposition which had absolutely no other basis but that of benevolence and friendship, he was rather satisfied to find himself aided in his difficulties by this new incident, which occupied and, at the same time, soothed the minds of his officers. He thought, too, that this institution would be one instrument the more for strengthening the Federal bond and promoting Federal ideas. The institution was formed. They incorporated into it the officers of the French Army and Navy, by whose sides they had fought and with whose aid they had finally prevailed.

"The uneasiness excited by this institution had very early caught the notice of General Washington. Still recollecting all the purity of the motives which gave it birth, he became sensible that it might produce political evils, which the warmth of those motives had masked. Add to this, that it was disapproved by the mass of the citizens of the Union. This alone was strong enough reason in the country, where the will of the majority is the law and ought to be the law. He said that the objects of the institution were too light to be opposed to considerations as serious as these and that it was become necessary to annihilate it absolutely. On this, therefore, he was decided. The first annual meeting at Philadelphia was now at hand and he went determined to use all his influence for its suppression. He proposed it to his fellow officers and urged it with all his powers. It met with an opposition, which was observed to cloud his face with an anxiety that the most distressful scenes of the war had scarcely ever produced. It was canvassed for several days and at length it was no more a doubt what would be its ultimate fate. The order was on the point of receiving its annihilation by the vote of a great majority of its members. At this moment their envoy arrived from France, charged with letters from the French officers, accepting, with cordiality, the proposed badges of the Society, with solicitations from others to be received into the order and with notice that their respectable sovereign had been pleased to recognize it and to permit its officers to wear the badge. The prospect was now changed. The question assumed a new form. After the offer made by them and accepted by their friends, in what words could they clothe a proposition to retract it, which would not cover themselves with the reproaches of levity and ingratitude? Which would not appear an insult to those they loved? Federal principles, popular discontent, were considerations whose weight was known and felt by themselves, but would foreigners know and feel equally? The idea revolted the whole Society. They found it necessary then to preserve so much of their institution as might continue to support this foreign branch, while they should prune off every other which should give offense to their fellow citizens, thus sacrificing on each hand, to their friends and to their country.

"The Society was to retain its existence, its name, its meetings and its charitable funds, but these last were deposited with their respective Legislatures. The order was to be no longer hereditary. The eagle and the ribbon were indeed retained, because they were worn and they wished them to be worn by their friends in a country where they would not be objects of offense, but themselves never wore them. They laid them in their bureaus, with the medals of American Independence, with those of the trophies they had taken and the battles they had won. But all through the United States, no officer is seen to offend the public eye with a display of this badge."

This narrative Mr. Jefferson called, "a short and true history of the Order of the Cincinnati." It furnishes a perfect answer to Jefferson's own criticism.

The general Society of the Cincinnati, shorn of its features which had been objected to, was continued, though not prominently, until the beginning of the nineteenth century. Some of the State societies had been disbanded and some had continued; among these, the Virginia Society. This Society, however, early in the century provided for its own dissolution.

It became known to the authorities of Washington Academy in 1802, that the Virginia Society, in anticipation of its dissolution, intended to bestow its fund of about $15,000.00 on some public institution. General Daniel Morgan, a member of the society, suggested that Washington College, of which he was a trustee, should apply for the fund. Whereupon, at a meeting of the board of trustees a committee was appointed to present their claim. Hampden-Sydney College was a lively competitor for this fund. The action of the society resolved, however, "That the object of appropriation of the funds of the Society be the Seminary of learning in the county of Rockbridge, denominated the Washington Academy."

In 1824, the fund was deposited with the state treasurer, subject to certain pensions. Soon after came the defalcation and suicide of the state treasurer, lawsuits and finally, the receipt of the money, principal and interest, in 1848. The fund when first deposited amounted to $15,000.00, but when finally received it was about $25,000.00.

In 1838, President Ruffner delivered an oration in honor of the Cincinnati Society.

For many years this fund has been doing fine service in the cause of education and the Society, which made this possible, will be remembered and honored for all time.

In recognition of this gift, the Cincinnati Professorship was established.

CHAPTER XII: JOHN ROBINSON

JOHN ROBINSON, a native of Ireland, a trustee of the college, a soldier under Washington, filled with veneration for his virtues and a laudable zeal to further promote the purpose of the Father of His Country, in 1826, bequeathed his entire fortune to Washington College. It must be remembered that when Lexington was bidding for the removal of the academy, in 1803, John Robinson subscribed a lot of his own ground on the edge of the town and, in addition, one hundred bushels of corn. His next offer was one of the noblest in the history of benevolence. In 1817, he offered his entire estate as an inducement to the State to adopt Washington College as a State University. Seldom do men give away their entire wealth while yet alive, but this he offered to do.

He was a rare character, this John Robinson, worthy and interesting and his memory should never be forgotten by Washington and Lee and Lexington. He was born in County Armagh, in the north of Ireland and was left an orphan in early life. He was bound out to a weaver to learn the trade. In some way he was released from his indentures and emigrated to America. It is said of him that he was a good lad, with a jovial nature. He was in his early twenties when the Revolution started, and participated in it. After the Revolution he found a good home with Colonel John Bowyer of Thorn Hill, near Lexington. His good behaviour and good temper together with a spice of Irish wit made him acceptable company with everyone.

He early added to his weaving business that of horse trading, at which he proved an adept. He maintained a good character for honesty and practiced none of the deceptions common among men of such a profession. He acquired much wealth from this business, later adding to it through the purchasing of soldiers' certificates, which, upon the establishing of the Federal Government, were redeemable and, from that time, he considered himself a rich man.

He now decided to buy land and fixed his eye on Hart's Bottom, as fertile a piece of property as could be found. This was the property of Colonel Bowyer, who gladly sold it to Robinson. For the operation of this new enterprise, he must have slaves. He owned many and was considered a very kind and reasonable master.

Hart's Bottom consisted of about four hundred acres, and a large section of the city of Buena Vista now occupies this lovely valley. After settling on his farm, Robinson added another line of business, the manufacturing of fine whiskey. This was one of the standard occupations of the country a century ago. His whiskey had the reputation of being the very finest that a "gentleman could buy."

The manufacturing of fine whiskey must have been looked upon as a very honorable business, indeed. It is claimed that during the building and early days of historic old Bethel Presbyterian Church, in Augusta County, when church meetings, for one cause or another, could not be held in the church, they were held in the office of the famous Bumgardner Distillery near by.

Old Barney one of Robinson's slaves, visited extensively about the neighborhood. After his master's death he would frequently come into Lexington, and as he, with all of Robinson's estate, belonged to the college, he considered himself the natural heir to all the old clothes of the students. He would come with bags to gather in his belongings. After loading himself with shoes, shirts and whatnots, he would increase his stock by passing on to the Arsenal (Virginia Military Institute), where the soldiers would dress him up in their old regimentals, including the tall cap and pompon. Barney would now come marching through the town, proud and happy, boasting of the advantages of belonging to a literary institution. Mr. Robinson lived a lonely, bachelor life at Hart's Bottom. His one indulgence was in riding his quiet, gray horse into Lexington, a distance of nine miles. About three times a week he would jog along in a meditative way until he reached the town. He would first visit the postoffice, later taking a chair on the sidewalk for the rest of the day. In those days, both chairs and benches ranged along both sides of Main Street, so that the talkers could pass over from the sun to the shade, or vice versa, according to the season and the time of day. No doubt Mr. Robinson found the wit and humor of Ben Darst, Sam Pettigrew, Archy Beard, and Jimmy Gold very welcome entertainment. Alex Sloan, the prince of humorists, also added to this "Main Street Free Entertainment."

A clause from Robinson's will typifies the man: "Having forborne to gratify the partialities of friendship in the bestowing of personal favors, I look for my reward to the diffusive and abiding benefits which must follow the judicious application of the legacy which I leave to the public. By adding to the means of public instruction I hope that some facilities have been given to the march of improvement and some contribution made to the welfare of society in having its members inspired at an early age with the salutary and conservative lessons of knowledge and virtue. And, though a foreigner by birth, without a child to provide for, I rejoice in the trust that I have done something to protect the sons of others from ignorance and vice, something to confirm the political institutions of the country by enlightening the public will upon which they rest. For these ends I cheerfully give up the earnings of my life and entreat as my last wish that they be so husbanded as to carry forward the benevolent results which I contemplate."

Mr. Robinson died June 26, 1826, at the age of seventy-three. Attended by a large number of his neighbors and a whole retinue of his slaves, his body was brought from Hart's Bottom to Lexington, where it was met by the faculty and trustees of the college. These were later joined by the college societies, the Franklin Society, ladies and citizens. The interment was on College Hill, on the spot now occupied by Dr. Howe's home. Years later his remains were removed from their original burial place to the concrete base of the monument, which marks his permanent resting place on the campus. In the box containing his remains was placed a sealed bottle containing a brief Latin legend, a number of college documents, newspapers, an extract from his will and the title page of the Holy Bible. This inscription is on the monument:

Honor to whom honor
Sacred to the memory of John Robinson
a native of Ireland
a soldier of
Washington
and a munificent benefactor of
Washington College
Born A.D. 1754
Died A.D. 1826
Erected 1855

The Valley Star of February 23, 1854, reported that the committee appointed to communicate with the alumni of Washington College and solicit from each the sum of one dollar for the purpose of having a block, with a suitable inscription, inserted in the Washington monument, in the nation's capital, wrote to every alumnus whose address was known, and from nearly everyone has received the amount asked for.

The contribution of such a block in the monument, by the alumni of the college, is an appropriate testimonial of their appreciation of the benefits conferred upon their Alma Mater by the Father of His Country, in bestowing upon her so magnificent an endowment, and will be a perpetual memento of their gratitude and veneration for his memory when they themselves shall have passed away. This block may be seen on the eleventh landing in the monument, on the east side, stone No. 67 and marked: "From the alumni of Washington College at Lexington, Va. The only college endowed by the Father of His Country." The stone is one hundred and thirty feet from the ground.

CHAPTER XIII: THE VIRGINIA MILITARY INSTITUTE

ASTLE-LIKE, on a great eminence overlooking some of the most beautiful country in the Valley of Virginia, and suggestive of Lichtenstein, the Robber Castle, or some other Old World stronghold, stands historic Virginia Military Institute, with its finely proportioned battlements and towers of Gothic design. Second only to the United States Military Academy at West Point, in age and rank in America, the school was founded by those with a keen eye for the beautiful as well as the practical. In the early days of Lexington, the land on which Virginia Military Institute now stands was owned by the Walkup family and was known as Walkup's Mount. The Walkups came from Ireland and were good Presbyterians, therefore, Lexington was good soil for them. Their ancestors, spelled Wauchope in Scotland, and Wauchope Hills are mentioned in *Scottish Chiefs*.

The real originator of Virginia Military Institute seems to have been Claude Crozet, a native of France, a soldier under Napoleon and a wearer of the Cross of the Legion of Honor, received at the hand of the Emperor himself. After Waterloo, Crozet came to America in 1817 and was almost immediately associated with the academy at West Point, where he was the first to teach the higher branches of mathematics in that institution. With the exception of the seven years spent there and a few years in Louisiana, he spent his long and useful life in Virginia, as engineer and teacher. He left many evidences of his skill. One outstanding is the Chesapeake and Ohio Railroad tunnel under the Blue Ridge at Afton.

In 1816 the Legislature of Virginia established arsenals throughout the State and one was at Lexington, where they maintained State Guards. Colonel J. T. L. Preston, a young lawyer of the town, advocated establishing a military school instead of the arsenal and the State Guard. The Virginia Military Institute, thus established, is the brilliant result.

Under Crozet, the first president of the board of visitors, the school was developed along the same lines as the academy at West Point and the uniforms of the two schools have always been that of the French Guard. The cadets wear their uniforms at all times and lead the very rigid life of the soldier. All cadets, during their first year, are assigned to one of the units of the R.O.T.C. maintained by the United States War Department. These units, cavalry, infantry, and field artillery, are well equipped and furnish excellent training. The school has the highest rank of the War Department. Graduates are commissioned as second lieutenants in the Officers' Reserve Corps.

The curriculum for the first two years of cadetship embraces mathematics, history, chemistry, physics, drawing, and elementary engineering, and a choice of one language: German, French, Latin, or Spanish, thus offering an opportunity for broad culture. After this the cadet elects his own course for the next two years, either civil engineering, electrical engineering, chemistry, or liberal arts.

Members of the first board of visitors included Claude Crozet, General P. C. Johnson, General Thomas Botts, General C. P. Dorman, Captain J. F. Wiley, Governor James McDowell, Dr. Edward Leyburn, and Hugh Barclay. A long line of distinguished men have served on this board and through the years there have been only five superintendents, each with many years of faithful and devoted service. Those who have guided its destiny from the beginning in 1839:

General Francis H. Smith: 1839-1889.

General Scott Shipp: 1889-1907.

General Edward West Nichols: 1907-1924.

General William H. Cocke: 1924-1929.

General John Archer Lejeune: 1929-——.

General John Archer Lejeune, the present superintendent, is a former Commander of the United States Marines and is internationally known and honored as a great soldier and Christian gentleman. Following General Lee's noble example, he chose, rather than ease and retirement, to come to Lexington to spend many of his most useful and most fruitful years in the moulding of life and character of young men. By precept and example he is accomplishing this worthy end. He is greatly beloved, and as was said of General Lee and Commodore Maury, he lives among his friends with simplicity and neighborliness.

Among the early professors were: General G. W. Custis Lee, Colonel Williamson, Colonel Semmes, Colonel Gilham, Colonel Brooke, and Colonel Maury.

For nearly a century Virginia Military Institute has been true to its motto: *In pace decus, in bello praesidium.*

In times of peace it has always stood for the highest in mental, moral, and physical development of manhood, and in times of national stress has stood second to none in the quality of its leadership. It has been well said that energy, efficiency, and reliability have been characteristic of Virginia Military Institute in every pursuit in life.

Bombarded and burned in 1864 by the Federal forces under General Hunter, himself a Virginian, the institution soon rose to a finer and better state. Since the Valley was the granary of the Confederacy, he was bent upon destruction of property and crops. Cannon balls imbedded in the sidewalls of barracks, left as souvenirs by Hunter's men, may still be seen. When they departed, leaving the school, the governor's home, and other buildings in blackened ruins, the college ransacked, and the town generally in chaos, they carried with them Houdon's statue of Washington, which had long stood in front of the main arch of barracks. This was the only time that Washington was ever a prisoner. Years later the United States Government returned it to its proper place and here he is saluted about as often as the clock ticks. On one occasion, a cadet who had "run the block," seeing the sentinel approaching, crouched behind the statue. On this cold, winter night, in the wee small hours, when all cadets were supposed to be reposing in the arms of Morpheus, the sentinel addressed the Father of His Country: "George, did you ever feel such a cold night?" when, from behind the statue came: "Hell, this ain't cold weather, you should have been with me at Valley Forge." Hurriedly the sentinel saluted and "made tracks."

The burning of the institute could be seen for many, many miles due to the large amount of barrels of rosin which was used to make gas for lighting the buildings.

Virginia Military Institute's first commencement was July 4th and was held in the Presbyterian Church. There were sixteen graduates, and a feature of the exercise was the reading by one of the graduates of the *Declaration of Independence*.

The first society was the Society of Cadets and was organized in 1840, and was followed in 1849 by the founding of the Dialectic Society.

During the first seven years of the institute, the cadets studied chemistry at Washington College and a class of Washington College students, uniformed and known as the Cincinnati Class, drilled with the cadets. Beginning in 1844, there arose and continued for some years, a lack of harmony between the institute on the one hand, and the college and the townspeople, with their Presbyterian Church, on the other. Removal of the institute to some other place was considered. This alarmed the college and the townspeople and they then exerted themselves to have it remain where it was and, as some one said: "Let it be Episcopalian."

In the beginning there were four rooms to accommodate the thirty-odd cadets and because of this condition, only a small percentage of applicants could be admitted.

The corner stone of the new barracks was laid July 4, 1850, and that year the corps was present in the City of Washington for the laying of the corner stone of the Washington monument. The band about this time was composed of Ruben and Mike, two very black men who dressed in scarlet uniforms. Ruben was short and round, like his drum, and Mike was tall and slim like his fife. At the church fairs in the community, the ladies would make and sell dolls dressed like Ruben and Mike, and they were great favorites with the children.

Shortly after the founding of the institute, came the War with Mexico and there we find many of the early graduates in service, mostly as commissioned officers. Then came the War Between the States and there we find a long and honored list in places of leadership and importance. What glory Stonewall Jackson, Scott Shipp and the boys at New Market shed upon Virginia Military Institute's scroll of fame and upon the Southland! These boy heroes immortalized themselves on that eventful, memorable day, May 15, 1864. The battle is vividly portrayed in Clindenst's painting in Jackson Memorial Hall. It is a masterpiece and depicts the horrors and reality of war as graphically as any of Meissonier's works. An elderly Englishman stood before this great portrayal and with emotion said: "What horror! this is the greatest argument against war that I have ever seen." The battle is further memorialized by the statue, Virginia Mourning Her Dead, by Sir Moses Ezekiel (himself a New Market cadet), on the parade ground. This statue was made in his studios in the Baths of Diocletian in Rome and was presented by Ezekiel and Thomas F. Ryan to the institute in 1912. Under it sleep several of the boys killed at New Market and their memory and their deeds are kept forever fresh in the minds of those who come after them. At the celebration by the corps each May 15th before the monument, the names of those lost in battle are called and reported, "died on the field of honor." Such a scene Crozet doubtless often witnessed in Napoleon's Army, where the name of Latour d'Auvergne, the first grenadier of France, continued to be called to the end of the Empire.

> "Sleeping, but glorious,
> Dead in fame's portals.
> Dead but immortal!
> They gave us great glory,
> What more could they give?
> They left us a story,
> A story to live."

In the World War the Honor Roll of Virginia Military Institute is a long one and their leadership conspicuous.

Not only does it have a glorious and honored past, which is greatly preserved as a priceless heritage; Virginia Military Institute is much alive to today and its needs, and annually graduates men who take their places as leaders in the world of thought and action.

The institution is a national, as well as a State pride, and draws its students from every state in the Union, and from many foreign countries.

The Memorial Garden, designed and given by Mrs. William H. Cocke, of Claremont Manor on the James, is a place of real beauty and interest. At the entrance to the garden is this arresting inscription from the pen of Colonel J. T. L. Preston:

> "The healthful and pleasant abode of a crowd of honorable youths pressing up the hill of science, with noble emulation. A gratifying spectacle. An honor to their country and their State. Objects of honest pride to their instructors and fair specimens of citizen soldiers. Attached

to their native State; proud of her fame and ready in every time of deepest peril to vindicate her honor and defend her rights."

In the garden are four handsome oaks, memorials to the four past superintendents: Smith, Shipp, Nichols, and Cocke. Many fine art treasures are displayed in the library and the museum.

The sentimental Old Guard tree is loved by every alumnus and friend of the Institute. It has seen every stage of Virginia Military Institute life from the beginning. What a story it could tell!

Until the leveling of the parade grounds a few years ago, there stood on the west end a huge boulder which had tremendous sentimental·value to many, for here were founded two national Greek-letter fraternities, Alpha Tau Omega and Sigma Nu. The Sigma Nu fraternity has marked this spot.

When General Pershing was recently a guest in Lexington someone said to him: "General, this school is often spoken of as the West Point of the South." "Yes," replied the General, "and West Point is just as often referred to as the Virginia Military Institute of the North."

The alumni of this great school, numbering thousands, are scattered throughout the world and will be found in every high calling in life. Every one of them acknowledges a debt of gratitude to his Alma Mater and it would be difficult to find anywhere greater alumni spirit than among these men. Should an alumnus of the early days return, he would hardly recognize the old place. Barracks would be familiar, but not the many magnificent new buildings, the enlarged parade ground and officers' quarters, and the fine athletic field. A great institution! With a glorious past, present, and future! A glory to the South, to the Nation, and to the world!

In pace decus, in bello praesidium.

During the latter years of the nineteenth and the early years of the twentieth century, there lived in Lexington, adjoining the grounds of the Virginia Military Institute, a very unusual woman, Miss Maggie Freeland. Ask any old cadet or friend of the institute of those years and many expressions of gratitude and appreciation will be heard. She commanded a unique position, something of an unofficial vice superintendent of the institute. A woman of rare culture and charm, combining the hospitality of Louisiana and Virginia in her home, where every cadet and his friends had free and easy entrée, she always kept open house for them, giving them a taste of home life when so far from their homes. Many will testify that when overtaken by homesickness and a longing "to go," that to stop in and see Miss Maggie, who was something of a fairy godmother, generally helped them over the hard places and they could return to the grind of barrack life, knowing that just across the parade ground was a real friend. Never before or since has there been anyone to so dedicate their all to the pleasure and happiness of the cadet life. In her lovely home was another woman of charm and personality, Miss Betty Clarke, who had been Miss Maggie's chaperone many years before. At all Virginia Military Institute dances she would be seen, despite her four-score and maybe ten, dancing with the boys and having the time of the sweet-sixteens and just as popular as any of them. Miss Freeland's niece, Miss Marie Lewis (Mrs. St. Julian Marshall) completed this interesting home circle.

Old cadets will tell of the lonely nights on guard, when at some wee hour of the night, Miss Maggie's servant would arrive with sandwiches. What a bright spot on a dark and lonely night!

Forest Inn near Natural Bridge

Iron Furnace, Rockbridge County
(Note men standing at base)

General Lee's home as it was during his residence

Interior of General Lee's home

The Virginia Military Institute cadets (Photograph made just after the war showing repairs to the barracks after Hunter's Raid in 1864)

Old packet boat, until 1883 the only passenger and freight transportation into Lexington. (Stono and Virginia Military Institute in background)

CHAPTER XIV: ANN SMITH ACADEMY

THE ANN SMITH ACADEMY, a classical school for females, was opened in Lexington in 1807 and incorporated in 1808. Many men instrumental in the establishing and success of the Franklin Society were equally responsible for the founding of the academy. Following its incorporation, the trustees purchased a lot which lay just outside the town limits, extending to the Franklin Society property at Jefferson and Nelson Streets. The same year, Colonel John Jordan, the ubiquitous builder of early nineteenth century Lexington, erected on this property a brick structure of rather pretentious proportions, which was considered the handsomest building in the town.

Reading, writing, arithmetic, grammar, geography, chemistry, belles lettres, natural philosophy, French, painting, music, and embroidery were included in the curriculum. Tuition was $25.00 a year and the young ladies ranged in age from thirteen to sixteen years and came from many sections of the South to receive the finishing touches to their education.

This was the only school of its kind in the State and its capacity was one hundred students. It was named for its first principal, Miss Ann Smith, a woman of culture, education, and executive ability, who gave of her time and talents, gratuitously.

Miss Smith has always remained about as mysterious as Melchisedek. Where she came from and her subsequent history is unknown. After five years of intelligent and sympathetic leadership, she severed her connection with the academy. After her departure, two of her students, Betsy Alexander and Sally Lyle were in charge. In 1811 Hyacinth Crusolles, a Frenchman, taught French in the academy and, for a while taught French in Washington College. In those days there were many Frenchmen and Germans in Lexington, but Englishmen were rare.

Adversity, as well as success, was experienced by the academy. One such time was in 1824, when its financial condition was so bad that the doors of the institution would have been closed, but for the aid of John Robinson, the friend and benefactor of Washington College. He lifted the mortgage and started the school again on its rosy path to usefulness, thus saving it from the sheriff's hammer.

In 1839 arrangements were made for the young ladies who were advanced in science to attend classes at Washington College, accompanied, of course, by their chaperones. The Lexington *Gazette* of August 3, 1854, contains this advertisement: "The duties of this school will be resumed on the first Monday in September next. The institution being well known, the pledge of the Principal and teachers is simply given to facilitate the mental and moral culture and improvement of all pupils entrusted to their care. Special attention is given the health and comfort of the young ladies boarding at the Academy.

E. NOTTINGHAM."

The Misses Nottingham were Englishwomen of rare culture and ability. They were in charge for many years. At the same time the Misses Baxter, talented daughters of the Presbyterian minister, were responsible for the education of the younger children of the community. It is said that these Baxter sisters were as homely as they were talented. On one occasion, their brother, a student at the college, was standing on the street corner with some other students, when his sisters, three in number, passed by. Not knowing who they were, one of the students asked young Baxter who that d— ugly woman on the outside was. "That's my sister," said Baxter. "No, I mean the one on the inside," said the embarrassed student. "That's my sister, too," said Baxter. "O, you don't understand me, I mean the one walking in the middle," said the student, more embarrassed. "Well," said Baxter, "all three of them are my sisters," to which the student, in desperation said, "Well, I do say you have the d— ugliest sisters in the world."

Another announcement of the Academy's efficient work appeared in the *Gazette* about this time:

"The pupils of this institution passed their public examinations on Tuesday and Wednesday. Their prompt and accurate answers to the difficult and searching questions pronounced, gave evidence of a degree of efficiency which excited our surprise and gratification and reflected credit alike upon the diligence with which they had prosecuted their studies and the ability with which their teachers had discharged the duties reposed in them. We have not, in the course of our college experience or since, witnessed a more rigid examination, or one conducted in a manner better calculated to make a true exhibit of the capacity and acquirements of the students and we do but justice to the young ladies in saying that we have never been present at one where the students acquitted themselves with more credit and we felt a sincere pleasure at the evidence thus furnished of the zeal and industry with which they have been exploring the fields of science and literature to gather the charms of a cultivated mind and associate with them the attractions which beauty of person and grace of manner give to the accomplished woman.

"The patrons of this school owe a debt of gratitude to the worthy lady, who fills the place of Principal, for a faithful discharge of the trust confided in her and the school merits a patronage more extensive than that which it has hitherto received.

"We wish it success."

Boys were first admitted in 1877.

Miss Madge Paxton, whose administration ran from 1879 to 1892, was the last principal, as after that date the building was leased to private individuals, who conducted the school under the same name.

About 1890 the public school was proving lively competition. The *County News* of February 6, 1885, contained this item of interest, regarding the fine work done in the free schools:

"On Wednesday we visited the school. Professor J. H. B. Jones, Principal, assisted by Misses Annie White, Nannie Jordan, Katie Estill, Maria Effinger and Sallie Davidson. We went into Miss Nannie Jordan's room and found it very comfortable, but not a map or chart of any kind on the wall. One side of the room was tastefully decorated · with small pictures and evergreens, gathered by pupils and teacher and tacked against the wall. Except by these and a large blackboard, the plastering of the room is unrelieved.

"We had geography, a map of Asia, a large class and we are free to confess that they knew a great deal more about it than we did. Then we had arithmetic, per cent, and in this they were well up. Here we saw several maps and charts drawn by the pupils. These were highly creditable, not only to the pupils but to the teacher, under whose direction they were made.

"We took a ballot to ascertain who were the three in the room most distinguished for good conduct and attention to their lessons. Votes were cast, of which Master Jimmy Withrow received eighteen, Lucy Withrow received fifteen, Laura Woodward and Nettie Banker received thirteen. The tie was decided in favor of Laura Woodward. We next went to Miss Annie White's room, where we were reminded of a visit we once made to an iron furnace in the Blue Ridge. We went into a little room, 8 x 10 feet, where there was not a single convenience and, after talking with the manager a few minutes, we told him that we would like to see the place. 'Well,' he said, 'we have nothing to show, but we sure do make good pig iron.'

"Miss Annie White has nothing to show in her room, not a map, chart, globe, motto or picture of any kind, but the work they do is first class. The exercise was mental arithmetic and was about perfect. The distinguished pupils were Annie Middleton, Annie Riley and Nellie Middleton. Professor S. T. Moreland delivered a lecture on Electricity. After this a number of pupils' maps were exhibited and a committee of Jacob Fuller, John Carmichael and the Reverend A. P. Boude were judges.

"Irene Beeton, Lula Grinstead, Agnes Root, Oliver Agnor, from the first department and Nettie Banker, Gertie Chittum, Lydia Wilborne, Laura Woodward, Sam Dold, James Withrow, from the second department. Maps displayed were of Virginia, Louisiana, the Gulf States, the Pacific States and the United States. Work was all so well done that it was difficult for the judges to make a decision. Finally, Laura Woodward and

Lydia Wilborne were the winners. Besides these maps was one very large one, very fine, of Rockbridge County, drawn by Miss Nannie Jordan and a basket of flowers drawn by Lizzie Markley, ten years old, who had never had a drawing lesson. These drawings and a number of charts will be sent to the Superintendents' Conference in Richmond and later to New Orleans.

"In Miss Annie White's room we heard a concert-reading lesson, which was perfect in both time and pitch.

"Next week we will visit the other departments, including Miss Deaver's school and the one at Levisia."

The last trustees of the Academy were: John L. Campbell, Addison Hogue, W. C. Stuart, Scott Shipp, and William T. Shields. In 1910 the academy property was turned over to the Lexington School Board as part of its educational equipment and in return for this gift, two perpetual scholarships were established in the high school to be known as the Ann Smith Scholarships. Thus closed the more than a century of the cultural influence of this grand old school.

Men and women throughout the world rise up and call blessed the old academy, where so many happy years were spent. Friends of Ann Smith Academy should never forget John Robinson. But for his aid in the early days, this institution might have ceased to exist.

CHAPTER XV: THE FRANKLIN SOCIETY

THE FRANKLIN SOCIETY is believed to have been in existence as early as 1796, longer than any like organization in America, and it did much toward moulding the thought and character, as well as the action of this community for more than a century. It was first called the Belles Lettres Society and in 1804 it was changed to the Union and, again in 1807, it was changed to the Republican Society. In 1808 it became the Literary Society of Lexington, and in 1811 the Franklin Society, and on January 30, 1816, was incorporated as such.

Conspicuous among its early members we find John Alexander, John Caruthers, Andrew Alexander, Dr. Samu'l L. Campbell, Layman Wayt, James Caruthers, John Leyburn, Alexander Shields, Cornelious Dorman, Thomas L. Preston, and others who were men of first importance in the community life.

In 1813 the first books were purchased for the library and consisted of thirty-eight volumes, mostly historical, as would have been expected. They were eventually housed in Franklin Hall and for more than fifty years the librarian was John Fuller. The books went through the Civil War unscathed. For ten years following its incorporation, the meetings were held in Washington College. By this time the society had grown in interest and membership to such an extent as to warrant a home of its own. Therefore, ground at the corner of Jefferson and Nelson Streets was bought and on it was built Franklin Hall, costing eighteen hundred dollars. This old landmark was destroyed by fire on January 8, 1915.

While primarily a debating society, with literary and scientific emphases, no question of local, state or national importance, secular or religious, escaped the thoughtful and scholarly consideration of this group of illustrious men.

The establishing of the Virginia Military Institute was first discussed by this society. Among other questions debated in those early days were: Would a separation of the states be preferable to a limited monarchy? Are theatrical amusements prejudicial to morality? Does man consist in two substances, special and distinct in each other? Can any heathen be saved who never heard the name of Jesus? Should the Scriptures be used as a textbook in our schools? Would it be right to repeal the hog law in this town?

On December 12, 1884, the *County News* reported that the Franklin Society disposed of the divorce question on Saturday night, and that next Saturday night the question for debate would be: Would it be a good policy for the United States Government to subsidize steamship lines? Wit and humor, satire and intelligence characterized the personnel of the membership.

For a century the Society might have been titled the graduate school of Washington College. So closely akin were the cultural aims of the two that the transfer to the college of the holdings of the society, including its library, guaranteed in perpetuity its ideals and purposes. The Franklin Society Scholarship, established in appreciation of this generous gift, is still one of the coveted honors of the college.

CHAPTER XVI: LEYBURN'S MEMORIES

THE WITHROW HOUSE, on Main Street, is one of the most picturesque and interesting structures in the town. In its early days it contained extensive grounds. The following extracts from Leyburn's *Memories,* written about fifty years ago, give a good picture of life in the old town a century ago.

"Our old house occupied a conspicuous place in the village. It was diagonally opposite the court house and on the corner of two principal streets. It was square, hip-roofed, with a tall chimney towering up from each corner and built of brick, some of which were glazed and so set in the walls as to form a succession of diamonds. Its elevated and isolated position exposed it to the full blasts of the winter winds, which came rushing down from the snow-clad mountains, roaring in the chimney tops and rattling the windows, moaning like so many spirits in distress through every crevice and keyhole, and throwing a gloom over our little circle.

"The village, years agone, had been destroyed by fire and often had we young people been thrilled with horror, whilst listening to the recital of the scenes of that terrible day, when the devouring flames turned the entire population out of doors and left their homes in ashes. Hence, there was a hereditary dread of fire among our villagers. When the appalling cry rang through the streets, waking them from their slumbers, every heart was smitten with terror, and men, women and children hastened from their beds to join the panic and confusion, which was sure to ensue.

" 'A dreadful night for fire,' my honored father would say, as the old northwesters roared and rocked the old homestead. Our house was rendered somewhat remarkable from being the resort of a great number of curious residents, which did not exactly belong to the family. In the summer evenings, as twilight began to fall over the neighboring mountains, millions of swallows would assemble from nobody knew where and, after floating for a long time in a wide, revolving circle around one of the high chimneys which was seldom used, would descend into its funnel and take up their lodgings for the night. When winter approached, they disappeared, but with the return of spring they regularly, year after year, came back to their old quarters. Strangers who visited our village seemed to regard our swallows as amongst the most notable objects of interest. From an opposite corner, they would stand and gaze at them, commenting upon their graceful circle until every bird had plunged into his narrow home. Usually they were blameless tenants, rarely making more disturbance than an occasional flutter and clatter of angry voices when crowded for bedroom. On one occasion we attempted to burn them out, by setting fire to some straw in the fireplace, but they were too many for us and we paid dearly for our inhospitality. They made such an ado with their wings and sent such a current of air downward that the flames were driven out into the chamber and we barely escaped a conflagration."

On summer evenings still these swallows return and are watched with interest, when anyone has time to stop long enough from the mad twentieth-century hurry to watch such a sight.

"The old house was in most respects a pleasant abode. Its apartments, for that day, seemed spacious and airy; the prospect of the surrounding hills and majestic mountains was beautiful and grand and the great piles of blazing hickory on the capacious hearth glowed with comfort and cheerfulness, as we cosily gathered round it. The long winter evenings, when the wind did not blow too hard for our tremulous nerves, were seasons of innocent joyousness never to be forgotten. Children from the neighborhood came in to join us in our playroom, and here the embryo amateur artist, with pencil and paint, made pictures for a laughing group or ludicrously besmeared their faces withal; here, pretended letters to great personages, detailing the petty affairs of the village, were penned; here, the cast-off habiliments of a former generation, or the military adornment of a country trooper, left here for safe keeping, were brought out and carefully arranged upon a hero of ten summers, to the great hilarity of the crowd; here, villainous gunpowder, clandestinely procured, sometimes burnt off eyelashes, sending the little circle screaming from the room; here, the story of 'rawhead and bloody bones' or the man that years ago had been hung on the neighboring hill, filled our young hearts with terror. Our evenings, whatever may have been their previous occupation, were invariably closed around the family altar."

Home life in this home was typical of old Lexington. Chess playing occupied a large part of the interest of the older people. Chess clubs went from house to house and spent long winter evenings in absorbed silence.

Dr. Archibald Graham was the Achilles of the town until Dr. Vethake, the new president of Washington College, arrived in 1835.

The Eagle Hotel, which stood where the McCrum Drug Company now stands, was the scene of many long drawn out chess matches between the intelligentsia of the village.

One of the few recorded accounts of trouble between a student and a professor took place at the Eagle Hotel. This is recorded by Dr. William Henry Ruffner:

"A student had been dismissed from school; he returned the next day and assaulted President Vethake in his office. Professor Farnum heard the scuffle, and seizing a pair of iron-tongs ran to the aid of the President, whom he found on the floor with the athletic young man standing over him. Professor Farnum sent the young man reeling from the blow of the tongs. This was the middle of the forenoon. The student vowed vengeance, and summoning a party of his friends, waited Professor Farnum's arrival at the

Eagle Hotel, where the Professor boarded. A lady, seeing him coming along with an ordinary cane in his hand, dropped a note at his feet, warning him of his danger. The Professor touched his hat and walked on. When near the Hotel door, the assailing party, armed with clubs, rushed out and attempted to surround him, whilst the student aimed a hard blow at the Professor's head, but the slender chemist, with the utmost coolness and grace, disarmed his adversary and with his cane gave him a thwack that must have reminded the gentleman of the tongs-salute he had received in the President's office. The friends of the offender now seemed determined to punish the object of their attack, but the Professor, who proved to be an adroit fencer, placed his back against the wall and kept the whole party at bay until the constable arrived. All were taken to the court house before the Bench of Gentlemen Justices. The scene in the court room was somewhat boisterous, until someone said something about jail. Professor Farnum preserved his dignity and gentlemanly manner perfectly and was discharged by the Court without censure. The students were required to enter into bonds for their good behavior.

"It was this occurrence which loosened the connection of President Vethake with the College and had something to do with Professor Farnum's resignation a year later."

In connection with the visitation, annually, of "millions of swallows," is another curious and interesting migration, that of the blackbirds. Records show that for over a century they have "hovered nightly" over the Lexington cemetery, making themselves quite a nuisance. Every conceivable means, from tying cowbells in the trees, to be rung at night, having the fire company turn their streams of water on them during the night, shooting them and every other idea that the mind of Lexington man or woman could conceive, has been tried, but the blackbirds are still with us.

The Scotch-Irish of Lexington proved too much for the Indians, but not for the swallows and the blackbirds.

CHAPTER XVII: THE IMPENDING CLASH

URING the 50's much was heard on all sides regarding slavery and secession and the impending clash, especially among the young men in the schools in Lexington, since they represented every section in the South, where were held very decided views and opinions about the questions at stake. In the fall of 1859 occurred a most spectacular affair, in which Lexington played a major part. A force of 1,500 armed men assembled at Charles Town for the execution of John Brown. Lexington was represented by General Francis H. Smith, who was in full charge of the execution and by Colonel J. T. L. Preston, with the cadets of the Virginia Military Institute.

In a letter written to his wife in Lexington Colonel Preston gives a vivid picture of the affair:

"The execution is over and we have just returned from the field. The weather was fine and between eight and nine o'clock the troops began to put themselves in motion to occupy the position assigned them on the field. To General Smith had been assigned the superintendence of the execution and he and his staff were the only mounted officers on the field, until the Major-General and his staff arrived. By ten o'clock all was arrayed and the general effect was most imposing and picturesque. The cadets were immediately in the rear of the gallows, with a howitzer on the right and on the left, so as to sweep the field. They were uniformed in red flannel shirts, which gave them a gay, dashing, Zouave look, exceedingly becoming, especially at the Battery. They were flanked obliquely by two corps, the Richmond Grays and Company F, which, if inferior in appearance to the cadets, were superior to any other company that I ever saw outside the regular Army.

"Other companies were distributed over the field, amounting to eight hundred men, and the military force was about fifteen hundred. The whole enclosure was lined with cavalry troops, posted with their sentinels and their officers, one on a peerless black horse and the other on a wonderful looking white one, continually dashing around the enclosure. The jail was guarded by several companies of infantry.

"Shortly before ten o'clock the prisoner was taken from the jail and the funeral cortege was put in motion. First came three companies and the criminal's wagon, drawn by two large white horses. John Brown was seated on his coffin, accompanied by the sheriff and two other men. The wagon drove to the front of the gallows and Brown descended with alacrity and without assistance and ascended the steep steps to the platform. His demeanor was intrepid, without being braggart. He made no speech; whether he wished to or not, I do not know. But had he so desired, he would not have been permitted. Any speech of his must of necessity have been unlawful, as being directed against the peace and dignity of the Commonwealth and, as such, could not have been allowed by those who were engaged in the most solemn and extreme vindication of Law. His manner was free from trepidation, but his countenance was not without concern and it seemed to me to have a cast of wildness. He stood upon the scaffold but a short time, giving brief adieus to those about him, and when he was properly pinioned, the white cap drawn over his face, the noose adjusted and attached to the hook above, he was moved, blindfolded, a few steps forward. It was curious to note how the instincts of nature operated to make him careful in putting forward his feet, as if he were afraid he would fall off of the platform. The man who stood on the brink of eternity was afraid of falling a few feet to the ground.

"It was now all ready and the sheriff asked him if he should give him a private sign before the fatal moment and he replied, in a voice that appeared unnaturally natural, that it did not matter to him, just so they did not keep him waiting long. He was kept waiting, however. While the troops were being put into position, he stood there blindfolded ten or fifteen minutes, the rope about his neck, expecting every moment the fatal act, but he stood motionless as a soldier. I was close to him and watched to see if I could detect any signs of flinching; once I thought I saw his knee trembling, but it was only the wind blowing his trousers.

"His firmness was subjected to still further trial by hearing General Smith announce to the sheriff, 'We are all ready, Mr. Campbell.' The culprit stood steady until the sheriff, with a sharp hatchet, severed the rope that held the trap-door, which sank beneath him and he sank three feet.

"The man of strong and bloody hand, of fierce passions, of iron will, of wonderful vicissitudes, the terrible Partizan of Kansas, the capturer of the United States Arsenal at Harper's Ferry, the would-be Cataline of the South, the demigod of the Abolitionists, the man execrated and lauded, damned and prayed for, the man who, in his motives, his plans, his means and his successes, must ever be a wonder, a puzzle, and a mystery—John Brown was hanging between heaven and earth.

"There was profound stillness during the time his struggle continued. At each feeble effort at respiration, the arms sank lower, the legs hung more relaxed and, at last, straight and lank he dangled, swaying slightly, to and fro, by the wind.

"It was a moment of deep solemnity and suggestive of thought that made the bosom swell. The field of execution was a rising ground that commanded the outstretching valley from mountain to mountain, with the white caps resting on them, suggesting the Alps. Before us was the greatest array of armed forces ever seen in Virginia—infantry, artillery and cavalry combined, composed of the Commonwealth's choicest sons and commanded by her best officers, and the great canopy of the sky overarching all, came to add its solemnity—ever present—but only realized when great things are happening under it.

"But the moral of the scene was the great point. A sovereign State had been assailed and had uttered but a hint and her sons had hastened to show that they were ready to defend her. Law had been violated by actual murder and attempted treason, and to uphold the law this armed force was assembled. Greater still, God's Holy Law had been vindicated. Thou shalt not kill; whoso sheddeth man's blood, by man shall his blood be shed.

"And here the gray-haired man of violence meets his fate, after he had seen two of his sons cut down in the same manner of violence into which he had introduced them. So perish all such enemies of Virginia! all such enemies of the Union! all such foes of the human race! So I felt and so I said, without a shade of animosity, as I turned to break the silence, to those about me. Yet the mystery was awful—to see a human form thus treated by men—to see life suddenly stopped in its course and to ask oneself the question without answer, 'And what then?'

"In all that array there was not, I suppose, one throb of sympathy for the offender—all felt in the depths of their hearts that it was right and, on the other hand, there was not one word of insult or exultation. From beginning to end it was marked by the most absolute decorum and solemnity. There was no military music, no saluting the troops as they passed by. The criminal hung upon the gallows about twenty minutes, and after being examined by the staff of surgeons, was deposited in a neat coffin and delivered to his friends and transported to Harper's Ferry, where his wife awaited it. She is described, by those who have seen her, as a large masculine woman, of absolute composure and manner. The officers who witnessed their meeting in the jail said that they met as though nothing had happened and that they enjoyed a good supper together.

"Brown would not have the assistance of a minister during his last days nor on the scaffold. He said that he was not afraid and that never in his life had he known fear. Brown was twice married and was the father of twenty children."

About this time the Lexington *Gazette* made this comment on the foresightedness of the women:

"We believe it is an historical fact that the ladies of the South have, from the beginning of our trouble, been in favor of secession. They see by the virtue of their superior intuition the propriety of the measure long before the dull and slated brain of man could perceive and respond to the necessity. Whilst men were reasoning upon the subject and striving in vain to solve the difficult problem, the intuition of the ladies had cut the Gordian Knot."

CHAPTER XVIII: THOMAS J. JACKSON ENTERS LEXINGTON

A MOMENTOUS DAY in the history of Lexington was March 27, 1851, when Thomas Jonathan Jackson, afterwards immortalized as Stonewall, was elected professor of natural and experimental philosophy and military tactics in the Virginia Military Institute. Many names were considered for this position, but he was unanimously elected, with a salary of $1,200.00 and commutation for quarters. Already marked by high character, scholarship and a brilliant career in Mexico, he was destined to go to greater heights than is given to many. He was born in Clarksburg (now West Virginia), January 21, 1824, of Scotch-Irish ancestry dating back to a parish near Londonderry. One of his ancestors, Colonel George Jackson, a contemporary of General Andrew Jackson of Tennessee, traced their ancestry back to the same parish and judging from the qualities of courage, energy and greatness, so similar in Stonewall and Andrew, the two who immortalized the name, it is logical to believe that they sprang from the same common ancestor.

Like General Lee, Jackson was left an orphan at a tender age, and his childhood was spent mostly with an uncle and other relatives, until his eighteenth year, when he rode horseback to Washington to receive, in person, his appointment to West Point.

From his earliest youth he demonstrated the spirit of Emerson's "The will is free; strong is the soul and wise and beautiful; the seeds of God-like power are in us still.—Gods we are, bards, saints, heroes, if we will."

Of his saintly mother it was said when she died, that "there were few women of equal, none of greater heart." Her only legacy, her prayers, but what a legacy! They shielded him through all his orphaned years and throughout his brilliant life. They were constantly answered in glorious endowments of virtue and grace.

Jackson made several unsuccessful attempts to locate his mother's grave. Many years after the surrender, Captain Ransom of Staunton, a close friend of Jackson, located the grave near Anstead, West Virginia and erected a stone to her memory.

Machiavelli said: "Virtue and richness seldom settle on the same man." How true in the case of Jackson.

After West Point and a splendid service in Mexico he came to Lexington, where he spent ten years. On June 4, 1853, he married Eleanor, daughter of Dr. George Junkin, President of Washington College and in whose charmed and beautiful home circle the Jacksons remained during their all too brief married life.

Mrs. Preston says: "Eleanor had many lovers before coming to Lexington, but her girl heart remained untouched until she met Major Jackson.

This was a surprise to the family, but they soon learned to love him, too. In early life Jackson was worldly and pleasure-loving. He goes to Lexington and it is generally thought that the earnest Presbyterianism of its Scotch-Irish laid hold on him. But a stronger power than the influence of a godly community had laid hold on him. Love, the Magician! He found Eleanor the sweetest woman he had ever known—a charming companion and the highest type of Christian. Hers was the staunch God-fearing faith of the old Covenanters. No wonder the soldier-professor, tossed hither and thither since boyhood, found in her the rest and joy of a satisfied heart. He adored her purity, reverenced her convictions and gave himself up to her spiritual guidance."

This lovely young woman, the idol of his life, passed away after fourteen months of perfect happiness. Major Jackson remained a member of the Junkin home and Mrs. Preston says further: "His early life, his lonely orphanage, his struggle with disease, his West Point life, campaigning in Mexico, his services in the Everglades of Florida and his life at various posts were topics upon which he often talked."

Jackson always maintained that his career would be that of a soldier, war being his true vocation, and that he only accepted a scholastic position for peace time. He was, however, a lover of peace. In one of his letters he said: "I greatly desire peace and I am persuaded that if God's people will earnestly and perseveringly unite in imploring His interposition for peace, that we may expect it."

It is known that he was not a popular teacher, and when one recalls the difficult subjects which he taught, such as the theory and practice of gunnery, the science of mechanics, optics and astronomy, some taught by experiment and some by application of mathematical analysis, it is not surprising that he was unpopular with students. When he would talk of the theory of light and motion and the doctrines of astronomy and employ the most abstruse and defined application of geometry and calculus of fluxions, one can easily believe that a large proportion of the class was overcome by the demands made upon them. Doubtless they floundered along in the rear of their teacher, with only a rare and occasional glimpse of the recondite truth that he was trying to impart.

When asked if he found teaching difficult, since it was not his chosen profession, he replied: "One may do whatever he resolves to do." This quotation was used so often by him that it has become synonymous with his name. It has been immortalized at Virginia Military Institute where it is emblazened on the wall of one of the halls. A fine reminder to those who are preparing for life: YOU MAY DO WHATEVER YOU RESOLVE TO DO.

No one ever doubted his ability and the better intellects recognized his scholarship, but the lesser lights and the laggards found him extremely hard and unreasonable. He lacked that peculiar tact of the born teacher, though he possessed all the endowments of the great soldier. He would give a question, to himself so simple and clear, and the student, not grasping it, would ask for a repetition of the question and Jackson would repeat verbatim, not making it one bit plainer for the poor student, for he would say, "If a boy was unable to comprehend a question, he was equally unable to answer it." To an officer, whose orders are given to be obeyed, this may be all right, but to a teacher, whose business is to instruct weaker minds, it seems a defect. The very force and clearness of Jackson's mind, moving from premise to conclusion, made it hard for him to appreciate this lack in others. However, he always used words perspicuous and without unnecessary phrasing.

One of the most painful consequences of ill health experienced by him for many years was the weakness of his eyes, which prevented any reading by artificial light, those reading hours so precious to most scholars. The only reading that he did at night was a short portion of the Scriptures, with which he invariably closed the day. His daylight hours were so full and his reading time so limited that he was forced to resort to an individual system of his own for study. In this connection, Mrs. Preston recorded: "His habits of study were very peculiar, but then, what was not peculiar about this exceptional type of humanity? Nothing but absolute illness ever caused him to relax his rigid system of rules. He would rise in the midst of the most animated conversation, like the very slave of the clock, as soon as the hour had struck and go to his study. He would, during the day, run superficially over large sections of French's mathematical works and then at night, with his green silk shade over his eyes and standing at his upright desk, on which a light always burned, with neither book nor paper before him, he would spend hours in digesting mentally what he had taken in during the afternoon in a mere mechanical way. His power of concentration was so great that he was able wholly to abstract himself from whatever was extraneous to the subject at hand. It became the established custom, unless otherwise engaged, I would go to his study at nine o'clock for an hour of relaxation and chat. But, if I knocked before the clock had struck, I would find him before the shaded light, as silent and dumb as the Sphinx. Not one moment before the ninth stroke had died away, would he fling aside his shade, wheel round and give himself up to such delightful nonchalance that one questioned whether this could be the same man that a moment before seemed to have neither motion, sight nor hearing."

In the classroom he never used a textbook, so accurately had he memorized his subject, and considering his subjects, this seems all the more remarkable. Most teachers would find difficulty in handling subjects dealing with the most refined mathematical analysis, the discussions of figures, dimensions, motions, and relations of bodies in space, even with many books and diagrams and other helps. Scholars will appreciate how great was his power of concentration and his exercise of memory, his imagination and his logical power. Some have thought him prosaic and unimaginative, but if imagination means the ability to express the creative power of the mind, to reproduce in the chambers of the soul, then it must be admitted that Jackson had great imagination. There is probably no better way to cultivate this faculty than through the study of applied mathematics in their higher branches.

A mathematician can map out in conception great circles of the heavens, equinoctial and ecliptic, with the orbits of the planets, and grasp the related movements of the worlds in his thought, as they wheel in intricate, yet orderly, labyrinths, while the feeble mind of the poetaster would collapse in utter confusion. The former can so produce before his own thoughts the things that are not seen with the reality of the things that are seen. This is that faculty of the intellect which raises man towards the all-knowing Spirit, in whose image he is made. Such a faculty in the great statesman or commander supplies that profound judgment which enables him to comprehend vast and multiplex affairs and to administer to his soul that stimulus of grand resolves.

Meditation over his meditation was a great aid to Jackson later, as a soldier. Command over his attention became a habit with him, which no tempest of confusion could disturb, and his power of abstraction became unrivalled. His imagination was so trained that it became competent for the grouping of the most intricate and extensive considerations, giving his mind power to endure its own tension. Having fixed in his mind the position of his own forces and those of the enemy in the field and the position of the rivers, streams and roads, he would study all the possible movements as he rode, rapt in thought, at the head of his column. No commander ever gave more scope to his own versatility and resources, yet there was never one whose foresight was more complete. Nothing emerged which he had not considered in his own mind. He was never surprised. His life at Virginia Military Institute was regular and marked by few incidents. He was ambitious and aspiring, which seemed to be stimulated by the memory of his early life and poverty. He once said to a friend: "An officer should make the attainment of rank supreme, within reasonable bounds, over every other consideration." His rule was to obtain advancement whenever possible, but never unless merited. He drew quite plainly the mark between fame and notoriety.

In June, 1854, the University of Virginia held an election for a professor in mathematics and Jackson applied for the place and produced many fine testimonials as to character, scholarship, and devotion to duty. Among these testimonials was one from Lieutenant Colonel Robert E. Lee, Superintendent of West Point. Jackson was not elected, however, and he acquiesced with perfect cheerfulness.

In politics Jackson was a Democrat and voted with his party, but he was never given to political discussions. His opinions were honest and without egotism and were his very own. "Be sure you're right, then go ahead," was one of his rules of conduct.

His closest friends never heard him boast of his military career nor of the many prominent members of his family. He knew, as did Plutarch, that "it is a desirable thing to be well descended, but the glory belongs to the ancestors." He was as cautious in his expressions as he was loyal in his principles. He did not boast of his ancestors, nor did he have reason to blush for them. They reflected virtue upon their posterity and their descendants have reflected back this virtue upon the old Scotch-Irish, whose noble blood coursed their veins, many of whom it could well be said, "they retained to their last days that elegance of manner and urbanity of speech so characteristic of these people."

One of the hardest things that Jackson ever had to do was to master the art of public speaking. Shortly after coming to Lexington he became a member of the Franklin Society, "a respectable Literary Society of Lexington, where the gentlemen of the town met for forensic debate." He was always punctual and spoke in his turn, but his first essays were as painful to his hearers as to himself. Confused and halting and often ending in silence and embarrassment, he would sit down. After awhile he would make another attempt and another and another until he finally expressed what was on his mind. Only by dogged perseverance did he overcome this diffidence, to the end that he became one of the most forceful speakers in the society, with a manner direct, forceful, emphatic and convincing. During his entire life in Lexington, he was a valetudinarian. He preferred the simplest foods and went entirely without stimulants, never using tea, coffee, wine or tobacco. In the winter of 1862, when prudence forbade the use of fire in camp, his medical adviser insisted that he have a stimulant, which he finally accepted. His attendant asked if it was unpleasant to take, to which he replied: "No, I like it and always have and that is the reason I never use it." On another occasion, when he and one of his officers were worn and weary, he was offered some brandy, which he refused, saying: "Thank you, but I am more afraid of that than I am of the Federal bullets."

Thus this great man, knowing his own weakness, kept free from temptation, for he said: "One break in my rule would not hurt me, but it would become a precedent for another and the whole conduct of my life would be weakened." A precedent embalms a principle.

Tall and erect and peculiarly English in his bearing, every movement quick and decisive, he practiced a military exactness even in his social relations. He was fond of ladies and said they were all angels. Opinions differ as to his comeliness. Stern and unbending, we think of him, but, when guest or host and occasion demanded, his serious and constrained expression gave way to a smile, so sweet and sunny that he appeared quite another person. But hearty laughter was a complete metamorphosis. His blue eyes fairly danced and his countenance rippled with glee. This could hardly be appreciated by those who never saw it, for it is certainly not the picture that most people have of him. If an artist could have put on canvas, side by side, his countenance as he played with a child upon his knee and then, that other countenance as he gave the command "to sweep the field with the bayonet," he would have accomplished a miracle in art.

On November 22, 1851, he joined the Presbyterian Church in Lexington; not, however, until he mastered thoroughly the Shorter Catechism and the Confession of Faith and was satisfied with its interpretations, and then only after long seasons of prayer did he make his decision.

He was interested in most community affairs and took a lively part in them. January 12, 1854, he was elected a director in the Lexington Bank. On that date, the *Valley Star* reported that the following were elected directors: General Francis H. Smith, Samu'l McD. Moore, James Compton, John L. Campbell, J. M. Pettigrew, Major Thomas J. Jackson, S. Vanderslice, and G. A. Baker, treasurer.

One of Jackson's outstanding interests in Lexington for which he will always be remembered was his Sunday School for the slaves of the community. Here he taught them Bible truths and helped them memorize and sing hymns. The African character is dilatory and, in his native state, he has little idea of time and he has retained much of this trait in his civilized condition. They were prone to drift along and to arrive at any and all hours at the school. This did not suit Jackson and such a condition could not long prevail. He warned them one Sunday that thereafter the bell would ring, then the door would be locked and no one admitted thereafter. This warning was necessary only once. It served to bring them on time. His prayers were very attractive to the slaves and he was often spoken of in Lexington as the "black man's friend." Jackson inculcated punctuality; like Rabelais, he considered nothing so precious as time and, like Sam Johnson, he thought nothing impossible to diligence and skill. To his own slaves he was methodical and exacting, but a kind and conscientious master, obedience being the rule of his household.

He was a deacon in the Presbyterian Church and no one ever performed more conscientiously his church obligations. His pew in the Lexington church is marked with a silver plate.

To get away from the grief caused by the untimely death of his devoted wife, he was persuaded to travel abroad. He visited England, Belgium, Switzerland, France, and Italy, returning after many months, greatly benefitted. July 15, 1857, he married Mary Anna Morrison and to them was born one child, Julia. Major Jackson was a home lover and all his interests centered there. His tongue, so guarded elsewhere, seemed, at home, to luxuriate in playful terms of endearment, borrowed often from the Spanish, which he claimed was more expressive than the English. The law of love reigned in his home. He entertained a great deal and was exceedingly generous and hospitable.

> In hospitality boundless
> In energy indominable
> In friendships ardent
> In good will to all, a model.

While it is generally felt that he was possessed of unlimited ambition, those who knew him in the privacy of domestic life, knew another and a different side. They knew of his aversion to some of the aspects of the soldier's life, its nomadic character, its want of domesticity, its stagnation in times of peace, and its interference with the ordered routine of a religious life. He advised a brother-in-law against entering the career of a soldier, for these reasons.

His was a sensitive nature, with an incredible impatience with, and shrinking from pain. The sight of a mangled body on a Mexican battlefield filled him with sickening dismay. Once when suffering from a slight attack of neuralgia, he said: "I could easier die than endure this for three days." Those who knew him in the home knew one side, and those who knew the soldier knew quite another side. In the home he was buoyant and cheerful, fond of children, rolling with them over the carpet, playing all manner of tricks and amusing them with his Spanish baby-talk.

When Jackson made up his mind upon a certain course, there was no changing. An authentic story illustrating this is told by Miss Nannie Jordan, whose father was Jackson's physician in Lexington. Jackson decided upon this method of keeping cool on hot summer nights: He would soak his shirt in ice-cold water and then put it on and go to bed, despite his physician's warnings. He always rose at dawn and, in spirit, if not in words, this must have been his salutation to the sunrise:

> Look to this day!
> For it is life, the very Life of Life.
> In its brief course lie all the
> Realities and varieties of your existence.
> The bliss of growth, the glory of action,
> The splendor of beauty.
> For yesterday is but a dream and
> Tomorrow is only a vision.
> But today, well lived, makes
> Every yesterday a dream of happiness and
> Every tomorrow a vision of hope.
> Look well therefore to this day!

His first occupation of the morning was secret prayer, followed by a brisk walk. Family prayers followed at seven, summer and winter, and all domestics were required to be present. Then breakfast and eight o'clock always found him in his classroom. He was truly a man of prayer, regarding which Dabney tells us that his was an intense sincerity of purpose and motive, knowing that faith teaches divine answer to prayer. No collisions of guilty desire with conscience, no side views of selfish ambitions, no itchings of avarice, no sensuality, no cravings for notoriety, no weakness of moral cowardice remained to disturb or jostle the steady adjustments of his judgment. The functions of his understanding were actuated by one supreme emotion, the sentiment of duty, a motive power as pure as forceful. Hence they were almost perfectly correct and true and, at the same time, full of intense vigor. Prayer implied to Jackson a Providence, with power to hear and answer prayer, otherwise, it was useless to petition. One of his most striking characteristics was that he prayed often and with much delight. Morning and night he bent in secret prayer, as well as in public with and for others.

This spirit of prayer was manifest by the change which was wrought in his whole manner. Everywhere in his speech he was curt and decided. At the throne of Grace, all was different. His enunciation was soft and deliberate, and his tones mellow and supplicatory, marked at once by profound reverence and filial confidence, abounding much in ascriptions of praise and thanks and the breathings of devout affection toward God.

"It would be unfair and unjust to the memory of one of God's most honored servants in Lexington to omit the mention of the chief instrument for the cultivating of this spirit of prayer in Jackson. When Jackson became a member of the Presbyterian Church, there was among its presbyters a man of God, whose memory yet lingers sweet, John B. Lyle. He was a bachelor, a bookseller, a man of middle age, well connected, but with small fortune, who devoted nearly the whole of his leisure to the spiritual interests of his charge. He was constantly the friend of the afflicted, the restorer of the wayward, the counsellor of the doubting, a true shepherd of the sheep and his inward Christian life was elevated as his outward was active." To him Jackson early learned to turn for counsel, for his spiritual state was not, at first, marked by that established comfort and assurance which shed such a sunshine over his later life. He confessed to Mr. Lyle his spiritual anxieties and seasons of darkness. His pious counsellor taught him by his example, by his instructions, and by suitable readings, which he placed in his hands, to cherish a high value on prayer and to expect, according to the scriptural warrant, a certain answer to it.

Two letters written to Mrs. Preston in Lexington show how genuine was his interest in his servants. From Centerville, October 23, 1861, he wrote thanking Mrs. Preston for her attentions to Amy and Emma (two of his slaves), and for the material comfort and spiritual care she had given them. He asked her to continue this and to assure them of his interest in, and prayers for them. He advised that he would keep a fund in the Lexington Bank upon which she was to draw for their needs. In this letter he said that his earnest prayer was for a speedy termination of the war.

In another letter, which was a reply to the news of Amy's death, he showed real grief at the passing of this faithful soul. He said that her devotion to the cause of her Redeemer had always impressed him and that she had gone to a better world, where he hoped that he and the redeemed of the Lord would be privileged to meet her. He also expressed gratitude that Amy had had a respectable funeral and that many had followed her remains to the grave: adding, "though such numbers cannot affect the dead, it is gratifying to the living."

It is told that Jackson was once saluted by a negro man, who raised his hat. Jackson, in return, did likewise. When spoken to about it he replied that he would not be less polite than the negro. He was practicing something of the teaching of the Koran, "when saluted with a salutation, salute the person with a better salutation, or at least return the same, for God taketh account of all things."

Such is a brief picture of Thomas J. Jackson, citizen, teacher, father, friend, and master as he went forth from little Lexington, in 1861, to fill the world with his fame. He left Lexington with the Virginia Military Institute cadets for Richmond, where they were engaged as drillmasters, many of them becoming officers in the Confederate Army.

CHAPTER XIX: THE BREAK COMES

NOW comes a critical time in the history of Lexington and the South. For many years there had existed between the free states and the slave-holding ones rather tense feelings, but Virginia had remained quiet and slow of expression. The winter of 1860-61 was a stormy one in Lexington. The cadets at the institute and the students at the college, being mostly from the seceded states, wore their badges and swore they would die rather than be coerced. The Lexington people, with a strong attachment for the Union which they had helped create and maintain, being slow to express their sentiments regarding secession, many word battles resulted between the young life and the older people. The following illustrates the affairs locally:

A great throng had assembled in the courtyard for the raising of a Federal flag and Francis T. Anderson was to make the oration. After much impatient waiting for the speaker to appear, his son, William A. Anderson, went to his office to see what was detaining him and found him closeted there with about twenty-five other leading citizens, seriously considering the latest developments. Finally, the speaker went to the court steps and the crowd cheered. He told them that the flag they had intended raising had been his flag, that he had helped bring it into being, had lived under it and had loved it, but that now it was in the hands of the enemy and would not be raised in Lexington. At this the crowd hissed and jeered, but when order was finally restored, he explained that a message had just been received from the governor of the State to the effect that Virginia had seceded, and there remained nothing left for Lexington but to follow the State's lead.

Not until President Lincoln called upon Virginia for a quota of soldiers to invade the seceded states did Virginia act, but now Unionism had come to a sudden stop in Lexington. The hissing and the jeering turned to cheering, and when a vote was taken on secession there was only one negative vote in the 1,728 cast. It is plain that these people took up arms with regret. Many thought that the war would be of short duration; some thought otherwise. Few indeed would have thought that more than thirteen hundred engagements would be fought on Virginia soil and that the dead and wounded would exceed a million men. General Sherman, upon leaving Louisiana, when that State seceded, said, that, though he was a West Pointer, he did not expect ever to take up arms against the South, for the reason that the war would not last long enough for him to be called into service. The Southern people can bear testimony as to the error of his judgment. He is credited with the phrase that "war is hell" and surely no one could have more thoroughly executed its reality.

When Virginia seceded, General Lee appeared before the Virginia Assembly, in session in Richmond, and offered his sword to his State and his Southland.

April 17, 1861, was a memorable day in Lexington. On that day Lincoln called on Virginia for men and the governor communicated Virginia's refusal to the President. Four days later the governor ordered Major Thomas J. Jackson and a number of the Virginia Military Institute cadets to Camp Lee as drillmasters and soon the call came for volunteers, and almost immediately appeared the Rockbridge Rifles and the Rockbridge Dragoons, headed for Harper's Ferry. Among those who acted as officers were Letcher, Edmondson, Lewis, Paxton, Hopkins, Boude, and others. The streets of Lexington took on a lively appearance. The citizens, including many of the colored ones, pledged their whole support to the Southern cause.

The Washington College students, known as the Liberty Hall Volunteers, under Captain James J. White and carrying a flag made and presented to them by the ladies of Falling Springs Presbyterian Church, was pronounced the best looking company of the time. The college, with only sixty-nine students, now closed its doors.

For weeks the ladies were busy making all kinds of garments for the soldiers and the local newspapers announced that within a few weeks after the governor's call the Rockbridge quota was ready for service. Among its contributions were two batteries of artillery, four companies of cavalry, seven companies of infantry, one of rangers, and many other men in miscellaneous lines of duty. The Rockbridge Battery was considered one of the very best in the Army of Northern Virginia. It served from the beginning to the surrender. The Liberty Hall Volunteers served with the Stonewall Brigade and participated in thirty-two engagements.

In the Rockbridge Artillery were forty-seven Washington College students, fifteen young men from the Episcopal Seminary and many graduates of the University of Virginia. Dr. William Nelson Pendleton, rector of Grace Episcopal Church in Lexington and a graduate of West Point, was their captain. When he ordered his men to fire, he would say: "Fire, boys, and may the Lord have mercy on their souls." Captain David E. Moore, long the Commonwealth's attorney of Rockbridge, fired the first shot in the Valley of Virginia. Most of the men from this section were in the Stonewall Brigade and of this company, Jackson said: "They are a noble body of patriots and when this war is over, the survivors will be proud to say that they were members of the Stonewall Brigade." He also said: "The name, Stonewall, should be attached to them rather than to me, for it was their heroism that won it at First Manassas."

Residents of Lexington claimed that all day long on the 21st of July, 1861, they could hear the guns at Manassas, one hundred and fifty miles away. That night the stagecoach came, bringing news of the battle. Colonel Cameron was on the stage. A man got off, carrying two guns; one of them accidentally went off and Colonel Cameron was killed. There were some who believed that this was not accidental, but nothing could be proven and, therefore, nothing was done about it.

Colonel Cameron, being a large land owner, with hundreds of slaves, was ordered to remain at home and produce food for the Confederate Army. He had four sons, who served throughout the four years in the Confederate Army and none of them received a wound and he, who stayed at home, was killed. General William A. Anderson, long the rector of the Washington and Lee University board of trustees and titled "Lexington's First Citizen" was a member of the college company; he was wounded at Manassas and crippled for life.

In the summer of 1861 many of the University of Virginia students came to Virginia Military Institute to be drilled.

Some may think that daylight saving time is something new, but the local newspapers reported in 1862 that candles were selling for seventy-five cents per pound and suggested, "why not substitute an hour in the morning for an hour in the evening?"

Popular foods (when obtainable!) included corn-pones, spoonbread, batterbread and spongebread all cooked on the fireplace. Cook stoves were introduced about 1850, but very few were in use during the war. Most of the gardens boasted of boneset, sage-ditny, catnip, horsemint, horehound, "old man" and "old woman," used for every kind of sickness by the old granny-woman, who could produce a tea or salve for almost any ailment. She used lobelia, white walnut bark, snakeroot, elder-blossom, bark of dogwood, cherry-poplar steeped in whiskey for fever. May apple root, walnut bark and slippery elm were also used with effect. Treatment for a cold was to warm the feet thoroughly before an open fire and get in bed and cover up. Many beautiful dyes were made by these women, copperas being the essential element used with root and bark of sassafras produced yellow and orange. With kalmia it produced a drab, and with leaves and berries of sumac it produced black, and so on.

Entertainments were simple, but evidently satisfying. Frolics or corn-husking contests, log-rolling contests, singing schools, shooting matches, hunting with hounds and many other sports were popular with old and young. Christmas was made much of and "bring your knitting and spend the day" was a general invitation.

The Odd Fellows' Hall, corner of Main and Henry Streets, was long the entertainment center of the village. It was the only public hall and here the delighted audience witnessed Wyman, the magician and ventriloquist, the celebrated Boone family, the famous Swiss bell-ringers and the wonderful Bohemian glass-blowers, who spun glass into beautiful tails for birds of paradise and peacocks. This hall later became the shoe factory of Thomas

H. Deaver. In 1885 roller-skating had an inning and this hall was converted into a skating rink.

During the earliest days of the "movies" in Lexington, this hall served the thrilled public with the old flickering Vitagraph pictures, featuring John Bunny and his gang. The hall, one of the very old buildings of Lexington, is still doing service. It is the property of the college and serves as the Troubadour Workshop.

CHAPTER XX: JACKSON AFTER CHANCELLORSVILLE

AFTER a brief though brilliant career in the service of the Confederate Army, about which so many biographers have written, Jackson was wounded and died at Chancellorsville. Riding hurriedly, at dusk, toward his own men who, thinking the enemy was approaching, opened fire. Several Confederates fell dead and many more were wounded, among them General Jackson, his right hand penetrated by a ball; his left forearm lacerated by another, and the same broken a little below the shoulder by a third which not only crushed the bone but severed the artery. His horse dashed, panic-stricken, toward the enemy line, carrying him beneath the boughs of a tree, inflicting severe blows and almost dragging him from the saddle. His bridle hand was powerless, but he seized the reins with his right hand and brought the animal under control. Before he could dismount, he fainted into the arms of his men, who bore him into the woods to shield him from the expected advance of the Federals. The blood was streaming when his two aides, Lieutenants Smith and Morrison, arrived. Morrison, the general's brother-in-law, was agitated by grief, but Smith was full of tenderness and self-possession, so valuable at such a time. With the skillful direction of General Hill, they effected an arrest of the hemorrhage and adjusted a sling to support the mangled arm.

Jackson immediately directed Smith to bring him some writing material and dictated a letter to General Lee. In the most unpretending words he stated that he had been disabled and that he had demitted his command to General A. P. Hill. He congratulated the commander-in-chief upon the victory which God had vouchsafed to his arms. He received soon after a note from General Lee: "Could I have directed events, I should have chosen, for the good of the country, to have been disabled in your stead. I congratulate you upon the victory which is due your skill and energy." Jackson remarked upon hearing this: "General Lee is very kind, but he should give the glory to God." At a later hour he remarked: "Our movement yesterday was a great success; I think the most successful military movement of my life. I expect to receive far more credit for it than I deserve. Most men will think that I had planned it from the first, but it was not so. I simply took advantage of circumstances as they were presented to me in the providence of God. I feel that His hand lead me. Let us give Him the glory." These words give the most exact representation of the character of his strategy.

His last military order was to General Pender. The Federals were pushing hard and Pender said: "My men are in such confusion that I fear I cannot hold my ground." To this Jackson replied: "You must keep your men together and hold your ground."

How fit was the termination of such a career as his and how expressive

Stonewall Jackson
(Note button out of place, sewn on by Jackson himself.)

A log house, Rockbridge County. The house still stands.

Castle Hill Hotel and tresle bridge

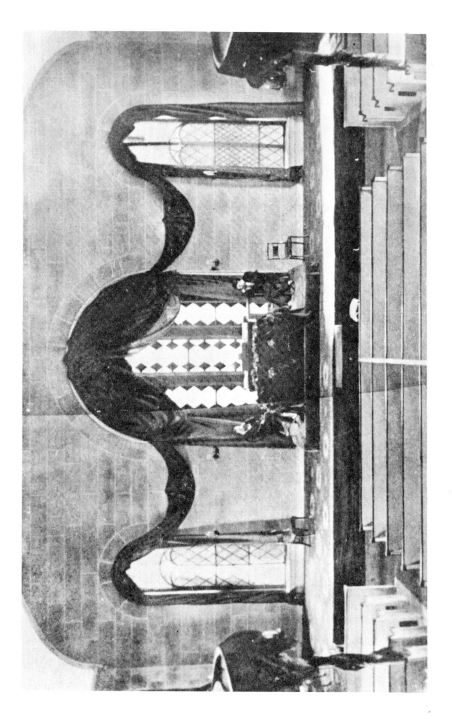

Washington College at the time of Robert E. Lee's arrival as president

"Virginia Mourning Her Dead" by *Sir Moses Ezekiel in original
location in front of Virginia Military Institute barracks*

of the resolute purpose of his soul! He now complained of faintness and men were obtained to bear him, despite the enemy's fire, through the tangled underbrush. The foot of one of the men bearing his head caught in a vine, he fell, and the general was thrown heavily upon the ground on his wounded side, inflicting painful bruises upon his body and intolerable agony on his mangled arm and renewing the flow of blood from it. As they lifted him again to the litter, he uttered one piteous groan, the only complaint which escaped his lips during the entire scene. Under a continuous shower of shells and cannonballs he was carried some distance to the rear, where he was met by an ambulance. This carried him to the field hospital near Wilderness Run, where he received care and attention. Dr. McGuire explained to him that he feared amputation of his arm would be necessary, to which he replied: "Dr. McGuire, do for me whatever you think best: I am resigned to whatever is necessary."

Preparations were made and chloroform was administered by Dr. Coleman. Dr. McGuire, with wonderful skill, performed the operation and Dr. Walls secured the arteries. Dr. Black watched the pulse and Lieutenant Smith held the light. Smith watched beside him during the remainder of the night. Early in the morning he was given some coffee, which he took with relish and said that it tasted good and refreshing.

Looking at the stump of his arm, he asked how he had acted through the operation under chloroform and added, "it was the most delightful physical sensation I ever enjoyed; I imagined I was hearing the most beautiful music that ever greeted my ear. I believe it was the sawing of the bone. I should dislike, however, above all things to enter Heaven in such a condition." He later said to a friend: "What an inestimable blessing is chloroform to the suffering."

The history of Jackson, as he turns from the battlefield to the quiet of the sick room gives an intimate glimpse into the real character of the great warrior. So eager a spirit would have been expected to chafe under his enforced inactivity at such a time, to have been like an eagle with broken pinions, beating against the bars of his cage, with a tumultuous struggle to soar again into the storm-cloud which was his natural air. But such anticipation did injustice to his Christian temper, which he constantly cultivated. From the moment he felt the hand of God laid upon him and his efforts, in the form of those wounds, he dismissed all the cares of command and the heat of his soul sank into a sweet and placid calm. He, who so recently had been pursuing victory with a devouring hunger, was now all acquiescence. He cast upon God all anxiety for his country and seemed unconscious of the grand designs that the day before were burning in his heart.

When he awoke from his slumber on the Sabbath morning, the sounds of a distant cannonade told his experienced ear that a great battle was raging. But the thought did not quicken his pulse nor draw from him a single expression of restlessness. He waited for news of results with full faith in God and in the valor of his army.

When a friend visited him and saw the stump of his arm and expressed sorrow at the misfortune, Jackson first thanked him and then proceeded with deliberation and emphasis, as though delivering a sermon on God's dealing with him: "You see me severely wounded, but not depressed, not unhappy. I believe that this was done according to God's Holy Will and I gladly acquiesce in it. You may think it strange, but you never saw me more perfectly contented. I am sure that my Heavenly Father designed this affliction for my good. I am satisfied that either in this life or in that which is to come, I shall discover that this which now seems a calamity, was a blessing. I can wait till God, in His own good time will make plain to me his object in thus afflicting me. But why should I not rejoice in it as a blessing and not look upon it as a calamity at all? If it were in my power to replace my arm, I would not dare to do it, unless I could know it was the will of my Heavenly Father."

He declared that he was in possession of perfect peace and that it had been a precious experience to be brought face to face with death and to find that all was well; that he had learned an important lesson "that one who had been the subject of converting grace and was a child of God could, in the midst of severe suffering, fix his thoughts upon God and Heavenly things and thereby obtain comfort and peace; but that one who had never made his peace with God, would be unable to control his mind, under such sufferings, so as to understand properly the way of salvation and belief in Christ; that if one had neglected the salvation of his soul before, it would then be too late."

Religion had long been his great concern and during these last hours seemed more than ever to occupy his mind and heart. He said that the Christian should carry his religion into his every enterprise; that it would make better any worthy calling; it would make a general a better commander and a shoemaker a better mechanic. So prayer, he said, would aid any lawful business, not only by bringing down the divine blessing, which is its direct and prime object, but by harmonizing his mind and heart.

On Monday morning he began to show signs of weakness and as the days passed this was more and more evident. Wednesday brought a cold, drenching rain, with a chilling atmosphere, bad for his enfeebled condition. That night Dr. McGuire, who had not rested for nights, but had stayed constantly by his patient's side, retired for the night. During the night the patient was overcome by severe pains in his side and by morning pneumonia had clearly developed.

When General Lee was informed of the critical condition he said: "Give him my affectionate regards and tell him to make haste and come back to me. He has lost his left arm, but I have lost my right arm. And tell him also, that I have wrestled in prayer 'for him' as I have never done for myself."

On Sunday morning, May 10, 1863, the doctor notified Mrs. Jackson that the end was near. She, remembering that the general had always said he would like a few moments' notice before the last struggle, decided to tell him. This she did with perfect calm. "Do you know that you will soon be in Heaven? Are you willing to acquiesce in God's allotment, if He wills you to go today?" He looked her full in the face and said: "I prefer it." Mrs. Jackson added: "Well, before this day closes you will be with our precious Saviour." He replied with distinctness, "I will be an infinite gainer to be translated."

He had often expressed the wish that he might die on the Sabbath day and this wish was granted. Just before the end came, Mrs. Jackson asked him where he wanted to be buried and he said, "In Lexington; yes, in Lexington." In his restless sleep he attempted to speak and finally said quite audibly: "Let us pass over the river and rest under the shade of the trees." These were his last words and Margaret J. Preston penned these lovely lines, based on this utterance:

THE SHADE OF THE TREES

What are the thoughts that are stirring his breast?
    What is the mystical vision he sees?
"Let us pass over the river and rest
    Under the shade of the trees."

Has he grown sick of his toils and his tasks?
    Sighs the worn spirit for respite and ease?
Is it a moment's cool halt that he asks
    Under the shade of the trees?

Is it the gurgle of waters whose flow
    Oft-time has come to him, borne on the breeze,
Memory listens to, lapsing so low,
    Under the shade of the trees?

Nay, tho the rasp of the flesh is so sore.
    Faith that had yearnings far keener than these,
Saw the soft sheen of the Thitherward Shore,
    Under the shade of the trees.

Caught the high psalms of ecstatic delight,
    Heard the harps harping, like soundings of seas,
Watched earth's assoiled ones walking in white
    Under the shade of the trees.

O, was it strange he should pine for release,
Touched to the soul with such transports as these,
He who so needed the balsam of peace,
    Under the shade of the trees.

Yea, it was noblest for him—it was best
(Questioning naught of his Father's decrees)
THERE to pass over the river and rest
    Under the shade of the trees.

Mrs. Jackson, prostrate with grief, leaned over him, with the only voice that had the power to recall him once more, for one brief moment, from the very threshold of Heaven's gate. He opened his eyes fully and gazing into hers, with a look of allegiance and love, closed them forever. His breath soon ceased and the great soul had taken its flight.

General Lee issued the following announcement to the Army:

"Headquarters Army Northern Virginia

May 11, 1863

General Orders No. 61

With deep grief, the Commander General announces to the Army the death of Lieutenant-General T. J. Jackson, who expired on the 10th, inst. at quarter past three P.M. The daring, skill and energy of this good and great soldier, by the decree of an all wise Providence, are now lost to us. But while we mourn his death, we feel that his spirit still lives and will inspire the whole Army with his indomitable courage and unshaken confidence in God and our hope and strength. Let his name be a watch-word to his corps, who have followed him to victory on so many fields. Let his officers and soldiers emulate his invincible determination to do everything in defence of our beloved country.

R. E. LEE, General"

How beautiful are Tennyson's lines here—"O iron nerve to true occasion true; O, fall'n at length that tower of strength which stood four-square to all the winds that blew"—"Other countries and ages might have witnessed such a national sorrow, but the men of this generation never saw so profound and universal grief as that which throbbed in the hearts of the Confederate people at the death of Jackson."

On the following day began the sad journey to Richmond. Upon reaching the outskirts of the city, Mrs. Jackson was met by Mrs. Letcher, wife of the governor, who took her through the most retired streets, to the Executive Mansion. Kind friends had provided for Mrs. Jackson a mourning outfit, which was gratefully appreciated.

The funeral cortege proceeded to the Governor's Mansion, followed by thousands of people. Business of all kinds had been suspended and the whole city went forth to meet the dead chieftain. Amid a solemn silence, broken only by the boom of minute guns and the wails of a military dirge, the procession finally entered the gates of the Executive Mansion. The casket, enveloped in the Confederate flag and laden with spring flowers, was placed in the center of the reception room. The Congress of the Confederate States had, a short while before, adopted the design for their flag and a large and elegant model had just been completed, the first one ever made, which was intended to be unfurled from the top of the capitol. This flag, the President had sent, as the gift of the country, to be the winding sheet for General Jackson.

In honor of the dead, the next day a great civic and military parade took place through the main streets of the city. The pallbearers were six major and brigadier generals in full uniform. The hearse, draped in mourning and drawn by four white horses, was followed by "Old Sorrel," led by a groom. This was followed by his staff officers; regiments of infantry and artillery; a vast array of officials; the President, cabinet, and all the general officers in Richmond, after which came a multitude of dignitaries and citizens. The avenues were thronged with spectators and a Sabbath silence brooded over all.

Upon reaching the Capitol, the pallbearers, headed by General Longstreet, comrade of the departed, bore the casket to the place prepared for it in the lower house of Congress, where it lay in state for the remainder of the day. Thousands upon thousands came to pay honor to the fallen hero. At the hour of closing the doors, came an old wounded soldier, pressing forward to have a last look at his beloved commander. Upon being told that he was too late, he remonstrated and was threatened with arrest, whereupon he lifted the stump of his mutilated arm and, with tears streaming down his face, exclaimed: "By this arm, which I lost for my country, I demand the privilege of seeing my General once more." The kind heart of Governor Letcher was so touched that the soldier's wish was granted.

The tears shed over Jackson's bier by strong men and gentle women bespoke the true and genuine affection and admiration in which he was universally held.

On Wednesday began the tedious journey, via Gordonsville to Lynchburg. No stop was made in Lynchburg, but a vast throng was there to attest their interest and affection. From Lynchburg to Lexington, the trip was made by canal boat to Alexander's Landing. Here the party was met by the Virginia Military Institute cadets, who conveyed the casket to barracks, to the classroom in which Jackson had taught during his ten years in Lexington.

The next day, it was taken to the Presbyterian Church, where Dr.

White, Jackson's pastor, in simple, but loving remarks, conducted the service, which was concluded at the village cemetery. He was laid to rest in the family plot, surrounded by boxwood and shaded by magnificent trees. This spot soon became the mecca for visitors from everywhere and today is visited by countless thousands, who admire true goodness and greatness.

In the early days of photography, it was considered quite the thing to be photographed at Jackson's grave and people came long distances for this purpose.

In 1891, Valentine's heroic statue of Jackson facing his beloved Southland, was erected and unveiled on the 21st of July. His remains were removed from their former resting place to the crypt under the statue, which marks forever the sacred spot where sleeps the great man and soldier surrounded by so many of those he loved in life. "Asleep till the day dawn and the shadows flee away."

July 21st dawned bright and clear, cool and bracing. Fleecy clouds floated about the sky, frequently obscuring the sun. The people of the village were pleasantly aroused early in the morning by the arrival of the Stonewall Brigade Band, marching to the strains of martial music, first to the cemetery and then to their headquarters at Franklin Hall. Fifteen guns, fired by the old Rockbridge Artillery, under command of its old Captain William T. Poague, ushered in the eventful and long to be remembered day. The guns were a part of the cadet battery formerly used by Jackson at the institute and later by the Rockbridge Artillery when it won immortal fame on the historic plains of Manassas, just thirty years before. From early morning till noon, thousands of visitors arrived from everywhere, coming by train, by carriage, buggy and wagons of any and every description, improvised for the occasion, by horseback and on foot. The entire population of the town and county contributed food and drink and comfortable quarters for the multitudes. Never was Lexington more heartily hospitable.

The streets were lined with people and the little town put on a holiday appearance. It was estimated that 30,000 visitors were present. Business houses, homes, horses and carriages were gaily decorated in bunting and Confederate flags, intermingled with State and national flags. At the cemetery the graves of the old soldiers were neatly decorated, with a Confederate flag placed on each. At the college, the tomb of Lee was beautifully and appropriately decorated by Miss Mary Pendleton. The main building and the Virginia Military Institute barracks were also very elaborately decorated in the emblems of the Confederacy. Jackson's lecture room at Virginia Military Institute was arranged by Miss Mercer Williamson for visiting sightseers. Here were on display many interesting souvenirs and relics pertaining to Jackson. Another object of interest to all visitors was Jackson's home, ornamented by festoons and flags, arranged with exquisite taste by Mrs. Nichols and Miss Annie White.

Arches, with mottoes and legends spanned the streets. The one at Main and Washington was of the mural-tower order. Over the keystone of the arch was a large Confederate flag, flanked by smaller flags. Along the crown of the arch on the obverse was: "Welcome to all who live—tears for all who died." On the reverse, over the crown was:

"From the field of death and fame
Borne upon his shield he came."

Portraits of Lee and Jackson were also on the arch. Stretching across the street in front of the courthouse was a snow-white banner: "Maryland, my Maryland." A block away another banner: "God bless old North Carolina."

Upon an airy and graceful arch in front of the school building another arch with an eagle perched thereon, holding the motto: "Hail, veterans, hail."

The grand arch was in front of the cemetery and modeled after the Arch of Titus. Along the attic, of the obverse and between the dates 1824 and 1863 was the word JACKSON and underneath this, encircling the crown, CHANCELLORSVILLE. From top to bottom hung banners of the Southern States and the names of Jackson's battles. On the reverse side was STONEWALL BRIGADE and the names of those who commanded it! Jackson, Garnett, Winder, Baylor, Grigsby, Paxton, Walker, and Terry.

The procession, forming on the Virginia Military Institute parade ground, moved slowly to the college campus. General Walker, chief marshal, headed the procession, followed by the Maryland Line and the Washington City veterans, headed by the great forty-piece Southern Band of Baltimore. In front of the speaker's stand, on the campus, the procession halted. Here was seated as distinguished an assemblage as was ever witnessed in the Old Dominion.

Lieutenant General Wade Hampton presided. After a very lengthy prayer by the Rev. A. C. Hopkins, of Charles Town, Colonel Thomas M. Semmes, professor of modern language and rhetoric at Virginia Military Institute read three poems: Stonewall Jackson's Way, Slain in Battle, and Over the River. This was followed by the oration of the day by Lieutenant General Jubal A. Early. He spoke "loud and long," ending with this rather striking paragraph: "Generals Lee and Jackson fully appreciated the character of each other, and there was the most perfect harmony between them. No man, in all the land, felt more keenly the loss of his great co-adjutor than General Lee. When anyone desires to find a defense of the justice of the cause for which they fought, let him point to the characters of Lee and Jackson. I conclude now, with the declaration I have made before; I trust that every faithful soldier of the Army of Northern Virginia is ready to exclaim with me, 'If ever I disown, repudiate or apologize for the cause for which Lee fought and Jackson died, let the lightnings of heaven blast me and the scorn of all good men and women be my portion.' "

At one o'clock, the roll of a dozen drums called the veterans and the volunteers to their positions and the procession started towards the cemetery, where the real event, the unveiling of the statue, took place. The procession marched around to the rear of the cemetery, by way of the old fairground road, and was massed in a field south of the center of interest. In the foreground was arranged column after column of veterans, until a solid phalanx was formed.

The unveiling was by Julia Jackson Christian, Jackson's only grand-daughter.

Lexington was never more hospitable. Free lunches were served to thousands and barrels of ice water were on every street corner.

The first sight of the statue gave real satisfaction to everyone. One veteran was heard to say, as he gazed upon the face and form of the statue: "That is Old Jack! May God preserve it."

The statue cost $9,000.00 which was raised by popular subscription. The first money raised locally for the fund was $2,000.00 from a bazaar, held in the Ann Smith Academy building, by the ladies of Lexington. It lasted a week and resulted in this large sum for the fund. The Jackson Memorial Association, organized in 1875, in Lexington, after sixteen years, realized the fruits of its efforts in this unveiling. Much of the success of the association was due Judge J. K. Edmondson, its chairman.

❧ ❧ ❧ ❧

Jackson's home in Lexington, the only one ever owned by him, has very fittingly become a memorial to his memory. Some years ago, the United Daughters of the Confederacy purchased it and converted it into the Jackson Memorial Hospital. Under wise and competent guidance it has become Lexington's indispensable institution, where the citizenry of the town and county and the students from every State in the Union receive medical and surgical attention of the highest order.

Souvenir hunters all but carried the house away piecemeal before it was rescued by these noble women. Among those who were instrumental in the accomplishing of this creditable achievement were: Miss Sue Davidson, the guiding hand and spirit, Miss Mary Davidson, Mrs. Clara D. Estill, Mrs. D. C. Humphreys, Miss Annie White, Mrs. Matthew W. Paxton, Mrs. Robert R. Witt, Mrs. W. A. Anderson, Mrs. Morgan Pendleton, Miss Mary Pendleton, Mrs. Gadsden, Mrs. Susan P. Lee, Mrs. W. C. Stuart, Mrs. J. McD. Adair, Mrs. Thomas M. Semmes, Mrs.

Wm. G. McDowell, Mrs. James Smith, Mrs. John H. Latane, Mrs. E. W. Nichols, Mrs. Wm. T. Poague, Mrs. W. LeC. Stevens, Mrs. John H. Moore, Mrs. A. T. Barclay, Mrs. A. L. Nelson, and Mrs. Belle Bruce. Many thought that they were attempting the impossible and with a less resolute group it might have been, but not so with them.

At a meeting of these ladies at the home of Mrs. Estill, they decided to undertake the proposition. On June 4, 1904, the property was bought from the widow of Stonewall Jackson. Without a penny in sight the ladies obligated themselves to pay Mrs. Jackson $2,000.00. Some of the first money raised for this purpose was from a speech by William Jennings Bryan (in the old skating rink), in Lexington in 1905. He was introduced by Frank T. Glasgow.

It is interesting to note that this house was built by William Alexander, a merchant of the town, and that he sold it to Major Jackson in 1858; thus it belonged to the Jacksons for more than a half century. As the ladies were leaving Mrs. Estill's they met Henry St. G. Tucker and he, in his jovial manner, asked, "Well, what mischief are you women up to now?" Miss Mary Pendleton told him what they had just undertaken, without a penny in sight. He handed her five dollars and said, "Well, here's a starter." This was the first money contributed toward this great undertaking and greater accomplishment.

Through the succeeding years Mr. Tucker and his wife proved to be the best friends that the association had. They protected the hospital property by buying and giving the buildings on either side, buildings that since have been greatly needed and are connected with the main hospital, one as nurses' home and the other the laboratory, equipped by William M. McElwee in memory of his wife.

Though photography was new in Jackson's day, only one photograph was ever taken of him. This was in 1862, just before the Valley Campaign. The circumstances were: At a dining given by Dr. McGuire, in Winchester, Miss McGuire requested that Jackson have his picture made for her. "All right," said the General, "I will go now and have it taken." Accompanied by Dr. Graham, he went to the studio of Mr. Roatzand and when getting ready for the sitting, the photographer said: "General Jackson there is a button off your coat." "I know it," replied the General, "and if you will give me a needle and thread, I will sew it on." This he did and sewed it out of line, as shown in the picture. This small defect, in an otherwise perfect likeness, has often been commented upon.

Like General Lee, Jackson liked fine horses. "Old Sorrel," his favorite war horse, spent his last days as an honored guest on the blue grass of the Virginia Military Institute parade ground. He was gentle and a pet of everyone, including the children. Souvenir hunters pulled so many hairs out of his tail that, before he died, at the advanced age of thirty-five, he hardly had enough tail left to "shoo the flies away."

The *Rockbridge County News* of November 7, 1884, notes: "Mrs. Jackson had given her consent for 'Sorrel' to be exhibited at the Hagerstown (Maryland) County Fair. Yesterday, toward the close of the races, it was announced from the judges' stand that Stonewall Jackson's old war horse would be brought upon the track. In a few minutes, 'Old Sorrel,' led by a small boy on a Shetland pony, came upon the track. The band struck up *Dixie,* followed by *Maryland, My Maryland.* At the sound of these familiar strains, 'Old Sorrel' threw his venerable head in the air, as if sniffing the scent of distant battles and pranced over the track with his old-time fire, which seemed to survive his thirty-four years. As he passed the grandstand he was greeted by handclapping and a round of applause and the waving of ladies' handkerchiefs. The whole scene caused much enthusiasm."

Another horse of which Jackson was very fond, was "Molly Jackson," a beautiful bay. At the outbreak of the war, the citizens of Augusta County made up a purse and bought and presented this fine horse to the General. After the death of Jackson, the horse came into the possession of Fielding Templeton and after the surrender, Mr. Templeton brought her to his farm near Fairfield, where she spent the remainder of her sixteen years, at the homeplace of J. McD. Adair, one of Lexington's most honored citizens. Mr. Adair, having passed the four-score mark, still hale and hearty, delights in telling of Molly Jackson's mean disposition. He says that she would not work and that she remained a fighter to the end of her days, and that no one dared to cross the pasture lot when she was there. She was as fearless as her great master. Mr. Adair says that he rode her many times to the local store and to the postoffice.

CHAPTER XXI: YANKEES ENTER LEXINGTON

ONE day, early in June, 1864, Lexington was startled by the arrival of a courier with the news that Hunter and his men were advancing and that they were only a few miles away. Cattle, horses, and sheep were hurriedly driven to the mountains for safety, family silver and other valuables were hidden and everything put in readiness for the coming of the enemy. On June 10, the town knew that he had arrived. From Shaner's Hill, just beyond the river, he bombarded the town, his shells striking more than forty houses, many of them striking the Virginia Military Institute barracks, which was his real target. Then, by the use of a pontoon bridge over the river (the Confederates had burned the wooden bridge, in their efforts to keep the Federal forces back), he entered the town without opposition, as only a feminine population, with a slim line of small boys and a few octogenarians was present.

A woman still living, who remembers this far-off day, recalls that from her home, on an elevated site near Lexington, she witnessed more than a dozen barns in flames at the same time.

The unwelcome visitors remained in Lexington three days. They made beefsteak of all the town cows and sausage of the hogs. They left very little in the way of food. Acres of onions, which had been planted for the Confederate Army, were gathered by Hunter. In their pillaging they took a sword from the Glasgows, at Tuscan Villa, and many years later Mr. Glasgow located the sword and it was returned to him. Tuscan Villa has been in the same family ever since the original grant from the King.

The negroes were afraid of the visitors, but when the Yankees left Lexington, many of the negroes followed them. Some months after Hunter's occupation of the town the Synod of Virginia met in Lexington and it was reported that "what Hunter did not get, the preachers did."

Mrs. Preston gives this picture of Hunter's call on Lexington:

She recorded that Sunday, June the 12th was a day she could never forget. "I slept undisturbed during the night, but was called down early the next morning by the servants who told me that they could not keep the soldiers out of the house. I went down and appealed to them as a lone woman, with no protection, but I might as well have appealed to the bricks. I had left the smokehouse door open to let them see that every piece of bacon had been taken. (I had some hid under the porch, which they had not yet found.) They came into the dining room and began to carry away the china, when a young fellow from Philadelphia took the dishes from them and made them come out. I told them that I was a Northern woman, but that I was not proud of my lineage, when I saw them come on such a mission. They demanded to be let into the cellar and one threatened to burn the house unless I did as they demanded. I told him to burn it, that we were at their mercy, but I would not give him the key. They took our arms and broke them up and then broke into the cellar. They carried away the molasses, lard and other things, but did not find the bacon. They asked if I had any more and I told them that I did, but that it was in the mountains. They pressed into the house and two of them searched my dressing room and what they took I do not know. They seized our breakfast and even snatched the toasted bread and egg that had been begged for a sick man's breakfast. My children were crying for food and I had nothing to give them but crackers.

"They set fire to the Institute about nine o'clock and flames are now enveloping it. The towers have fallen and the arsenal is exploding as I write. Governor Letcher's home has been burned and they told me that all the professors' homes would be burned, including Colonel Preston's. By and by an officer came and told me that I had been annoyed and that he would send me a guard, though he had no authority to do so. Let me note here and I do it with chagrin and shame that the only really civil men have been those from Western Virginia and from Philadelphia. Invariably those from Virginia were polite. One offered some silver for bread. I had nothing but crackers, which I gave him, remarking that he was on the wrong side for a Virginian. He looked decidedly ashamed. It was twelve o'clock before we got our breakfast. They carried off the coffee pot and everything else they could lay their hands on and while the guard, a boy of seventeen, was walking around the house, they emptied the corncrib. General Hunter has ordered the burning of all the professors' houses. Mrs. Smith pled that hers be spared because of her very ill child and, for this reason, it was not burned and Hunter used it for his headquarters.

"This has been an awful day and it might be worse before night. One cavalryman said that if all talked as I did they would fire the whole town.

"News has come that General Smith, General Williamson, and General Gilham have been taken prisoners. Where is my husband? If he is taken prisoner and our home is burned, what will life be worth? (Three o'clock in the afternoon) I am in despair — forty thousand troops are marching on Richmond, through here. A guard told me that Richmond must fall. How can it withstand such numbers! I am astonished that in the midst of our troubles we can be so calm. How awful is war! Who would think that this is Sunday and our intended communion?

"One of our overseers has just come to tell me that every sheep has been killed and every cow and horse been carried away."

The next day Mrs. Preston had a long talk with one of the officers and he asked her for some trifle that had belonged to Stonewall Jackson, saying, "we think as much of him as you Southern people do."

It had been reported that every house would be searched for arms and

Mrs. Preston hid Jackson's sword in Mrs. Jackson's piano; that sword that had flashed so victoriously over many a battlefield.

Her last entries of these hectic days were: "A report has come that the cadets have been captured and that the servants are flocking away and that she is heart and soul weary." The Northern guard said in parting: "Well, in the next world there will surely be someone made to suffer for all this." With the departure of the uninvited guests the spirits of the people began to rise and they ceased feeling subjugated.

During the war the investments of the college suffered along with the common calamities of the South and its financial condition was crippled. Though it was private property and hallowed by the association of Washington, it did not escape the havoc and ruin of wartime. The trustees, however, appealed to the general public throughout the country and immediately came contributions from Texas, Louisiana, Tennessee, Kentucky, Ohio, Maryland, Missouri, New York, and Philadelphia. Though poor in finances, it was and always has been rich in the things that money cannot buy. Its hallowed associations give it a place unique among all American universities.

CHAPTER XXII: APPOMATTOX

WORN down and shut off from supplies, the Army of Northern Virginia gave up the struggle at Appomattox, April 9, 1865. Mrs. Preston records in her diary of April 10th: "News has come that General Lee has surrendered. We are struck dumb with astonishment! Why then all these four years of suffering, of awful bereavement, of separation, of horror, of blood, of havoc? Why these ruined homes, these broken family circles, these scenes of horror that must scathe the brain of those who witnessed them till their dying day?" Just before the fall of the Confederacy, means of subsistence became narrower and narrower, disaster thickened, starvation for the whole country threatened. The only gleam of brightness was the courage of the soldiers in the field and the suffering people at home, both with entire readiness to keep up the fight as long as "Marse Robert," the Confederacy's idol, stood at the head.

The winter of 1864-65 was remembered by the Lexington people as the dreariest of the century.

It is easy to believe that the feeling of the Southern people, upon learning of the surrender, was that life was over. This feeling did not conquer, however, for they were not the kind to quit, but, with that indomitable spirit, which had brought them through those four hard years of warfare, they immediately faced the future and the gigantic task of rebuilding, and the results are well known. In the full tide of success and victory the South had given General Lee its fullest allegiance, but when it saw him yield the sword, it seemed more than ever to cement the love and confidence of the entire South for him. The men of the Confederacy had done their best, and a noble best it was; and had they forgotten, the women of the South would have kept that memory alive. The old soldiers often contended that they were never whipped, but that they wore themselves out whipping the Yankees!

Lee's farewell to his worn and tattered army is sympathetic and characteristic:

"Headquarters Army Northern Virginia,
Appomattox C. H. April 10. 1865

"General Orders No. 9

"After four years of arduous service, marked by unsurpassed courage and fortitude, the Army of Northern Virginia has been compelled to yield to overwhelming numbers and resources. I need not tell the survivors of so many hard fought battles, who have remained steadfast to the last, that I have consented to this through no distrust in them, but feeling that valor and devotion could accomplish nothing that would compensate for the loss that must have attended a continuance of the contest, I determined to avoid the useless sacrifice to those whose past services have endeared them to their countrymen.

"By the terms of agreement, Officers and men can return to their homes and remain until exchanged. You will take with you the satisfaction that proceeds from the consciousness of duty faithfully performed and I earnestly pray that a merciful God will extend to you His blessing and protection. With an unceasing admiration for your constancy and devotion to your country and a grateful remembrance of your kind and generous consideration of my self,

"I bid you all an affectionate farewell.

ROBERT E. LEE."

Apropos of the men being permitted to return to their homes and to retain their sidearms and horses is this interesting heart-story: Ben Cox, with his superior officer, Colonel Fleming, had withdrawn from Petersburg, two or three days in the van of Lee's retreat. At the time of the surrender, they had reached Amherst Heights, near Lynchburg, and were pressing westward, hoping to join Johnston in Tennessee. A courier overtook them and ordered them back to Richmond for parole. They rebelled and could hardly be persuaded that the surrender was a reality. Finally, they broke down the wheels of their cannon and spiked it and each got astride a horse, which, by the way, were U. S. Army horses, previously captured and branded U. S., and started for Richmond. In Buckingham County, they came upon the Federal force, and a young officer from Massachusetts engaged young Cox in conversation, seeing that he was riding a U. S. horse. After the facts regarding the capture of the horses were related, they introduced each other in friendly manner. Cox said, "Why we have had a governess by that name in our family for years." "And that is my sister," said the officer from Massachusetts. As they rode along together like two cronies, Cox was asked the whereabouts of his father's plantation. Upon learning that they would pass through the very edge of it, the officer suggested that Cox change clothes with a Union man and, as they neared his father's place, he slip out and go home and thus avoid the long trip to Richmond and return. This Cox did and reached his home early in the night. The preceding days had been hard ones. For weeks they had had very little food and the confusion and heartache incident to defeat had cut deep lines on the faces of the most robust. So when young Cox knocked at his father's door and stood face to face with his old black mammy, who had reared him, he was not recognized. But this was not surprising, for he had spent ten months in the trenches around Petersburg, those terrible months upon nerve stamina. Instead of the vigorous, stalwart, optimistic youth, who so recently went forth in defense of his country, stood a gaunt, unshaven, undernourished, sad-eyed man, and to add to mammy's confusion, he looked for all the world like a Yankee. As she professed no love at all for the enemy of her white folks, she was about to slam the door in his face, when suddenly she recognized him and throwing her black arms about him and with tears of joy, she exclaimed: "for Gawd's sake, if it ain't ma li'l Marse Ben. How come you got them Yankee clothes on? Come in dis house and git 'em off you."

Young Cox was not permitted to take his horse, as all horses had to be taken into Richmond. Many years passed and the incident was all but forgotten. One of the kind concessions of General Grant to General Lee was that the horses were to be kept by those in whose possession they were at the time of surrender. About 1915, there was a bill passed in Congress reimbursing those from whom horses were taken after the surrender and Mr. Cox, then the beloved and honored business manager of the State Teachers' College at Farmville, was able to make an affidavit to the effect that his horse had been taken from him. With the money he received, he bought a diamond ring for his lovely wife. The ring was later bequeathed to their daughter, Miss Mary White Cox of the Teachers' College.

It has been said that earth has known no lonelier spot than Lee's tent on the night of the surrender. His feeling of utter helplessness was shared by the Southern people. Four long, hard, bitter years—and defeat at last. Here, however, he turns his back to the past and faces the future. How appropriate the Lee crest: *Non incautus futuri.*

General Lee was never known to indulge in arguments about the war, but carried in his own bosom his disappointment and loss. Light griefs speak out; great ones are silent. After the surrender Lee retired to the home of friends in Cumberland County. While there, many invitations came to him as well as offers for the use of his name, to which he replied: "My name is not for sale." Admirers in England offered him ease and retirement to which he replied: "No, I will never leave my people in their extremity. I will stay with them. We will endure together. I am ready to break with them my last crust."

Soon after the surrender the trustees of Washington College met for the purpose of electing a president. Their unanimous choice was General Lee. It was reported that one of his daughters had said that, though many offers had come to her father, nothing had been offered him whereby he could earn a living for his family.

The trustees decided to extend the invitation of the presidency of the college to General Lee and to present it in person. Judge Brockenbrough was appointed to go on this very important mission. But owing to the exigencies of war time, he had no suitable clothes in which to appear before the great general. Another member of the board, Hugh Barclay, had some respectable clothes which he offered, and thus equipped, Judge Brockenbrough made the successful trip.

General Lee took the matter under advisement. His letter of acceptance, written from Powhatan County, August 26, 1865 follows:

"Gentlemen;

"I have delayed for some days, replying to your letter of the 5th inst, informing me of my election by the Board of Trustees to the Presidency of Washington College, from a desire to give the matter due consideration. Fully inspired with the responsibilities of the office, I have feared that I should be unable to discharge the duties to the satisfaction of the Board or to the benefit of the country. The proper education of youth requires not only great ability but, I fear, more strength than I now possess, for I do not feel able to undergo the labor of conducting classes in regular courses of instruction. I could not, therefore, undertake more than the general administration and supervision of the Institution.

"There is another subject which has caused me serious consideration and is, I think, worthy the consideration of the Board. Being excluded from the terms of amnesty in the proclamation of the President of the United States, on the 29th. May, last, and an object of censure to a portion of the country, I have thought it probable that my occupation of the position as President might draw upon the College a feeling of hostility. I should, therefore, cause injury to an Institution which it would be my highest desire to advance. I think it is the duty of every citizen of the country, to do all in his power to aid in the restoration of peace and harmony and in no way to oppose the policy of the State or general Government directed to that object. It is particularly incumbent upon those charged with the instruction of the young to set them an example of submission to authority. I should not consent to be the cause of animadversion upon the College.

"Should you, however, take a different view and think that my services in the position tendered me by the Board, will be advantageous to the College and to the country I will yield to your judgment and accept it. Otherwise, I must respectfully decline the office.

"Begging you to express to the Board of Trustees of the College my heartfelt gratitude for the honor conferred upon me and requesting you to accept my cordial thanks for the kind manner in which you have communicated your decision,

I am, Gentn with great respect
Your most obedient servant

R. E. LEE.

"To Messrs

John Brockenbrough, Rector
S. McD. Reid   Alfred Junkin
Horatia Thompson   Bolivar Christian
J. L. Kirkpatrick

Committee."

CHAPTER XXIII: ROBERT E. LEE ENTERS LEXINGTON

PROBABLY the most important day in Lexington history was the 18th of September, 1865, when General Robert E. Lee, after four days en route from Cumberland County, rode Traveller up the long Main Street into town. Unlike the great Homer, who in life had to beg his daily bread, but in death was claimed and honored by many cities, General Lee had the hearts and homes of the entire Southland tendered him. This community realized the honor and distinction that came to it on that eventful day, which forever set it apart. As he rode, alone with his thoughts, over the beautiful Virginia hills and across the Blue Ridge, he must have halted on the pinnacle of these lovely mountains and taken a farewell glance eastward. What memories must have surged in his breast! Then looking westward, Lexingtonward, he must have sensed it as his promised land, where his golden years were to be spent and where he would be loved and appreciated for all time. How grand must have been his resolve as he bade farewell to the past and now, at the age when most men sought retirement, faced the gigantic task of rehabilitating an almost defunct college, of rebuilding a chaotic South, of reuniting a severed nation. History plainly reveals his monumental success.

With his coming, the college doors again opened and, more than ever, were thronged with eager and ingenuous boys from every section of our common country, whose zeal and devotion in search of knowledge won the commendation of both the community and the college authorities. The homes of the village were also opened, for General Lee preferred that the boys stay in the Lexington homes, where they would come in contact with the best society and its wholesome influence.

General Lee was a great college president. He exemplified in his daily life the principles upon which his fame rests. Many claim that he was second to none. During his first year he broke away from the long prescribed course and inaugurated the elective system, which Harvard and other schools came to later. Journalism was stimulated (the Lexington *Gazette* gave free instruction to students), as was agriculture and engineering. The first pronouncement of the Honor System appeared during his regime. The college catalogue of 1867 says: "The discipline has been placed upon the basis on which it is believed experience has shown it can most safely be trusted, upon the honor and self-respect of the students themselves." He knew and called all the students by name and manifested a peculiar and an individual interest in them. Walking from chapel one morning, in deep meditation, he was asked by a friend why he was so serious. "I was thinking of my responsibility to Almighty God for all these young men," he replied.

A student asked General Lee for a copy of the college rules. "We have no printed rules here, we have but one rule and that is that every student be a gentleman."

Student orators often indulged in compliments to General Lee and the ladies, and just the reverse towards the Yankees. General Lee sent them his criticism. "You young men speak too long and you make three other mistakes. What you say about me is distasteful to me, and what you say about the North tends to promote ill feeling, and your compliments to the ladies would be more appreciated if paid in private."

The following extracts from a recent autobiography by an alumnus of General Lee's régime gives a fine picture of student life at that time:

"The only college to be thought of was, of course, Washington College at Lexington, Virginia, where my two brothers had been before me and of which our great Southern hero, Robert E. Lee, was President. In August, 1869, I left home for an absence of three years and no more home-sick youth was ever landed on a college campus for an absence from home of three years. I will give the itinerary of my journey from Mt. Holly, Arkansas, to Lexington, Virginia, as illustrative of the one thousand years, measured not by the almanac, but by the rate of the world's progress previous to that time, which have intervened between that date and now. Leaving home on Monday morning, I traveled one day by private conveyance to Camden, then two days by stage-coach to a point on the Mississippi, one day and night by steamer to Memphis, and two days on the railroad, the first I had ever seen, to Lynchburg. Arriving there late, we missed the Saturday evening canal boat to Lexington and had to wait till the following Wednesday for the next boat. The entire journey, which could be made now in ten hours by airplane, consumed ten days.

"The morning after my arrival, I had my first meeting with General Lee. With my friend, Drake Haislip, another Arkansas boy, who had been at college the year before, we were passing the chapel door as the General was coming up the steps from his office. My natural timidity was aggravated by having been recently placed in an unaccustomed environment and I had looked forward with dread to the experience of meeting so great a man face to face. But when I had a full view of his countenance my timidity vanished and with no embarrassment whatever, I responded to my friend's introduction and extended my hand and said, 'Good morning, General Lee.'

"I have a little faded photograph of General Lee taken while I was at college, which preserves the sweetness and gentleness, combined with strength and dignity, which impressed every member of the student body.

"General Lee taught no classes, but confined his labors to the general direction of college affairs and the administration of discipline. His government of the college was entirely paternal. His first administrative act was to abolish all rules, except the general and comprehensive one that every student was expected to attend faithfully to his college duties and to conduct himself as a gentleman. His own character, as the ideal gentleman, was deeply impressed on all who were capable of being impressed.

"One impression that I retain of General Lee was his sobriety. Lexington was a wide-open town in those days. He never touched ardent spirits, nor did he use tobacco. His breath was as immaculate as the clothes he wore; yet, he had a way of reaching the boy who happened to drift into dissipation. It is said that he went through the Mexican and the Civil Wars without touching a drop of ardent spirits. I had a friend and fellow student, who one day stepped out of a bar-room just as General Lee passed on Traveller. He hoped that the eagle-eye of the President had not seen him. There was a custom of posting all names of students whom the President wished to see. It might be business, or news from the boy's home or social. Everyone so posted reported immediately at the office of the President. It was nearly a week before my friend's name appeared on the bulletin board. He went to the office in fear with a conscience disturbed. General Lee greeted him by saying that he had had occasion to write his mother and had told her how well he was doing in his classes. Such a statement surprised the boy who replied: 'I hope I may always live worthy your good opinion.' Then the wise President said: 'Did it ever occur to you, Mr. —— that when you reach middle life and old age, you will need stimulants and, if you get accustomed to them in your youth, it will take so much more to have the necessary effect?' To this the boy replied: 'General, I did wrong, but I promise not to do so again.' On the wall of the boy's office, in later years, hung the letter, which the General had written the boy's mother—it controlled his business life. But this was fifty years before national prohibition and, while General Lee never touched ardent spirits, his home was not an exception to what was then the practically universal custom in the South of serving light wine with refreshments at entertainments. This leads me to relate a somewhat remarkable incident, the place and the time being considered. It was General Lee's custom early in each school year to invite all the new students to an entertainment in his home, when he would talk with them personally and learn their names, which he would never afterward forget. At these gatherings we were introduced to the members of the family and thereafter any student was welcomed as a visitor in the home, without any inquiry into his social or genealogical antecedents, provided only that he knew how to conduct himself as a gentleman. It was a home in which true aristocracy and true democracy were shown to be entirely compatible.

"At the entertainments referred to, was some dilute sherry wine seasoned with spices and lemons and about the color of weak tea. Before going to Lexington, I had never seen either sherry wine or cold tea. As I was being served, the sophisticated boys mischievously called it cold tea, which I innocently thought it was, only I thought it had a more pleasant flavor than the cold tea that was served at our boarding house and I allowed my glass to be refilled many times. Presently, I began to have a queer feeling of elation and found myself much more fluent in conversation than usual. Turning to a young lady, I asked if she had observed that I could not stop talking. She said she had. I replied that I knew what I was saying now, but that I did not know how long that would be the case—that I had thought I was drinking cold tea, but that whatever is was, it had gone to my head and that I was losing my self-control. She advised that I had been drinking sherry cobbler. I suggested that she and I take a promenade in the fresh air. This we did and my equilibrium was soon restored and I was a wiser, if not a better man.

"The Lee family living in the home in Lexington as I knew them consisted of General and Mrs. Lee, their son, George Washington Custis, who succeeded his father as President of the College, and three daughters, Mary, Agnes, and Mildred. Agnes was an invalid and was away from home on health trips most of the time and I saw very little of her. The oldest daughter, Mary, was a person of strong, but somewhat eccentric character. She was wholly devoid of fear and was fond of taking long walks in the country alone. On one of the walks, on the road leading to House Mountain, she came upon a mountaineer, bringing a load of apples to town, who was savagely beating his horse in trying to extricate his wagon from a mudhole. She walked up to him and demanded that he stop beating his horse and that she would show him how to get out of the hole. The mountaineer asked, 'And who are you?' 'Never mind who I am,' she replied. Under her direction he succeeded in getting on firm ground. On returning home and learning the man's name and where he lived, she wrote me the following note:

" 'The name of the vivid illustration of cruelty to animals is John Moodispaugh and he lives near House Mountain on Kerr's Creek. I saw him drive by this morning with a good team and he was driving carefully. So perhaps there are capabilities of improvement which might be developed. We might hunt him up on Sunday and persuade him to come to Sunday School or church, (we had a Y.M.C.A. Sunday School on House Mountain) though every one agrees in pronouncing him a hard case.'

"He was persuaded to come and bring his family and he did not miss a Sunday in three years. The whole family was taught to read, and after three years, they were hardly recognized as the same people.

"All of this is related to show that along with the masterfulness of character, for which she became rather widely known, she also had a kindly heart and a mind set on doing good.

"One of the loveliest features of the Lee home was the motherly attitude of Mrs. Lee toward the student body. She took a special interest in those far from their homes. She several times asked me to bring to her any article of clothing that might need mending and once gave me a little sewing case furnished with the facilities for sewing on buttons.

"My acquaintance with the youngest daughter, Mildred, developed into a warm personal friendship which lasted while she lived and while I live will abide with me as a precious memory. She inherited from her father a brilliant mind and true nobility of character and from her mother a charming personality.

"The longer I live, the deeper grows my appreciation of and my gratitude for the privilege that came to me as a student under this model leader of young men, 'this courtliest and most gracious gentleman' I ever met. Splendid as was his career as a general in the field, nothing in his life became him more than his end. His resolute refusal, in circumstances of great difficulty and temptation, to take part in any of the controversies the war engendered, his devotion to his work of training young men of the South to forget the quarrels of the past and to be good Americans, all displayed, even more truly than the tests of the battlefield, high courage, sincerity of purpose, devotion to duty and nobility of soul.

"When he died in the fall of 1870, his body lay in state in the College Chapel. A guard of honor of twenty-one students, selected by the family, was appointed by the faculty to watch by his bier. It would be impossible to describe the emotions we felt, when removing the cloth from the casket to allow visitors to gaze on the face as calm in death as a summer lake, his battles over, and his soul enjoying the rest which God gives the faithful soldier.

"Five thousand people attended the funeral, which was conducted on the campus, by General W. N. Pendleton, who had been General Lee's Chief of Ordnance and was then Rector of the Grace Church in Lexington, of which General Lee had been a vestryman. A never-to-be-forgotten feature of the funeral was the singing of the General's favorite hymn, 'How Firm A Foundation' by the great crowd of friends and Confederate soldiers present.

"It is pleasant to know that mostly through General Lee's influence the fires of sectional hate that burned so fiercely during the War and more fiercely, if possible, during the Reconstruction years, have almost entirely died out.

"There was nothing spectacular about my college career. I won no medals, although I was able to graduate with distinguished proficiency. I have regretted seeing the disappearance of Latin as a required subject in our public-schools and state supported college curriculum. It means that we are to have a generation of college graduates who have no adequate appreciation of the beauties of Milton and Wordsworth, of Tennyson and Browning. Thomas Nelson Page was a member of our Latin class and generally stood near the bottom of the class, and while not very socially inclined, he was respected by everyone for what he was—a fine specimen of the Virginia gentleman.

"Being in training for a career in public speaking, I joined the Washington Society and took part in the Friday night debates. Later, I was selected by my class as their valedictorian. That was the only honor that came to me and I would not have exchanged it for any scholarship conferred by the faculty, for it expressed the estimate of my fellow-students for me as their representative man. The delivery of the valedictory on commencement day, surrounded on the platform by the faculty and trustees and many distinguished visitors and with all the beauty and chivalry of the town, beside the student body, for an audience, was an occasion to test the nerve of a timid boy. I met it with a *sang froid* that was more apparent than real, and was quite flattered by the cards and flowers sent up by students and girl friends. Our commencement speaker was Dr. B. M. Palmer of New Orleans, one of the greatest orators of his day. His address followed my valedictory and before he had spoken ten minutes his audience was hypnotized and all interest in my performance was obliterated. My seat on the platform was between Commodore Maury and the Honorable John Randolph Tucker. Dr. Palmer's face in repose was the reverse of handsome. When he rose to speak, Commodore Maury spoke across me to Mr. Tucker and said; 'He is the ugliest man I ever saw, Sir.' A few minutes later he spoke again to Mr. Tucker, 'He is getting better looking, Sir.' Finally, being fully magnetized by the eloquence of Dr. Palmer and pleased by the Jeffersonian doctrine he was proclaiming, the Commodore again spoke to Mr. Tucker, 'He is the handsomest man I ever saw, Sir.'

"More influential on my life than all I learned from text-books were the personal contacts and friendships made while at college. Our Presbyterian pastor, Dr. John W. Pratt, was a very brilliant preacher, and to sit for three years under his ministry was no small part of a liberal education. The majority of the students from both the college and the institute were drawn by his eloquence to the Presbyterian Church. He had a very beautiful daughter, named Grace, who was very popular socially and whom the students were much given to looking down on from their seats in the gallery. Once at a meeting of the Episcopal vestry someone expressed the regret that Dr. Pratt's eloquence was drawing all the young men to the Presbyterian Church. General Lee, a member of the vestry, quietly remarked: 'I should not be surprised if Dr. Pratt's "Grace" had as much to do with it as his eloquence.'

"A warm college friendship, which lasted through life, was with Harry St. George Tucker, who succeeded his father both as professor in the Law School and in Congress for many years. I was fond of going with him to visit at Clifton, the home of Colonel William Preston Johnston, whose daughter he married. On one of these visits I met the daughter of Jefferson Davis, who seemed to have inherited from her father the meticulous regard for conventions and proprieties that sometimes interfered with the working of common sense in his appointments and dismissal of generals in the conduct of the Civil War. For instance, when I was turning the leaves of the music she was playing, although not dressed decollete, she would not allow me even to stand by her side, but required me to come entirely around in front of her.

"As I was not studying law, I did not come in contact with John Randolph Tucker in the classroom, but I attended some wonderful lecture courses he gave in the Presbyterian Sunday School; one especially, on the Ten Commandments and one on Hume's argument against miracles. His speech was not mere eloquence, it was logic set on fire. The Lexington Bar, composed of men like Mr. Tucker, Judge Baldwin, Governor Letcher and Judge Sheffey, was one of the finest in the country and it was no small privilege to be brought into contact with such brilliant men in the formative years of one's life."

The following extracts from an old letter, now in the possession of Miss Maude Houston, give an interesting picture of social life in Lexington, during the years that General Lee presided over Washington College. It was written by Miss Houston's father, a student at the college, to an aunt, telling her of the happenings in the village during the holiday season. It bears the date, January 14, 1869:

"Dear Aunt Sally; As I have a perfect antipathy for Sight Drafts, or anything pertaining thereto, I am willing to write my existence out in preference to coming in contact with anything resembling a Draft, and for fear from threats made in your last letter, that I might very soon be confronting one, I propose to avoid the unpleasant feeling, by sending you a small communication from this end of the line, even if I am at a loss to know the Calibre or direction that my Draft will take. It has been so long since I wrote and so many things have transpired since, that I could almost shoot out of a sixty-four pounder and every bit of it be interesting to you. I could tell you of the pleasant Christmas I spent in visiting our young lady friends, going to 'big parties,' how beautifully the girls were dressed, paying New Year calls, the magnificent receptions given, of pleasant rides on horseback, how pretty Miss Maria looked, how sweet Miss Mary appeared, what a tremendous impression one of your Richmond belles, Miss Turpin, made! And a thousand other things which I know would be relished by you beyond conception, but, unfortunately, man is not gifted with the power of particularizing and entering into the details of dress, looks, actions, etc., etc., to the entire satisfaction of woman, but even with this misfortune to contend with, I shall make a feeble effort, confining myself to my own actions.

"I was invited to several dinings on Xmas Day, but, having a horror for all dinings, I refused all invitations. During the week, Mrs. Mary Lou White gave a 'Smashin' party,' which was considered the party of the season. About one hundred were invited and all went and you can imagine the jam it was in those small rooms. She had both a meat and cake supper, gotten up in a style as only Mrs. White, or Aunt Sally, could do. Everyone had a pleasant time, which was attributable to a certain extent to Old Jim's pompous efforts to keep things moving.

"I will now tell you about New Year's day, when the best wishes of the day were being extended. Will Anderson and myself started out at noon. We first went to Jim Davidson's, where they had an elegant reception prepared, three or four tables groaning under egg-nog, punch, assorted wines, cakes, coffee and nuts, with the beautiful Miss Clara at one table, a charming widow at another and a daughter of the tropics at another. After the disappearance of a few glasses of egg-nog and wine, Will and I wished them a happy New Year and left, coming up to Dr. Waddell's, where no public reception was given. We staid a few minutes and then started for the Hill. taking General Lee's first. There they had a brilliant reception and the house was crowded all day. They had a center table filled with meats, breads, cakes, nuts, etc., whilst the side tables were filled with coffee and fine wines, which, with the continued efforts of Miss Agnes and Miss Mildred, Will and myself did full justice to. The old General, there, as everywhere, was acting the agreeable, as he only can, adding much to the ease and comfort of all the visitors. After repeating the salutations of the day, we journeyed onward. Going next to Mr. Nelson's, where everything was fixed up for a reception. We next went to the home of Captain David Moore. They, too, were receiving, but not on so large a scale. Then we went to the Myers', who were receiving and we found everything nicely fixed, though the only place we met with no drinkables. From there to Mr. Pratt's and to Dr. McClung's. Next to Governor Letcher's, but they were not receiving. Then to Charlie Estill's, where wine was seen and then to Colonel Reid's, where we again found cake and wine (the remains of the party). Here Will Anderson got tired and stopped and Cliff Gordon took his place.. Cliff and I then went down to General Moore's. It was then dark and we paid a long visit. Miss Sally had everything in apple pie order, with plenty to eat and plenty to drink. From there we expected to close out the day by going home, but, when we came up the street, we joined the Masqueraders, who were going the rounds and they wanted us to go with them, so that people would know it was a respectable party that was masked, being composed of students—Berkley, Harry McDonald, Pat Calhoun, and others. At a late hour we went to the Davidsons', where, even at such an hour, the house was crowded, with wine and egg-nog still circulating. We now found that it was 2 o'clock and time for everybody to be in bed, so we disbanded and went home. And that was the last of New Year's Day for 1869.

"Since then, nothing has happened."

During General Lee's presidency, one day was given as Christmas holiday. Some of the students signed a petition for a week's vacation, declaring they would not attend classes that week. The president issued a reply that, "any man whose name appeared on the petition, would be sent home and that if the whole student body signed it, they would all be sent home and he would lock up the college and put the key in his pocket." Such a scramble to get their names off the petition!

Like Stonewall Jackson, General Lee was in his office daily at 8 o'clock a.m.

It is hard for us of a later day to realize the intense enthusiasm that existed at the conclusion of the war for General Lee. Soldiers and citizens alike had for him the greatest affection and devotion. "Cromwell's Ironsides would march into a breach and die at his bidding; Washington's Continentals were content to serve and perish, inspired by the unselfish patriotism of their Chief; Napoleon's Grenadiers never ceased to feel the electric power of his name. Wellington's troops rushed upon death, proud to be sharers in their leader's glory, but, none of these commanders captivated and held the hearts of their men as did the grand soldier, who, possessing the calm dignity of Washington, united with a warmer heart and a far more gracious manner, was able to impress himself personally upon everyone under him. His character was perfectly poised, his blood and breeding gave him the highest tone as a man."

Born at Stratford, in Westmoreland County, January 19, 1807, of a long line of distinguished ancestry, many of whom were leaders and counsellors, both in the Old Dominion and in England, Robert Edward Lee was destined to be the greatest leader and counsellor of them all. He was the fourth son of Lighthorse Harry Lee. His three older brothers, Henry (only child by the first marriage), Charles Carter, and Sidney Smith, were all considered clever men. His two sisters were Mildred and Anne. His lovely mother, Anne Carter, of Shirley-on-the-James, was one of twenty-three children of Charles Carter and a granddaughter of King Carter.

The noblest blood coursed his veins. He was the culmination of all that is finest and best in the Anglo-Saxon people. Stratford Hall, the seat of the Lees in America, has the proud distinction over other historic American houses, for here were born five patriots of the Revolution; Richard Henry Lee and Francis Lightfoot Lee, two signers of the *Declaration of Independence;* William Lee, Arthur Lee, and Thomas Ludwell Lee. But its greatest distinction—it was the birthplace of Robert E. Lee, "the greatest soldier and captain of the English speaking people."

Stratford Hall has been called the most impressive pile of bricks on the American continent and looks as though "it had been built by Elizabeth and bombarded by Cromwell." For ages an old Roman Road, leading to London, passed through Essex. For many centuries Roman Legions,

Mediaeval Wayfarers, Canterbury Pilgrims and other travelers passed this way. The Strat, the Anglo-Saxon word for road, crossed the river, Lea, not many miles from London, by an ancient ford. Old maps noted this as the Strat-by-the-ford—hence, Stratford, the name of the Lee homes in England and Virginia. Houses of that period had to be strong, for they were both home and fort against the Indians.

Both Stratford Hall and Shirley, his paternal and his maternal homes, stand today as enduring monuments to a gracious and lavish hospitality of a day that is gone.

Born and reared in an atmosphere permeated by the spirit of Washington, it is only natural that he was greatly influenced and that through his life he bore a strong resemblance to Washington's character, poise and rounded completeness.

As Dr. Freeman has concisely said, "the home in which Robert E. Lee was trained, God came first and then Washington."

A band of noble women have undertaken the restoration of this famous home. It should and will remain a shrine, to which will go thousands who admire true greatness and nobility of life and character.

Stratford Hall will stand while the American nation stands and will always be symbolic of those undying principles which animated the Lees, especially Robert E. Lee. No one will visit this old Manor House, without a consciousness of Holy Ground and retrospection of a glamorous past. In 1829, Robert E. Lee was graduated, with honor, from the military academy at West Point, of which school he later served as superintendent. His four years' cadetship there were without demerits. General Scott loved him devotedly and predicted that he would be a great leader.

June 30, 1831, he married Mary Parke Custis. The ceremony took place in the grand drawing room at Arlington. This stately mansion, overlooking the nation's capital, was, until the war clouds gathered, the very happy home of the Lees and life there was idyllic.

In 1859, while at Arlington on leave, General Lee was ordered to capture John Brown, which he did.

It is interesting to note that General Lee made his will in 1846, twenty-four years before his death and never changed it. It was short and simple and followed by his valuation of his estate of $38,750.00 in stocks and bonds and some lands. A clause in his will freed all his slaves, in these words: "Nancy and her children at the White House, in New Kent, all of whom I wish liberated, as soon as it can be done to their advantage and that of others." His will reads:

"I, Robert E. Lee, of the United States Army, do make, ordain and declare this instrument to be my last will and testament, revoking all others.

"1. All my debts, whatever they may be and of which there are but few, are to be punctually and speedily paid.

"2. To my dearly beloved wife, Mary Custis Lee, I give and bequeath the use, profit and benefit of my whole estate, real and personal, for the term of her natural life, in full confidence that she will use it to the best advantage in the education and care of my children.

"3. Upon the decease of my wife, it is my will and desire that my estate be divided among my children in such proportions to each as their situations and necessities in life may require and as may be designated by her. I particularly request that my second daughter, Anne Carter, who from an accident she has received in one of her eyes, may be more in want of aid than the rest, may, if necessary, be particularly provided for.

"Lastly, I constitute and appoint my dearly beloved wife, Mary Custis Lee and my eldest son, George Washington Custis Lee, (when he shall have arrived at the age of twenty one) executrix and executor of this, my last will and testament, in the construction of which I hope and trust no dispute will arise.

"In witness of which, I have set my hand and seal, this thirty-first day of August, in the year one thousand eight hundred and forty six.

(Seal) R. E. LEE."

Fred A. Smith
Capt. Engrs.
R. Cruikshank.

General Lee's time of greatest decision came upon the secession of Virginia, his native State. Between his State and his country, he must choose and it was no small matter. He declined the offer of command of the U. S. Army. He could not draw his sword against his own home and people. He was opposed to slavery and said that if he owned all the slaves in America, he would gladly free them to preserve the Union. Mrs. Preston, who knew General Lee well, said, "as a man, physically, intellectually, morally and socially, we of the South think that his equal was never seen. He was a superb specimen of manly beauty, elegance, and grace. His tall, erect figure, his fine coloring, his sparkling hazel eye, his perfect teeth, his engaging smile, his chivalry of bearing, the musical sweetness of his perfectly true voice, were attributes never to be forgotten by those who had once met him."

His domestic life was ideal. The same devotion and attention he had shown his mother during his boyhood was now lavished upon his invalid wife. Heart to heart they had passed through mingled scenes of joy and sorrow, and hand in hand they were to glide down the evening of life together, in peaceful little Lexington.

"His attentions to Mrs. Lee were beautiful to see and his tenderness to his children, especially his daughters, was mingled with a courtesy which recalled the *preux chevalier* of knightly days. He had a way of addressing his daughters with the prefix Miss. 'Where is my little Miss Mildred?' he would ask, when returning from his daily ride at dusk. 'She is my light-bearer: the house is never dark when she is near.' "

Mrs. Tiffany, of Mount Custis Manor on the Eastern Shore of Virginia, an intimate friend of the Lees, claimed that Miss Mildred was not only her father's favorite, but the favorite of all.

General Lee loved children and they loved him. Many a little Lexington urchin, as well as the children of the campus, had the thrill and honor of riding with him on Traveller.

Mr. Charles Pole tells this story which illustrates the love of General Lee for children and his interest in their happiness. While Mr. Pole's father was building the Lee home on the campus, he would often follow his father to his work. One day the boy spied a very fine game rooster in the yard and the general noticed the boy's interest in the bird. The next day, when the boy returned home, his mother said, "look in the yard and see what General Lee brought you." There was the rooster, which the general himself had brought to gladden the heart of the boy. Mr. Pole's father and Mr. Walsh Shields built the chapel, also, under General Lee's supervision.

Lexington was full of interesting people during General Lee's residence, constituting a galaxy, of which he was the center. Conspicuous among these, we find his talented faculty members: Brockenbrough, Kirkpatrick, Harris, White, Campbell, McCulloch, Nelson, Joynes, Johnston and Allen, Commodore Maury, Colonel Brooke, General Francis H. Smith, General Pendleton, ex-Governor Letcher, Judge Edmondson, Dr. J. W. Jones, Colonel Ross, General William A. Anderson, Colonel Preston, and his gifted wife, Margaret Junkin Preston, Judge Houston, Colonel Poague, Captain Moore, W. C. Stuart, General Scott Shipp, Mrs. Stonewall Jackson, and scores of ex-Confederate veterans, everyone of whom held a large place in the general's great heart.

Lexington has always been a place of warm and lasting friendships and never more pronounced than at this time. It is safe to say that nowhere in the world could General Lee have found so congenial a home and certainly nowhere could he have been more genuinely appreciated.

The country people delighted in supplying him, gratis, with their choicest mellow apples, rolls of golden butter, fresh home-made cheese, cakes of maple sugar, blackberry cordial, Rockbridge sorghum, spring chickens and ducks. The universal love and admiration for him knew no bounds. By precept and example the people learned from him those lessons of patience, obedience, and loyalty during the hard days of Reconstruction.

No one knew better than General Lee, that want and chaos would be inevitable in the South. Nevertheless, he cast his lot with his people and there is no record that he ever regretted his decision. Never was poverty more honorable in the history of the world than in the South during these years. For anyone to have a semblance of wealth was looked upon with disfavor and suspicion, and even to this day, excessive worldly possessions are not coveted by Lexingtonians, though a substantial ease and comfort characterizes them. Visitors with money and money alone have never found Lexington a specially congenial place, while those with talent in music, literature or art, and interested in such worthwhile things, find it a happy environment. Many such "take root" and spend their days in this fine atmosphere. It would be difficult to find anywhere in America a more interesting, a more cosmopolitan population.

General Lee's funeral, October 15, 1870

Main Street, looking north, shortly after Hunter's Raid

Washington and Lee University, circa 1890

Old Lime Kiln Bridge, near Lexington

Virginia Military Institute cadets at Jackson's grave just after the surrender

CHAPTER XXIV: THE PASSING OF GENERAL LEE

AS the day that marked the entrance of General Lee into Lexington was its greatest, so the day that marked his passing was its saddest. On that day, October 12, 1870, a pall, exceeding all its former sorrow and loss, fell upon the entire Southland. He was the idol of the Southern people, was foremost in the rebuilding of the South and in reuniting the nation. His last public service was to attend a vestry meeting of Grace Episcopal Church. At this meeting he complained of not feeling well. At the conclusion of the meeting he went home, where he found his family waiting tea for him. He took his place at the head of the table, standing for grace. His lips could not utter the prayer of his heart and, being unable to speak, he took his seat. An expression of resignation was noticed by the family, as though he knew that his hour was near. After a simple supper, he decided to rest on the couch in the dining room, from which he was never removed. His physicians claimed that "the symptoms of his attack resembled concussion of the brain, without the attendant swoon. There was marked debility, a slightly impaired consciousness, and a tendency to doze, but no paralysis of motion or sensation and no evidence of inflammation of the brain."

In the words of his physician, "he neither expected nor desired to recover." His physician, trying to cheer him, said, "General, you must make haste and get well; Traveller has been standing so long in the stable and he needs exercise." The general made no reply, but slowly shook his head and closed his eyes.

On October 10, he showed signs of weakening and on the next day he was sinking rapidly. Shortly before nine o'clock, on the morning of October 12, the overtaxed heart finally gave way, and surrounded by those nearest and dearest to him, he slipped quietly away, murmuring at times, orders to his gallant lieutenant A. P. Hill, who had fallen at Petersburg, to "strike the tent." Thus the great leader of the battles of the Peninsula, of Second Manassas, Sharpsburg, Spotsylvania, Cold Harbor, the siege of Petersburg, and the campaign against Meade in '63, had fallen peacefully asleep, leaving to future generations the inspiration of example.

The English mystic Launcelot's beautiful prayer seemed consummated here: "Grant, O Lord, that the end of this life be Christian and without shame and, if it please Thee, without pain."

In war and in peace he had left his impress upon all who came in contact with him and great has been and is his influence. "He has achieved success, who has lived well, laughed often and loved much; who has gained the respect of intelligent men and the love of little children; who has filled his niche and accomplished his task; who left the world better than he found it, whether by an improved poppy, a perfect poem or a rescued soul; who never lacked an appreciation of earth's beauty or failed to express it; who has always looked for the best in others and gave the best he had; whose life was an inspiration, whose memory a benediction."

Elizabeth Barrett's beautiful poem, based upon that line from the Psalms, "He giveth His beloved sleep," applies so well here:

What would we give to our beloved?—
The hero's heart to be unmoved—
The poet's star-tuned harp to sweep—
The patriot's voice to be unmoved—
The monarch's crown to light the brow?
He giveth His beloved sleep.

Sleep softly beloved! we sometime say
And have no tune to charm away
Sad dreams that through the eyelids creep;
But never doleful dream again
Shall break the happy slumber when
He giveth His beloved sleep.

For me, my heart, that erst did go
Most like a tired child at show,
That sees through tears the jugglers leap
Would now its wearied vision close;
Would childlike on His love repose.
He giveth His beloved sleep.

Life's race well run,
Life's work well done,
Life's victory won,
Now cometh rest.

Through all the future years it will be said of Robert E. Lee: "Once in the flight of ages past, there lived a man!" His body lay in state in the college chapel for several days, the students acting as guards day and night; an honor and distinction they cherished for the rest of their lives. Mrs. Lee chose, of all the places offered her throughout the South, that he should be buried on the campus, the spot he so loved.

The quaint little ivy-covered chapel, graceful and dignified, designed by him and built under his supervision, as a place of assembly for the college students, became his last resting place. Here also sleep his noble wife, Mary Custis, great-great-granddaughter of Martha Washington, his distinguished father, Lighthorse Harry Lee, his mother, Ann Carter, of Shirley, and other members of the Lee family.

Through the years countless thousands have come to pay honor and to worship at his tomb and will to the end of time. Many stories are told of the impressions and expressions of visitors as they get their first glimpse of Valentine's superb work. Some kneel in prayer, others stand speechless, while others, in softened tones give audible expression to their feelings. To some must come the immortal lines from Thanatopsis: "Like one who wraps his robe about him and lies down to pleasant dreams."

Valentine reached the zenith of his skill and greatness as a sculptor in this work. It is of faultless Vermont marble and in accord with Mrs. Lee's wish, was modelled after the statue in Charlottenburg, of Louise of Prussia.

An elderly lady from New Hampshire, after examining the work, rather critically, said: "Well, General Lee was a greater man than I thought he was." A child of six stood gazing at the figure, and looking up at her father said: "Daddy, is the gentleman asleep?" Another child asked her mother "if it was God."

The handsome wrought iron grill and gates, which both ornament and protect the sacred spot, was a gift from Henry E. Litchford, of Richmond and Raleigh.

Priceless portraits, some having once hung in Mount Vernon and others in Arlington, adorn the walls. Memorial tablets to students of the college also adorn the walls. The quaint one-manual organ, sweet and harmonious in its setting, was a gift in 1872 from the ladies of Texas to the memory of General Lee. Formerly the motor-power was supplied by a janitor, who pumped and pumped to the nth degree of his strength. Happily now, for the janitor, the power is electric.

In the rostrum windows is lovely glass of unusual design and made in England. In the vestibule are interesting tablets to the Liberty Hall Volunteers and to the Colonial Dames of America.

In the lower part of the chapel, adjoining the tomb, is the general's office just as he left it sixty-five years ago. It contains some handsome old furniture, the envy of lovers of antiques. In the museum is a fine collection of portraits and relics pertaining to the Washingtons, the Custises, the Carters and the Lees. Here, also, is the Lee piano, a gem, made by Stieff and Sons of Baltimore, after the war, especially for General Lee. It bears his name inlaid in mother-of-pearl. The skeleton of Traveller, encased in glass, is also here.

It is claimed that some of the ivy on the chapel was brought from Washington's Tomb at Mount Vernon and that some of it was sent from England by an admirer of General Lee and planted by John L. Campbell, long the treasurer of the University who, like his brother, Dr. Harry D. Campbell, the Dean of the University for so many years, enjoyed the unbounded love and admiration of thousands of Washington and Lee and Virginia Military Institute men over a long period of years. Sons of Professor John

L. Campbell, a member of General Lee's faculty, they were born on the campus. These two Campbell brothers spent their long and useful years in the interest of Washington and Lee University. It is hard to think of the campus without them. They contributed much to its welfare and success.

Another campus figure, greatly beloved by every Washington and Lee man and by every resident of Lexington, during the past quarter of the century, was Dr. Delawar B. Easter. The happy, genial spirit of this good man, a type of the old school of gentility and courtesy, is greatly missed. Miss Annie White tells this story, which is typical of the sympathy and nobility of character of John L. Campbell. William Harvey, one of the college janitors, who had once been a servant in the Lee home, was very ill and Mr. Campbell visited him daily. Harvey, like all the college servants, was devoted to Mr. Campbell. While Harvey was breathing his last, the graduating exercises were in progress in the chapel and Mr. Campbell, instead of being there, was with Harvey, ministering to him to the last. When the commencement exercises were over, Miss Annie sent all the floral decorations from the chapel to Harvey's funeral.

The servants connected with the college have been of a very high order, especially those connected with the chapel. Harvey Myers, who so recently passed away, was for many years an institution in the chapel. Visitors delighted to hear his descriptions of the portraits, especially, when he would say: "Now, this here one is General George Washington and this here one is Miss Marthy, his wife." Gooch, the last of these old-time servant-guides about the college, is still on duty at General Lee's tomb. He, like all of his generation, is the embodiment of good manners and gentility, acquired through years of contacts with fine people.

One of the saddest changes noticeable about Lexington today is the absence of scores of these old-fashioned colored men and women of yesteryear, so beloved by the white people of Lexington and by the students and cadets. They belonged to a type, the like of which the world will never see again.

"Peace to their ashes and to their memory."

We loved them and were loved by them.

ROBERT E. LEE: 1807-1870

When the future historian comes to survey the character of Robert E. Lee, he will find it rising like a huge mountain above the undulating planes of humanity and he will have to lift his eyes to Heaven to catch its summit. He possessed all the virtues of the great commanders, without their vices.

He was a foe without hate,
A friend without reproach,
A Christian without hypocrisy
And a man without guile.
He was a Caesar without his ambition,
A Frederick without his tyranny,
A Napoleon without his selfishness
And a Washington without his reward.
He was as obedient to authority as a servant
And as royal in authority as a king.
He was as gentle as a woman in life;
Modest and virtuous as a virgin in thought.
Watchful as a Roman vestal in duty,
Submissive to law as Socrates
And as grand in battle as Achilles.
(Hill's tribute to Lee)

O Robert Lee, you paladine
I wonder how my words would strike you!
I know the portrait might have been
In many, many ways more like you.

But you would not have had me plan
To make the picture more heroic;
For you would rather be a man
Than just a marble-hearted stoic.

And I can often hear you say
When they condemn and when they flatter;
In your divinely tender way,
'Good friend, it really doesn't matter.'

In an autographed copy of his *Lee, the American,* sent a friend in Lexington, Gamaliel Bradford wrote the above original poem. He also wrote this friend that one of the great disappointments of his life was that he dared to write of General Lee without having set foot on Virginia soil, but that, after all, General Lee is an American heritage and as such he wrote of him.

General Sir Frederick Maurice, of the British Army, who wrote of Lee from a military standpoint, classed him with Alexander, Caesar, and Wellington. Later, when on a visit to Lexington, General Sir Frederick, speaking in the chapel, to a few people invited to meet him, expressed regrets that he had not first visited Lexington.

In McElhenney's *Recollections* is this reference to Lee: "He was strikingly like his portraits. His manner was the perfection of unassumed dignity. His air was cheerful and his whole appearance well suited to arouse the esteem and admiration of the public and the reverence and love of individuals. Grandfather was delighted with the Chieftain, whose simplicity and urbanity were akin to his own. With the exception of General Breckenridge, who was the finest personage I ever saw on horseback, General Lee came the nearest being the ideal commander. Joseph E. Johnston had a martial bearing and erect military figure. Beauregard, on the other hand, was low in stature and of a square build, which brought to mind the Emperor Napoleon the First."

Valentine's *The Man and His Work,* gives this intimate picture: He claimed that one of General Lee's outstanding characteristics was a total absence of the melodramatic in all he did and said. As an artist, Valentine would have been quick to detect any artificiality, posing, or attempt at vanity. When he remarked that his fortunes had changed since the war, General Lee said: "An artist should not have too much money." This artist certainly did not have too much money for, in a few days, he had to borrow the price of transportation from Richmond to Lexington. Some time later, General Lee, in conversation with Valentine quoted from Marcus Aurelius: "Misfortune nobly borne is good fortune."

In June, Valentine arrived in Lexington, via the stagecoach through Goshen Pass. He dreaded the thought of being closeted for days with the great general, but he was soon put at his ease, for he found that the simplicity, which he had heard characterized General Lee, was true and that he was exceedingly kind and considerate in all his relations.

Valentine said that in his profession he met many intelligent people from every section of the country and from abroad and that they were always genuinely interested in everything connected with General Lee, for they recognized that in him were blended the finest qualities of mind and heart. His early boyhood; swimming in the Potomac; his teacher, Weir, at West Point and his experiences in the Mexican War were among the interesting topics about which he talked with Valentine, during the days while sitting for the measurements for the bust.

The last time that Valentine saw General Lee was in the summer, when he called to say goodbye. A number of guests were present and they were startled to hear the general say: "I feel that I have an incurable disease coming on, old age. I would like to go to some quiet place in the country and rest." On April 1, 1875, after five years work, the statue was finished and ready to be delivered to Lexington. Accompanied by an escort of students of Richmond College, it reached its destination on April 17th, by the old canal boat. The students of Richmond College assumed all responsibility and expense of bringing it from Richmond to Lexington. All along the way, great deference was shown by the people, for was it not the idol of the Confederacy in marble, representing him asleep in camp, and perpetuating for all future generations the perfection of his features and his marvelous physique!

Mr. Thornhill, in appropriate terms, delivered it and ex-Governor Letcher accepted it. Addresses were also made by General Early and Colonel W. Preston Johnston. Albert Steves, of San Antonio, a student at the time, writing in 1934 says: "Vividly do I recall the day when the students of the College were asked to come to Alexander's Landing to help draw the wagon on which was placed Valentine's statue of General Lee. Upon a given signal, the one hundred and eighty odd students put their force in front of the cross-pieces attached to a cable and the statue was moved from the river to the campus, where it was walled in the north end of the old dormitory, "Purgatory," where it remained several years till its permanent place in the chapel was ready for it. On the 28th of June, 1883, the day after the Washington and Lee finals, the unveiling took place. The unveiling was by little Julia Jackson, only child of Stonewall Jackson. John W. Daniel was the orator of the day and spoke for three hours. This was followed by Father Ryan's reading of his own immortal poem, the *Sword of Robert E. Lee*:

> Forth from its scabbard, pure and bright,
>   Flashed the sword of Lee;
> Far in the front of the deadly fight,
> High o'er the brave in the cause of right,
> Its stainless sheen, like a beacon light,
>   Led us to victory.
>
> Out of its scabbard, where full long
>   It slumbered peacefully;
> Roused from its rest by the battle song,
> Shielding the feeble, smiting the strong,
> Guarding the right, avenging the wrong,
>   Gleamed the sword of Lee.
>
> Forth from its scabbard, high in air,
>   Beneath Virginia's sky;
> And they who saw it gleaming there,
> And knew who bore it, knelt to swear,
> That where that sword led they would dare
>   To follow and to die.

Out of its scabbard, never hand
   Waved sword from stain as free;
Nor purer sword led braver band,
Nor braver bled for a brighter land,
Nor brighter land had a cause as grand,
   Nor cause a chief like Lee.

Forth from its scabbard; how we prayed
   That sword might victor be!
And when our triumph was delayed,
And many a heart grew sore afraid,
We still hoped on, while gleamed the blade
   Of noble Robert Lee.

Forth from its scabbard; all in vain
   Forth flashed the sword of Lee.
'Tis shrouded now in its sheath again,
It sleeps the sleep of our noble slain,
Defeated, yet without a stain,
   Proudly and peacefully.

The Stonewall Brigade and other branches of the Army of Northern Virginia were represented at the unveiling ceremonies and many distinguished visitors from every section of the country were present. Among them were General Wade Hampton, General Jubal A. Early, General Fitzhugh Lee, General William Terry, General George H. Steuart, General M. B. Corse, General R. D. Lilley, Colonel William Norris, Colonel H. E. Peyton, Colonel T. M. R. Talcott, Colonel W. H. Palmer, Captain R. E. Lee, Major E. L. Rogers, Captain J. H. H. Figgatt, Judge H. W. Bruce, Judge J. H. Fulton, Father Ryan, Hon. C. H. Breckenridge, Rev. Dr. Alexander, Leigh Robinson, John J. Williams, C. W. Button, Guardner Tyler, Mrs. Carlisle, Mrs. Stonewall Jackson, and Mrs. General George E. Pickett. The venerable philanthropist, W. W. Corcoran, Esquire, of Washington and ex-Governor Smith of Virginia, honored the occasion with their presence.

A crowd of ten thousand gathered on the campus for this great affair and considering the facilities for traveling in those days, that was indeed a large assemblage. The day was bright and clear and the moment for the unveiling was announced by a salute fired by the survivors of the Rockbridge Artillery. Two guns, which had constituted a part of their armament at First Manassas, were used. These had been a part of the cadet battery used by Stonewall Jackson at Virginia Military Institute and are again in the institute's keeping. Fifty members of this famous company had assembled under their former commander, Colonel William T. Poague. What memories of the past did these guns recall!

As the guns were fired the chapel doors were thrown open and the vast throng began to move through the building to get a close view of the statue. This continued all day. The homes of Lexington were never more hospitable, practically every one of them entertaining visitors. There was also a lunch served on the campus by the citizens to thousands of guests, gratis. Among the floral tributes were two from Winnie Davis and made of immortelles to represent the Confederate battle flag. One was for Jackson's grave and the other for Lee's tomb. This was truly a great occasion and evening fell on a day forever marked in the history of Lexington.

✦ ✦ ✦ ✦

During the Reconstruction days a Yankee was not especially a popular person in Lexington. However, when Colonel Waite, of New York, came to visit the Davidsons, in 1873, he reported that he had been well treated and in a friendly and courteous way. He observed that the negroes flocked to the towns, although many of them were still with their former masters. He found slavery unregretted. In the opinion of the most thoughtful, the manner in which the enfranchisement of the blacks was accomplished was a political blunder.

Two years later, John Leyburn remarked that no well disposed Northerner need fear as to a kindly reception. And two years later, the shooting of President Garfield caused this to be printed in the Lexington *Gazette:* "No event in American history has so unified the American people as the shot at Garfield. We have discovered all at once that we are Americans. The Union has been restored. The Republic lives. Guiteau's bullets have done more to show the people of these United States what manner of men they are than anything that has happened in their history. The spontaneous outbursts of Southern indignation speaks too plainly to be misunderstood."

In announcing the death of the President, C. M. Dold, Mayor of Lexington, requested that all business be suspended for the day and that everyone assemble in the Presbyterian Church for a memorial service, which was largely attended.

CHAPTER XXV: TRAVELLER

WHEN the name of Robert E. Lee is mentioned, the natural second thought is of Traveller, his faithful companion of many years. What Bucephalus was to Alexander, Traveller was to General Lee. How close and intimate is the comradeship between a man and his horse! It is a silent, yet comprehensible friendship; an intercourse beyond the need of words. They drink at the same crystal spring and rest under the same shade tree. Unless a man is a pagan and an unbeliever, when he calls upon his God, it will be for a double blessing upon them both.

General Lee bought Traveller in Fayette County (now West Virginia), before the war, in which they served the four years together, and after the surrender together they came to Lexington and were constant companions until General Lee's death. It is safe to say that Traveller enjoyed the beauty of the countryside as did his master, for the general once said: "Traveller and I wander into the country and enjoy sweet confidences." On their daily outings they discovered all the lovely byways and bridlepaths about Rockbridge, occasionally accompanied by Miss Mildred on Lucy Long, but generally only the general and Traveller.

When the general passed away, Traveller evidenced a real understanding of his loss. He remained a pet on the college campus to the end of his days. His skeleton was mounted and is in the chapel museum. Before it was enclosed in glass it was the target for everyone's pencil. It is literally covered with names and initials. For many years it stood near a smaller skeleton. The students, in showing the freshmen about the place would point out the two skeletons; the small one was Traveller when a colt, they would say, and the larger one, when he was grown. "Amazing information!"

Rosewell Page tells this incident: His two brothers went to Washington College while General Lee was president, and once when the general rode over to the parsonage to call on his kinswoman, Mr. Page's mother, on a visit there, the boy was allowed to hold Traveller to graze on the high grass in the yard, and as any boy would have done, he climbed into the saddle. When the general returned the boy slid down and held the stirrup. General Lee said, "I hope, Sir, that you enjoyed your ride."

On the general's saddle were the letters R.E.L. in silver. An artist once wrote to General Lee for permission to paint a portrait of Traveller to which the general replied: "If I were an artist like you, I would draw a true picture of Traveller; one representing his true proportions, his muscular figure, deep chest and short back; strong haunches and flat legs; small feet, black mane and tail. Such a picture might inspire a writer, whose genius could then depict his worth and describe his endurance to toil, hunger and thirst, heat and cold and the dangers and sufferings through which he passed. He could dilate upon his sagacity and affection and his invariable response to every wish of his master. He might imagine his thoughts through the long night watches and days of battle. But I am neither an artist nor a writer and all that I can say is that Traveller is a true Confederate Gray."

CHAPTER XXVI: NATURAL BRIDGE

O NE is not long a resident of Lexington before he acquires a feeling of ownership in the scenic wonders of the place, particularly the world-famed Natural Bridge, Goshen Pass, Lover's Leap, Cave Spring, and the James River Water Gap. Like all such places of interest, they must be seen to be appreciated, as it is impossible to adequately describe them. John Marshall called the Natural Bridge, "God's greatest miracle in stone." Fourteen miles south of Lexington, on Route 11, through beautiful country, with superb mountain scenery in every direction, it is one of the long-remembered drives about the countryside. As far back as 1759 are records of those who visited the bridge, and through the years countless thousands have come to view this great natural wonder. It is fifty feet higher than Niagara Falls and spans Cedar Creek by an archway two hundred and fifteen feet high; its width is eighty feet and its length ninety feet, with a thickness of sixty feet.

This description was given by a very early writer: "The stupendous arch, constituting the bridge, is of limestone rock, covered to a depth of from four to six feet of alluvial and clayey earth and based upon huge rocks of the same geological character, the summits of which are ninety feet and their bases fifty feet asunder and whose rugged sides form a wide and awful chasm spanned by the bridge. The bridge is guarded as if by the design of nature, by a parapet of rocks and by trees and shrubbery firmly embedded in the soil; so that a person traveling the stage road running over it would, if not informed of the curiosity, pass it unnoticed. It is also worthy of note that the creation of a natural bridge at this place has contributed in a singular manner to the convenience of man, inasmuch as the deep ravine over which it sweeps and through which traverses the beautiful Cedar Creek is not otherwise easily passed for several miles either below or above the bridge. Consequently, the road running north and south, with an acclivity of thirty-five degrees, presents the same appearance in soil, growth of trees and general character as that of the neighboring scenery."

Thomas Jefferson was the original patentee, having obtained a large tract of land in 1754. He was very proud of having possession of one of the world's natural wonders and built a small cabin near the bridge for the entertainment of visitors and many prominent people came from far and near to view this grand creation and to be his guests.

Washington visited it and did the daring feat of climbing high up the sidewall and carving his name, which may still be seen. A few years later, a Washington College student decided that he would not be outdone by the Father of His Country and dared to go higher than did Washington. The author Caruthers tells of this attempt on the part of the college student:

"Mr. Piper, the hero of the occasion, commenced climbing on the opposite side of the creek from the one by which the pathway ascends the ravine. He began down on the banks of the brook so far that we did not know where he had gone and were only appraised of his whereabouts by his shouting above our heads. When we looked up, he was standing apparently right under the arch, I suppose a hundred feet from the bottom and that on the smooth side, which is considered inaccessible with a ladder. He was standing far above the spot where George Washington is said to have carved his name when a youth. The ledge of the rock by which he ascended to this perilous height does not appear from below to be three inches wide and runs at almost right angles to the abutment of the bridge. Of course its termination is far down the cliff on that side. Many of the written and traditional accounts state this to be the side of the bridge up which he climbed. The ledge of rock on which he was standing appeared so narrow to us below as to make us believe his position a very perilous one and we entreated him to come down. He answered us with loud shouts of derision.

"At this stage of the business, Mr. Penn and his servant left us. He would not have done so, I suppose, had he known what was to follow. But up to this time not one of us had the slightest suspicion that Mr. Piper intended the daring exploit which he afterwards accomplished. He soon after descended from that side, crossed the brook and commenced climbing on the side by which all visitors ascend the ravine. He first mounted the rocks on this side as he had done on the other side. The projecting ledge may be distinctly seen by any visitor. It commences four or five feet from the pathway on the lower side and winds round, gradually ascending until it meets the cleft of rock over which the celebrated cedar stump hangs. Following this ledge to its termination, it brought him thirty or forty feet from the ground and placed him between two deep fissures, one on each side of the gigantic column of rock on which the aforementioned cedar stump stands. This column stands out from the bridge, as separate and distinct as if placed there by nature on purpose for an observatory to the wonderful arch and ravine which it overlooks. A huge crack or fissure extends from its base to its summit; indeed it is cracked on both sides, but more perceptibly on the one side than on the other. Both of these fissures are thickly overgrown with bushes and roots project into them from trees growing on the precipice. It was between these that the aforementioned ledge conducted him. Here he stopped, pulled off his coat and shoes and threw them down to me. And this, in my opinion, is a sufficient refutation of the story so often told, that he went up to inscribe his name and ascended so high that he found it more difficult to return than to go further. He could have returned easily from the point where he disencumbered himself; but the fact that he did thus prepare so early and so near the ground and after he had ascended more than that height on the other side, is clear proof that to inscribe his name was not, and to climb the bridge was, his object. He had already inscribed his name above Washington's more than fifty feet. Around the face of this huge column and between the clefts he now moved, backward and forward, still ascending as he found foothold. When he had ascended about one hundred and seventy feet from the earth and had reached the point where the pillar overhangs the ravine, his heart seemed to fail him. He stopped and seemed to us to be balancing midway between heaven and earth. We were in dread suspense, expecting every moment to see him dashed in atoms at our feet. We had already exhausted our powers of entreaty in persuading him to return, but all to no purpose. Now it was perilous even to speak to him and very difficult to carry on conversation at all from the immense height to which he had ascended and the noise of the babbling brook as it tumbled in tiny cascades over its rocky bed at our feet. At length he seemed to discover that one of the clefts before mentioned retreated backward from the overhanging position of the pillar. Into this he sprang at once and was soon out of sight and out of danger.

"There is not one word of truth in all that story about our hauling him up with ropes and his fainting away as soon as he landed on the summit. Those acquainted with the locality will at once perceive its absurdity, for we were beneath the arch and it is half a mile around to the top and, for the most part, up a ragged mountain. Instead of fainting away, Mr. Piper proceeded down the hill to meet us and to get his hat and shoes. We met about half way and he lay down a few minutes to recover himself from his fatigue."

Those who long had a sentimental ownership feeling for the bridge, in the horse and buggy age, feared the changes that the passing years would bring. One could wander at will about its lovely wild and natural fastness, strolling to Lost River and Lace Falls, often without meeting anyone. It was truly the Natural Bridge and, except for the footpath, one was not conscious that man had ever before visited this unique natural wonder. One felt himself a pioneer, a Daniel Boone, a discoverer.

The quiet and restful hotel was alluring and the picturesque little gatehouse, where one man dispensed Coca-Cola and post cards and admitted guests to the glen, was a resting place, after a delightful walk of a few miles, under the bridge. Those old-timers felt some resentment when man-made inventions were added to the bridge, but these attachments have been so marvelously and faultlessly made that instead of resentment, everyone feels an added pride and enthusiasm and the glorious music and the Story of Creation, together with the superb and inspiring lighting effect, creates an unforgettable impression.

Those who know and love the bridge would unhesitatingly say that if only one visit could be made, this should be a night visit. If its majesty and grandeur can be accentuated, the lighting, the music, and the impressive Story of Creation does it.

The wild and woody pathway, under some of the oldest arborvitae trees in the world, leads under the great archway and ultimately to the bewildering Lost River and the delicate Lace Falls. Enchanting as ever, unchanged and unchanging, except for the throngs and throngs of visitors which the fine highways and motor cars today make possible. The picturesque, rambling hotel rates among the country's best. Riding, driving, tennis, golf, and swimming are among the entertainments offered guests. Scenery in all directions is superb and is protected by the Natural Bridge Company. A folder about the bridge says of the Singing Rocks: "Racial memories of primitive forgotten man—the inconsequence of time—a canvas of sky overhead—moonlight and shadow shot thru with the murmur of Cedar Creek—high overhead the dark span of the old Bridge—soft glowing of diffused lights moving as the music moves—mingle in an unforgettable, soul-stirring andante of all time in nature's own cathedral, out under the stars where one seems to walk alone with God."

"Through millions of years a giant whirlpool raced its way around the south wall of the Bridge, forming a mammoth sounding board surface capable of handling the mightiest of music with the sensitiveness and tone value of a fine violin. Through the day, appropriate cathedral music intermittently floods the glen and at the close of day a forty-five minute twilight concert is given, a beautiful, tender harmony matching the mood of a dying day and bringing back, as the shadows fall, the half-forgotten long ago. Each night at forty-five minute intervals the incredible Natural Bridge Symphony of Creation is given.

"Worshipped by the Monacan Indians, as the Bridge of God, Natural Bridge has stirred the emotions of men of all time. Its shadowed silence reaches deep into racial memories and the primitive within stands awed at the amazing miracle of its high arch of stone stretching across the sky."

"The bridge not made by hands, that spans a river, carries a highway and makes two mountains one."   HENRY CLAY.

Visit the Bridge in the daytime for the facts of its history, geology, proportions, flora and fauna. Also walk up the paths of the glen, beside the rapids of Cedar Creek, visit Saltpeter Cave, the Lost River and the Cascades. The bridge was once used as a shot tower and Saltpeter Cave supplied the saltpeter, processed with water from Lost River for use during our war with the British. The night program, with the Story of Creation, of simple but inspiring eloquence, spiritualizes the Bridge with living light which words cannot describe. Mountains become a vast stage and the scenes move and change with the mood of gripping music. The pageant takes possession of the onlooker and carries him back through eternities of silence to the first faint stirrings of life in the evening and the morning of the first cataclysmic day.

In the spring of 1782, the Marquis de Chastellux, a member of the French Academy and an officer who served under Count de Rochambeau in the French Army, traveled in North America and made a trip from Williamsburg, through the Valley of Virginia. According to the custom of the day, he kept a journal of his travels. He recorded a quaint description of the Natural Bridge and of local hospitality.

"We set out about nine o'clock in the morning and, to say the truth, rather heedlessly, for in the mountains where there are either too many or not enough roads, people always think that they have given sufficient directions to travelers, who seldom fail to go astray. This is the common fault of those who instruct others in what they themselves are well acquainted with; nor are the roads to science exempt from this inconvenience. After riding about two miles, however, we luckily met a man who had got his horse shod at a neighboring forge and was returning home, followed by two or three couples of hounds. We soon entered into conversation with him and, what seldom happens in America, he was curious to know who I was and whither I was going. My quality of a general officer in the French Army and the desire I expressed of seeing the wonders of his country, inspiring him with a kind of affection for me, he offered to be our conductor, leading us sometime through little paths, at others, through woods, but continually climbing or ascending mountains, so that without a guide, nothing short of witchcraft could have enabled us to find the road. Having thus traveled for two hours, we at last descended a steep declivity and then mounted another, during which time he endeavored to render the conversation more interesting. At last, pushing his horse on more briskly and then stopping suddenly he said: 'You desire to see the Natural Bridge, don't you, Sir? You are upon it. Alight and go twenty steps to the right or to the left and you will see this prodigy.' Chastellux was making drawings. His retinue of servants had learned from their conductor that he kept a public house seven miles from the place where we were and about two miles from the road which we must take the next morning to leave the mountains. Mr. Grigsby, the name of our guide, had expressed his wish to receive us and assured us that we would be as comfortable as at the tavern recommended by Mr. Paxton. But, had this been otherwise, we had too many obligations to Mr. Grigsby, not to give him the preference. We renewed our journey, therefore, under his guidance, through the woods, which were very lofty—strong robust oaks and immense pines, sufficient for all the fleets of Europe, here grow old and perish in their native soil.

"We arrived at Mr. Grigsby's a little before five o'clock, having met with nothing on the road but one wild turkey. The house was not large, but neat and commodious. Other travelers were there. A young man, his wife and baby, traveling on one horse from Pennsylvania to 'Kentucket' to make their new home. While supper was preparing and we were talking of our travels and tracing on the map the road our immigrants were to travel to 'Kentucket,' I recollected that we had one hour yet of daylight and it was just the time I had seen the wood-hens, of which they assured me there were plenty in the neighborhood and that 'there is a critical moment in hunting as well as in love.' "

The Marquis had a good supper, a comfortable night and breakfast and then Mr. Grigsby guided him to the right road, via Greenlee's Ferry. The Marquis was interested in the profusion of bird-life and of the rare and beautiful flowers. Especially did he enjoy the wild-plums and the Judas Tree.

Chastellux was of noble birth, born in Paris in 1734, son of a French officer. He entered the army at the age of fifteen and rose rapidly. He soon had a regiment named for him. In 1780 he came with Rochambeau's Army to America, in which he was a major general. Later he returned to France, where he died in 1788. He had cultivated a strong attachment for George Washington. After his death, with his wife's permission, some of his letters were published and are very interesting. This one from Washington:

"Mount Vernon, July 18, 1781.

"My dear Chevalier;

"You have taken a most effective method of obliging me to accept your caste of claret, as I find by your ingenious manner of stating the case—that I shall, by a refusal, bring my patriotism into question and incur a suspicion of want of attachment to the French Nation and of regard for you, which, of all things, I wish to avoid.

"I will not enter into a discussion of the point of divinity, as I perceive you are a master of that weapon. In short, my dear Sir, my only scruple arises from a fear of depriving you of an article that you cannot conveniently replace in this country. You can only relieve me by promising to partake very often of that hilarity which a glass of good claret seldom fails to produce.

"With much truth and affection, I am yours etc

G. WASHINGTON."

Another written to Chastellux from Newburgh, December 14, 1782:

"......................... I can truly say, never in my life did I ever part with a man to whom my soul clave more sincerely than it did to you."

Chastellux then returned to France and carried a letter from Washington to Lafayette.

It is certain that under old Rockbridge County are caverns as lovely as those found anywhere, but with so much beauty on top it is not necessary to explore beneath.

The royal James flows past the Natural Bridge and through the Balcony Falls Water Gap on its peaceful way to the Atlantic. Through this gap also runs the Chesapeake and Ohio Railroad and a magnificent highway, with superb prospects and sylvan scenes. The glory of its May day rhododendron and mountain laurel resplendence is a scene worth traveling many miles to see.

During the greater part of the nineteenth century, river navigation from Richmond to Lexington was through this gap. The old bateau, a narrow boat ninety feet long, with a canvas awning and propelled by long poles, handled by several negroes, transported wheat, flour, and tobacco from Rockbridge to Richmond. Balcony Falls was a nightmare to the operators of these primitive boats and high wages were paid anyone who could master a craft through Bal-co-ny. During high waters many bateaux were broken on the rocks. Later, the canal boats took the place of the bateaux. These were drawn by mules and horses on the tow-path and were changed every ten or twelve miles.

One mile south of the Natural Bridge is Forest Tavern. Here Mr. and Mrs. John D. Clothier dispense genuine old-fashioned hospitality. It is one of the loveliest places in the south, open all the year to guests. This historic house, standing amid a hundred or more magnificent century-old, virgin oaks, was built in 1790 by an uncle of Sam Houston. Young Sam often visited here. Another charming home open to guests all the year is Herring Hall, two miles north of the bridge and operated by delightful English people. In the early days this lovely old home belonged to one of the Grigsbys. Today, as always, it is famed for its generous hospitality, of which many have partaken. The house is filled with valuable antiques.

David Crockett's father kept a drover's stand on the road from Abingdon to Knoxville. Jacob Siler, a German, was moving to Rockbridge with his belongings, including a drove of cattle and he hired young David, a small boy and very poor, to accompany him to his new home near the Natural Bridge. Davy was well treated and paid five dollars for his time and service. Siler persuaded him to spend several weeks with him in his new home. Finally, some wagons came along, headed for Davy's home and they agreed to take him to his father, if he would meet them the next morning, seven miles ahead at the tavern and they promised him protection, in case they were pursued. The boy rose at dawn and walked the seven miles through the deep snow, arriving on time and thus making the trip to his father's home in safety.

CHAPTER XXVII: GOSHEN PASS

HERE is a place to inspire poetry and song! World travelers have always acknowledged the beauty of Goshen Pass. A great mountain gorge, of which there are many in the Blue Ridge and the Allegheny ranges, the Pass is several miles long, through the most verdant growth of rhododendron, laurel, ferns and mosses in great variety, vying with magnificent pines, hemlocks and other evergreens, maples, dogwood and the white fringe of the mountain ash. Whether in its May day or its October splendor, it is a place where nature's brush and palette have been lavishly used.

After threading its doubtful way from its head springs, behind interminable mountains, Maury River flows, sometimes furiously, sometimes leisurely, through the Pass, its huge boulders causing cascades great and small, as it glides along to mingle with the noble James, on to the Atlantic.

Much admiration is expressed by those who drive through this veritable fairyland, under towering mountains on either side, with the river far below. In the early springtime, Phlox subulata and trailing arbutus literally carpet the ground, while all about the roadside and over the sides of the mountains is the queen of the mountain, the rhododendron.

Longfellow must have written of the Pass when he penned:

"In all places then
and in all seasons,
Flowers expand their light
and soul-like wings;
Teaching us by most
persuasive reasons,
How akin they are
to human beings."

In the early days the Pass was known as Dunlap's Gap and later as Strickler's Pass, and prior to the coming of the railroads into Lexington about 1880, it was the stagecoach thoroughfare with the outside world. It was once the trail of the elk and the buffalo, as they went across the mountain in search of food.

The Pass remains as primeval as when traversed by the red man, despite the fact that a much used highway passes through it. New vistas open up with each turn of the road. Mountains tower a thousand feet on either side; bird-life is interesting and abundant. A real treat is to follow Laurel Run to its source—its crystal pools, filled with myriads of rainbow trout, and its miniature cascades are beautiful beyond description. A sure cure for the blues and twentieth century discouragement is an hour spent in this delightful spot with nature and nature's God, after which one has a finer appreciation of real values.

[151]

Wilson's Springs was for many decades known as Strickler's Springs and as far back as 1822 are records of great religious meetings held on "the green." One such meeting in 1822 was a memorable event in Rockbridge. The Reverend William Brown, in his *Reminiscences,* written four score years ago, gives a picture of the setting of this meeting. Traveling over North Mountain, by way of the Rockbridge Alum Springs, he entered the depths of Strickler's Pass (Goshen Pass) and taking into account the narrowness of the defile, the stupendous crags hanging over the sudden and surprising curves in the road, the bendings and interlapping of the ridges, suggested doubt as to whether he could find his way; it was a scene of wildness and grandeur unsurpassed. Riding as he did, on horseback, alone through the six miles of deep, silent shade, during the last hours of a hot summer day, the impression was indeed lasting.

As he emerged into the valley and caught a view of old Jump Mountain, with the last rays of the departing sun just leaving its peak, he was admonished to hasten on. But, no! Something seemed to grip and hold him—some magic power—was he not on Holy ground? Here on this spot, years before he had witnessed a scene of memorable interest, a great religious meeting and the administering of the Lord's Supper. The Sabbath was one of loveliness, such as the climate of old Rockbridge often gives in September, especially in the mountains. The assembly was immense. Carriages were rarely seen and the multitudes came on horseback and on foot, from Hayes' Creek, Kerr's Creek, Walker's Creek, from the Pastures, Timber Ridge, Fairfield, New Providence, and Lexington. It was a time of unusual religious awakening over the country, the hearts of the people being deeply moved by "power from on high." Order and solemnity marked the occasion and many were admitted to church membership and sat down for the first time at the "Table of the Lord."

In the great gathering were seen newly convicted sinners, the stricken penitent, the rejoicing converts and the older Christians, all mingling together, making a scene in which angels would have rejoiced. Negroes were there in large numbers and many were admitted to church membership. The preacher was the Reverend Baxter, a man of strong religious views and feelings, who early in life had made a complete surrender of his great talents to the ministry and to teaching. He had been a pupil of the Reverend Graham and had graduated from the "Log College" before it became Washington Academy. He was for thirty years the president of Washington College and, for thirteen years, was the minister of the Lexington church.

A great and good man, a man of genius, a distinguished scholar, with endowments of mind and powers as a preacher, he was surpassed by none and equalled by few of his contemporaries. In mathematics, logic, rhetoric, theology, and history his knowledge was extensive and profound. In the entire command of his thoughts, he excelled most men. As a preacher, he was esteemed a model. In style, taste, gesture and argument, he was the finished and consummate orator, mighty in the Scriptures, mighty in the knowledge of the "faith once delivered to the saints," mighty in the history of the church, mighty in sound wisdom and discretion. Yet, notwithstanding all, he was as simple as a child, confiding in his friendships, sincere in his profession, always charitable and forgiving, with humility real and unostentatious. Like Paul, Whitfield and others of the same spirit, his benignant face was bathed in tears as he appealed to the multitudes. The whole assembly was deeply moved and many of the "stout hearted" melted "like wax."

Passing from the shadows of the mountain and riding in the twilight toward the Rockbridge Baths, the reflection of Dr. Brown was a natural one: Where are now those who constituted that vast assembly! Gone to their reward. "Dear old Rockbridge! a place where any might be thankful to be born, with a scenery so bold and charming as hardly to allow a sister in the family to vie with her, with a region where indeed the Lord plentifully 'sendeth the springs into the valleys, which run among the hills,' with a people who, from the first, filled it with sanctuaries and schools—the home of Graham, Alexander, Baxter, Ruffner, McDowell and Stonewall Jackson—the great and the good and of multitudes unknown to fame 'whose record is on high.' May blessings be forever on Thee."

Matthew Fontaine Maury added to the fame of the Pass, which he claimed to be the loveliest spot in Virginia. He expressed the wish that his body be carried through the Pass when the rhododendron was in bloom. He passed away in the winter, and in compliance with his request, his remains were kept in Lexington until the Pass was bedecked in its glorious May day splendor and then, accompanied by the Virginia Military Institute cadets, as honor guard, he was carried through this mountain pass to his last resting place in beautiful Hollywood in Richmond.

On the day of the funeral, Mrs. Preston, unable to attend, sat in her home and penned these immortal lines:

THROUGH THE PASS

"Home, bear me home at last," he said,
  "And lay me where my dead are lying;
But not while skies are overspread
  And mournful winds are sighing.

Wait till the royal march of spring
  Carpets your mountain fastness over—
Till chattering birds are on the wing
  And buzzing bees are in the clover.

Wait till the laurel bursts its buds
And creeping ivy flings its graces
Above the lichened rocks and floods
Of sunshine fill the shady places.

Then when the sky, the air, the grass,
Sweet nature all, is clad and tender,
Then bear me through the Goshen Pass
Amid its flush of May-day splendor."

So will we bear him! Human heart
To the warm earth's dew never nearer;
And never stooped she to impart
Lessons to one who held them dearer.

Stars lit new pages for him; seas
Revealed the depths the waves were screening;
The ebbs gave up their masteries,
The tidal flows confessed their meaning.

Of ocean paths the tangled clew
He taught the nations to unravel;
And marked the track where safely through
The lightning-footed thought might travel.

And yet, unflattered by the store
Of these supremer revelations;
Who bowed more reverently before
The lowliest of earth's fair creations.

What sage of all the ages past
Ambered in Plutarch's limpid story,
Upon the age he served, has cast
A radiance touched with worthier glory?

His noble living for the ends
God set him (duty underlying
Each thought, word, action) naught transcends
In lustre, save his nobler dying.

Do homage, sky and air and grass,
All things he cherished sweet and tender;
As through our gorgeous mountain pass
We bear him in the May-day splendor!

Several years ago friends and admirers erected, in the Pass, a monument to his memory. It is a huge boulder, mounted with a bronze tablet, on which is his bust in relief and this inscription:

MAURY—THE PATHFINDER OF THE SEAS.

The genius who first snatched from ocean and atmosphere
the secret of their laws.
Born January 14, 1806
Died at Lexington, Va.
February 1, 1873.
Carried through Goshen Pass to his last resting place in
Richmond, Virginia.
Every mariner for countless ages, as he takes his chart
To shape his course across the seas will think of Thee.
His inspiration Holy Writ—
Psalms 8 and 107
Verses 8-23-24
Ecclesiastes 1—8
A tribute by his native State, Virginia—1923.

The anchors about the base of the monument are from the bottom of Hampton Roads and were given by the Virginia Pilot Association.

This place of beauty and history has been loved with a peculiar attachment ever since the coming of the white man. Doubtless, the red man loved it, too, for he certainly fought to hold it. It remains a favorite camping paradise, with innumerable cottages and cabins secluded among its forests of magnificent trees.

Thousands of visitors drive through the Pass in the early spring and thousands return for a repetition of this thrill. It is not infrequently titled "Little Switzerland." Before the coming of the motor car and good roads the Pass was considered quite a distance from Lexington, but now the twelve miles is only a pleasant drive after the evening meal and makes a grand climax to one's day.

I love the mountains wreathed in mist,
    The twilight skies of amethyst,
The groves of ancient groves sun-kissed
    In Old Virginia.

I love the gorgeous trumpet flowers,
    Wild rose and honeysuckle bowers,
The woodland incense after showers,
    In Old Virginia.

I love the laughter of the rills,
Cloud shadows stretched athwart the hills,
The jocund sound of him who tills
In Old Virginia.

I love the martial ranks of corn,
Their blades agleam with lights of morn,
The curtains of the night withdrawn
In Old Virginia.

I love the modest maidenhood,
The deference paid to womanhood,
The chivalric and gentle blood
In Old Virginia.

I love the love of native sod,
The simple faith that trusts in God,
The heads bowed neath the chastening rod
In Old Virginia.

CHAPTER XXVIII: OLD STORES AND QUAINT ADVERTISEMENTS

IN the early years of the nineteenth century there were many stores doing business in Lexington, but trading was on a small scale. From an old scrapbook is unearthed the following account of how the Lexington merchants did business a century ago: "The mode of doing business by the merchants in those early days was so different from the plan used today, that it will be a revelation to the modern shopkeeper to know how the method was ever successful. To do business then, required a capital of from five to fifteen thousand dollars, because a stock sufficient to supply the trade for six months was bought at one time, mostly in Philadelphia and Baltimore—twice a year. (No "drummers" on the road in those days.) The merchants carried memorandums of what their customers wanted and carried the cash to pay for their purchases as there were no banks. They saw their goods packed and shipped before they left the city. The city merchants were polite and attentive and often invited the country merchants to their homes.

"Merchandise was shipped to Richmond and from there forwarded to Lexington by wagons and was on the way several weeks. The merchants generally went to market on horseback and it took them about three weeks to make the trip. When the goods finally arrived in Lexington, the merchants and clerks worked day and night until they were exhibited to the trade. Sales were mostly on credit and very large, as most everyone bought a season's supply at one time. There were no porters or deliveries."

General merchandise was truly not a misnomer, for the average merchant handled everything that a family needed: dry goods, hardware, queensware, shoes, hats, groceries, stationery, etc. A typical advertisement of a general merchandise store in the Lexington paper of 1854 follows:

"Perry and Perry has for sale: lemons, oranges, prunes, gum-drops, perre sauce, sardines, Rio coffee, molasses, pepper, sugar, olive oil, ginger, powder, shots and shells, starch, foot-mats, brooms, turpentine, shaving and home-made soaps, vinegar, writing paper, torpedoes, thimbles, needles, thread, cotton, matches, hooks and eyes, Yankee soap, shoebuttons, slates and slate pencils, pipes and pipe stems, Florida-water, wax and common dolls, cologne, motto-wafers, Pomade, dolls and doll heads, fans, port-monies, tuck, side and pocket combs, canes, India rubber dolls, tops, breastpins, finger rings, fobs, chains, guards, fancy soaps, false faces, banjo and banjo strings and a stock of chewing tobacco and cigars and Mereweather's celebrated Denicitized Smoking tobacco. The subscribers respectfully request that the public give them a trial as they are determined to sell for 'cash' cheap, or on time to punctual customers. Fresh cakes and pies on hand."

It required some education to do business. Clerks had to serve a term of years before they were considered competent to do business. They were trained to practice rigid economy in the expenditures of the store. No waste of paper, boxes or twine or anything else was ever permitted. Above all things, clerks were required to be strictly honest in all their dealings with the public. A clerk who would take advantage of a customer by misrepresenting his goods was promptly discharged. As a consequence the customers had implicit confidence in the merchants.

The merchants also traded for country produce, paid in goods and sold the produce for the same they paid for it, their profits in the transaction being on the goods exchanged.

The merchants were considered an honest and reliable set of men, known for their fair dealings with the public. Most of them were among the builders of Lexington, Washington and Lee University, and the Virginia Military Institute. They were successful, some accumulating a competency for old age. Many had large families, which were educated and became valuable citizens in many parts of the world.

Just one hundred years ago, Horace Melcher was the first manufacturer of candy in Lexington. He lived where the *County News* is now located and his factory was in the back yard. He was an expert at his trade and his cakes, pies, and candies were unsurpassed and were very popular with the townspeople and the college boys. (Many decades later, this same location was the home of Mrs. Jaccheri's famous ice creams and cakes, oysters and pies.)

On Jefferson Street, near the Franklin Hall, old Miss Patsy Blunt kept a cake and cider shop and did "very little business." Archibald Beard, a saddler and harness maker, lived on the old Back Spring lot, where he raised a large family. He was a good workman, a great punster and wrote "poetry," but was too fond of the "over-joyful" and just would take his sprees!

In 1852 Dr. J. W. Paine was the ebullient bookseller of the village and had been for some years. He also conducted a private classical school. Most of the stores sold whiskey in those early days—12½c per quart and 37½c per gallon. All four of the hotels had bars and sold by the drink or otherwise, as the customer desired. The records do not state whether Dr. Paine sold whiskey along with books or not, but doubtless he did. Through the succeeding years this establishment has been operated by Lyle, Bowie, and Stuart and is now Boley's.

"John Blair Lyle lived in Lexington and conducted an 'automatic bookstore,' that is to say, one that was left often to itself, with a request lying on the counter, to the effect that if anyone wanted anything in the store, he could take it, provided he would make the proper entry on the slate. John Lyle was too fond of society, too jovial, too philanthropic to care much for money or to be an attentive business man. It made him happier to give than to make, and the size of his gifts was measured by his feelings rather than by his ability. Under a warm appeal, he would plunge his hand into his pantaloons pocket, which was his money-drawer, and bring out a handful of silver change and drop it in the collection basket. He died about the time he reached the bottom of his pocket. But while his chief book account was that of profit and loss, his moral record was rich in words and deeds. No church was ever blessed with a nobler elder; few richer voices ever led the music in the sanctuary; no better friend ever watched over the weak and erring. He was indifferent to money because of his greater regard for the salvation of men."

January 1, 1854, this store was proudly advertising for sale a book by a Virginian: *Flush Times in Alabama and Mississippi,* by J. G. Baldwin.

About this time, the following advertisement in the local paper shows a variety of offerings:

"Just received a large addition to my stock of books: The Lamplighter, Wide-wide World, This, That and the Other, Old Man's Bride, Party Leaves, Twenty Years in an American Slaver, Satanic Science (a Temperance Tale), Sketches of Ireland, Life and Work of Burns, Proverbial Philosophy, Six Weeks in Italy, Modern Philosophy, Foot's Sketches of North Carolina, Ruins of Nineveh, Gil Blas, Robinson Crusoe, Life of Dr. Alexander, Lady Huntington and Her Friends, Memoirs of Lady Colquhoun, Bate's Divine Attributes, Consolation, Moral Science, Daniel Boone, Genius of Scotland and many others. Also a large assortment of pens, paper, ink, blank books, sealing wax, wafers and wafer albums, Indian rubber flutes, flute music, courting and visiting cards, portfolios, tissue and drawing papers, paint boxes, brushes, pencils, Mer's Propelling Pencils (something new), surveyor's instruments, fine Bibles, Psalms and Hymns and Methodist's Hymnals.—J. W. PAINE."

In the same newspaper was advertised: "English stationery on sale."

In 1877 appeared this advertisement:

"Newspapers, magazines and wall paper;
Books for sale, hire or exchange.
Circulating library. Will be glad to supply
all your wants without buying."

Many stories are told of the bookstore of more recent times, when it was the pleasant rendezvous for the elderly gentlemen of the town, mostly ex-Confederate veterans, gentlemen of the old school, God bless their memory. Their like we shall never see again, and for this the world is the poorer.

Older residents recall that prior to the war, Major Thomas J. Jackson was a daily caller at this popular meeting place, where he was always assured a congenial assemblage, and that after the war, General Lee was a frequent visitor there, where he too met congenial friends.

Daily there assembled in the rear of the store, around a huge stove, which stood there summer and winter, as a focal point and a place to rest tired feet, a most unusual group of the intelligentsia of the day. Many a feast of reason and flow of soul took place in this sanctum sanctorum. Mr. Stuart, the proprietor, himself an ex-Confederate veteran, a leader in church and community affairs, and a perfect host at all times, supplied an unlimited number of easy and comfortable chairs "much worn."

On one occasion a daughter of one of the frequent visitors said to the proprietor's daughter: "I think your father needs some new chairs in his store." The immediate reply was: "Well, your father ought to buy them, then, for he helped to wear these out."

At these gatherings everything from Dan to Beersheba was discussed—pro and con—to and fro. The younger generation, always evident in the bookstore, came in for "plenty" of their attention and discussion. These men insisted that things were very different when they were boys. They noticed that young people did not obey their parents any more, and that unless some "curb be put upon them," they greatly feared for the future of the world. It was reported that boys were actually smoking vile cigarettes in the very presence of ladies and some of them did not tip their hat any more, when meeting a lady or a professor!

Arguments a-plenty! Many a battle was refought, many a question of local, state, national and international importance was "settled" at these meetings. The college boys, being both amused and enlightened, called these assemblies "bull-sessions." Customers would come and wait, and wait, and finally, in desperation, find what they wanted and leave either the cash or a charge slip and depart.

On one occasion it was said that the proprietor and his best friend were comfortably seated about the stove when a customer appeared. "There's a customer, Cal." "Be real quiet, Frank, and maybe he will go on out," said the proprietor.

It seems that this was one place where the spirit of commercialism was never paramount, but a place where leisure was enjoyed—more important than buying and selling was, it would seem

"the love of learning,
the sequestered nooks
and all the sweet
serenity of books."

It has always been a place where warm and lasting friendships have been formed. When in 1858, Mr. Lyle, the proprietor died, he was so beloved by his friends and particularly by Colonel Preston, that he had him buried in the Preston plot and erected a monument to his memory with this high tribute:

"He was the truest friend, the bravest man
and the best Christian ever known to him
who erects this stone to his memory."

The great Waterman Pen Company, the pioneer in the fountain pen industry, recently celebrated its fiftieth anniversary. The first year that this company made pens, this bookstore bought and sold seven of their pens. What luxuries they must have been in that far-off day!

In 1888 the Lee-Jackson Camp of Confederate Veterans was organized, and through the years most of their meetings were held in the bookstore, where their charter still hangs.

The Rockbridge Savings Bank was, for many years, operated here by Mr. Stuart. This institution later developed into the Rockbridge National Bank.

Another business of continuous operation since the middle of the nineteenth century is Pettigrew's. In the *Valley Star* of eighty-three years ago appeared this quaint advertisement:

"Just received—not gone—but going fast!
Imported cigars for sale cheap and for cash."

And a few weeks later this firm published this advertisement:

"Oranges, lemons, figs, prunes, perfumery, soda water, whips, sugar, toilet soap, double-barrel shot guns, molasses, etc. I have connected with my establishment a candy manufactory. Also a soda fountain and the best London ale. Call and see for yourself as I have a great variety of articles too tedious to mention."

Pettigrew's toy and candy store, as several generations of townspeople, students, and cadets have known it, has been a real institution in this community, famous for its attractive display of toys of foreign and domestic make. Here all the grown-ups as well as the children loved to go, fascinated both by the toys and by the happy, jovial, and entertaining Mrs. Pettigrew, a real personality, who retained the dress and manners of the ladies of a few decades past.

Mrs. Pettigrew loved children and they loved her, but they always knew that she was in authority. Famous also was the place for its wonderful display of fine candies, with quality and cleanliness "par excellence." The scales rarely ever had a chance, for after they had told their story, on would go a few more pieces for friendly good measure, along with some delectable tidbits, touching upon this and that, here and there, "me and you."

Years agone it was customary for stores of this type to have a huge statue of an Indian chief or maiden, resplendent in all the colors of the rainbow, stand in front of the store to let the world know that tobacco and cigars were on sale. Such a Minnehaha graced the entrance to this establishment. The college boys being intent upon carrying her away, the proprietor had to put her inside every night, as the streets were in darkness. One evening, the proprietor, trying to put her in for the night, had difficulty handling her. She toppled, and they had quite a tussle; he thought that she, too, had had too much "fire-water." This statue, probably the only one in Lexington, now graces the formal gardens of Mrs. Livingstone Smith.

Dold's has long been an institution and a landmark. It has been known and patronized by thousands of students and cadets, as their headquarters for smokes, eats, and drinks. Who does not remember the peanut roaster, the quaint little whistle, and the funny little man who operated it and turned out good-smelling and good-eating peanuts! The proprietor styled himself the "only Dold and the student's friend" and has traveled about the world, probably as extensively as any citizen of Lexington.

Samuel Pettigrew's daguerreotype studio, too, has survived the long years. In the *Valley Star* of July 27, 1854 appeared this rather lengthy notice:

"Ho, all who want good daguerreotypes, call upon the subscriber at the Sky-light room, opposite McDowell's Hotel, where he is now taking some of the best pictures ever taken—as good as any taken in the Northern cities. He studied under Tanner and feels authorized now to pledge to his patrons just as good pictures as Tanner could take.

"His gallery is neatly and tastefully arranged and is a place of fashionable resort to all who have a few minutes to spare pleasantly. He is always glad to see his friends, especially the ladies, whether they want pictures or not. He feels confident that his arrangements and specimens cannot fail to please. What is more pleasant than a promenade around a Daguerreotype Gallery, where you may again look upon the faces of those who are now far distant and perhaps almost forgotten? It calls us back to many scenes in which we have mingled and revelled, and for the time being, we live over the past again. Whether this is a profitable employment or not, he leaves the philosopher to decide, but it is a very pleasant one, even though some of the associations which it calls up may be very mournful indeed.

"To those who want pictures taken, he would say, 'secure the shadow ere the substance fade.' He does not require persons to take pictures unless satisfied and you cannot, therefore, lose anything by giving him a trial.

"He also has a stock of locket jewelry, which he will fill on modest terms. Since now, everyone has a chance to see himself as others see him, it is to be hoped that no one will fail to avail himself the opportunity to do so."

"It is of interest that Louis Mande Daguerre, the French chemist, made his first daguerreotype in 1839, and in the 1840's Pettigrew opened his studio in up-to-date Lexington. Pettigrew's continued until the war period. After the surrender, there came to the community an ex-Confederate soldier and an artist of unusual ability, Mike Miley, who perpetuated the picture business. Miley's contribution to the world was great. To him is due the credit for many of the best photographic studies of General Lee. Wherever these photographs have gone, has also gone—'photo by Miley.' He developed a formula for taking pictures in their natural colors, for which he received national recognition. Valentine sought Miley's artistic and authentic advice in his masterly work on the Lee monument. This interesting business continues under the guidance of his son, Henry Miley, likewise a real artist."

The following advertisements, picked at random from a local newspaper of eighty years ago, show real snap and originality on the part of the advertisers:

"Miss Annie Archibald takes this opportunity of returning thanks to the ladies of Lexington and vicinity for the liberal patronage she has received in the past and would respectfully ask for a continuance of the same. She is prepared to do all work entrusted to her, either in Mantua or Millinery, in the latest style. Her attention will be particularly paid to making silk and crepe bonnets. She may be found at any time on back street, next to the Methodist Church."

"Mrs. Moody wishes to inform the public that she is now prepared to attend to any work in her line of business that they may bestow upon her. She is prepared to whiten old hats and bonnets, such as went to seed last year and to rip them up and make young Democratic flats of them. You can find her next to Mrs. Riggons, opposite the Methodist Church."

"Murder, murder, murder!

"Take 'em off! Take 'em off!

"All persons indebted to the estate of Colonel John Jordan, dec'd, will—I was going to say, please—but I won't—come up and pay down by the first of February or I will certainly send the sheriff after them, without fail and no mistake. And let them know that I cannot poke my head out of my hole without having some one tramp on my toes, squeeze my hand, grunt or squint, and some go so far as to burrow into my hole to dun me, all asking the same question: 'Jim, can't you settle that little balance your father's estate owes me?'

"So, have mercy on my distressed condition and plank up the dimes without further notice.

"Yours in haste,

JAS. JORDAN, Exr for Col. John Jordan."

"N.B. I would say to creditors, 'hold on, be of good cheer, for I will certainly pay them as soon as I can killect.'"

This was supplemented a few weeks later by this rather urgent request:

"The devil is to pay! The devil is to pay! and naught to pay with!

"Since my first call on persons indebted to the estate of Colonel John Jordan, dec'd, some have come nobly up to the rack—others—sorter orter —as to the balance, who haven't paid a dime, you had better fork over soon or I will be after you with a sharp stick. I am writing no tomfoolery.

One more good lift and I can venture out of my hole, without being elbowed in my sore side, and breathe fresh air again.

"My pious regards to those who have come nobly up.

JIM JORDAN."

"Dr. William A. Graham offers his services to the public. He can be found at Dr. Marshall's Office or at his mother's home, near the Episcopal Church, when not professionally engaged."

Robert E. Lee — the last photograph (January, 1870)

Stono, built by John Jordan for his family

Virginia Military Institute barracks after Hunter's Raid, 1864

Lexington railway station

Robert E. Lee's funeral cortege, Main Street, (October 15, 1870)

Entertainment for Lexington's Elite in the "Gay Nineties". Virginia Military Institute vs the University of Virginia

CHAPTER XXIX: NEWSPAPERS AND TRAVEL

THOUGH Lexington has always enjoyed an isolated retirement from the great centers of population and the marts of trade, it has ever been interested in and intelligent about the affairs of the big world outside. Those agencies of education and enlightenment, books and newspapers, both secular and religious, have played a large part in the life of the community. The *Lexington Gazette* displays on its building, "Established 1804," and few experiences are more interesting than rummaging among its ancient files.

During the second decade of the nineteenth century, there lived at the east corner of Washington and Jefferson Streets, the Reverend Valentine Mason, a Baptist minister of Neriah Church, near the old Buena Vista Furnace. He was also the publisher of the *Rockbridge Intelligencer*. What is left of his old Lexington home, since being desecrated by the conversion of the first floor into shops, reveals his fine architectural taste. Later, he lived in Ann Smith Academy. From the century-old files of this paper is this item which bespeaks the alertness of old Lexington:

"The era of good feeling passed away in 1824-25. All the candidates for the presidency belonged to the Republican party. Rockbridge was largely Republican. The contest was between Adams and Jackson and was so nearly a draw race that it was decided in the House of Representatives in favor of Adams. Then began the era of bitterness between the friends of these leaders, which culminated in the Democratic and Whig parties. Rockbridge sided with the Whigs.

"The Intelligencer believed in Henry Clay against those who charged him and Adams with a corrupt agreement. There is no doubt that when the opponents of Jackson, led by Clay, Calhoun, and Webster took the name of Whigs in 1833, Rockbridge supported this party and did so until the rearrangement of the parties after the war.

"In other words, the people of Rockbridge in those days favored a Protective Tariff, internal improvements by the General Government and a United States Bank. The Democrats were opposed to all of these."

In this same paper appeared in 1826 a series on "Hard Times." "This is a subject most mysterious in political economy. Rulers, Parliaments and philosophers have all failed to guide the people in such habits of production and consumption as would establish a steady and permanent prosperity."

The files of both local newspapers show a cognizance of world events, domestic and foreign, with exceptionally well-written editorials. Typical is this rather detailed one in the *Valley Star* of August 31, 1854, on the death of a European monarch, the late King of Saxony:

"The death of this distinguished Monarch has been already announced. His demise appears to have been the result of an unfortunate accident, while traveling from Munich to his own Capital at Dresden. The carriage in which the King rode was, by some mismanagement, overturned and His Majesty, falling among the horses, received a kick, which terminated fatally almost immediately afterwards.

"The deceased Monarch was a son of Duke Maximillian, who was born in 1759 and died in 1838. His Majesty was born on the 18th of May, 1797, and succeeded in June, 1838, by virtue of the act of renunciation of his father to his uncle, King Anthony, having been co-regent from the 13th of September, 1830, to the period of his accession. The King of Saxony visited England in May, 1844, and was the guest of Her Majesty the Queen at the time of the unexpected arrival in London of the Emperor of Russia. The two Monarchs met at Buckingham Palace and Windsor Castle and were together at the Ascot Races of that year. The King, although twice married, has left no issue by either consort. His first wife was the Arch-Duchess Caroline Ferdenandine Theresa Joseph Demetrie, who was born in 1801 and died in 1832. His Majesty married secondly, Marie Anne Leopoldine, daughter of the late King Maximillian Joseph of Bavaria, who survives her royal husband. His Majesty is survived also by his brother, the Duke John Nepomucene Marie Joseph, who married in 1822, the Duchess Amelie Auguste, daughter of the late King Maximillian Joseph of Bavaria, sister of the present Queen Dowager of Saxony, by whom he has a family of eight children."

In the same issue of the *Valley Star* appears this note of the college commencement:

"Orators: Thomas L. Preston, William T. Price, Charles P. Estill, Benton Taylor, J. D. Morrison, with R. R. Houston as Valedictorian. The Salutatory was in Greek and Latin and the orations given were:

"Destiny of the English Language.
"Preëminence of Classical Study.
"Religious Tolerance Abroad.
"Internal Improvements.
"The Baccalaureate was by the President, Dr. Junkin."

The *Rockbridge County News* was established Friday, November 7, 1884, with Moore and Boude, editors, with this arresting caption:

"The clock strikes high twelve!
Pull the bell, we're off!"

Their first editorial:

"We shall print for the many, not the few. The partizan may smoke his pipe over his campaign paper, though it may slander his neighbor, cast firebrands everywhere in society and delude him with false hopes and visions of party triumphs, but while he is chuckling over his miserable caricatures and coarse jokes, his wife and children will want to be reading the County News."

This newspaper has, for these fifty years, been a power in moulding the thought and character of the people of Lexington and Rockbridge County, and is one of the strong and unfailing ties that binds many former Lexingtonians, scattered throughout the world, to the old home town. For the greater part of these fifty years, this paper had as its guiding spirit, the gifted and scholarly Matthew W. Paxton, whose wise judgment and brilliant intellect was greatly appreciated by the public.

Of interest to girls should be this "wise counsel," which appeared many years ago in the *County News:*

"A girl should learn to cook, sew, mend, be gentle, value time, dress neatly, keep a secret, mind a baby, avoid idleness, be self-reliant, darn stockings, respect old age, make good bread, keep a house tidy, be above gossiping, humor a cross man, control her temper, care for the sick, make home happy, sweep down cobwebs, marry a man for his worth, be a helpmate to her husband, keep clear of flash literature, take plenty of active exercise, see a mouse without screaming, read some books besides novels, be light-hearted and fleet-footed, wear shoes that won't cramp her feet, and be a womanly woman under all circumstances. This doing, she will have little time for idleness."

The following will prove the value of the Lexington papers as an advertising medium: In a recent issue Bobby Funkhouser advertised that he had guinea hens for sale. (He did not specify how many.) One week later he received an order from California, for one thousand to be shipped immediately. He promptly replied that he could not supply, as his "flock of three" had been disposed of.

Both the *Lexington Gazette* and the *Rockbridge County News* have always commanded the superior brains and wide experience of Lexington's outstanding citizens, who have never failed to champion the best and highest interests of mankind. Great has been their influence upon the thought and action of this people.

✓　✓　✓　✓

Throughout its long history, Lexington has seen every possible form of transportation and travel, from the courier on foot, the horse, ridden over Indian trails, the oxcart, the stagecoach, the canal boat, the train—the old Virginia Creeper, which came around the bend, "turned on the Y and backed into town, as if ashamed of itself"—up to the modern motor bus and airplane. Whatever form of transportation comes, regardless of its destination or speed, Lexington will share in it.

The most picturesque modes of travel, the stagecoach through the beautiful Goshen Pass and the canal boats on old North River, have never been surpassed in beauty and interest, as approaches to Lexington. They afforded magnificent scenery for travelers. A fine description of travel of that period is given by Albert Steves, of San Antonio, Texas. In 1934 he writes:

"About the 15th of September, 1874, my mother, by brothers, Ed, Ernest and myself boarded a stagecoach in San Antonio bound for Lexington, Virginia. Leaving San Antonio early in the morning, we drove to Austin and owing to the wet weather, it took two days and a night to make the ninety miles. Here we boarded the train for Houston, as the H. and T. C. Railroad had just been completed to Austin and, on reaching Houston, we boarded the I. and G. N. for St. Louis, taking ninety-six hours to make the trip. All engines were then wood-burners. Leaving St. Louis for Cincinnati, where we boarded the River Steamer, Skillinger, for Huntington. Owing to the drought then existing in that section, the Ohio River was very low and it took us six days and nights to make the trip, because of the sandbars in the river. This steamer took us to Catlettsburg, where we embarked upon a smaller boat. Upon leaving Catlettsburg, we were hardly out two or three hundred yards when a cog broke and we had to float back in to the Catlettsburg wharf and wait twenty-four hours to have the repairs made. Then boarding the boat again for Huntington, where we took the C. and O. train for Goshen, Virginia. Here we took stagecoach for Lexington, traveling through the Pass. The stage was crowded with college boys. After a hard two weeks, we reached our goal and were matriculated at good old Washington and Lee. After a year's routine of study, in 1875, we were headed for home for our summer vacation.

"Leaving Lexington at night, on the Yeatman packet boat, we arrived in Lynchburg the next morning. The night being a beautiful one, there was not much sleeping, as nearly everyone sat on deck, singing until the wee hours of the morning. This was undoubtedly the most beautiful trip then existing and cannot be surpassed now.

"In the summer of 1876, mother and father came to visit us in Lexington and they also came by canal boat from Lynchburg. We three boys walked to the first lock, early in the morning, to meet them at Alexander's Landing. After their visit in Lexington, we all took boat for Lynchburg and there took train for Washington and Philadelphia for the big Centennial.

"Well do I recall these wonderful trips up and down old North River and the James and the sounding of the driver's bugle for the opening and closing of the locks. I believe in the trip were encountered about sixty of these locks. In the winter months, when the old freezes were on, there was not much travel on the packet line and the raising and lowering of the water in North River, by the packets going through the locks, caused skating above the locks to be much interfered with. Yet, it was a common occurrence for us to skate eighteen or twenty miles down the river, as we walked around the locks and there was usually snow on the ground."

One of the oldest German families in Texas and largely responsible for the great city of San Antonio of today, the Steves family is one of the most outstanding Washington and Lee families in America. Several generations have received their training in this school, and their loyalty and devotion to it knows no bounds. Three generations of the Steves family have studied under three generations of the Campbell family, namely: Albert Steves under Professor John L. Campbell, Albert Steves, II, under Dean Harry Campbell, and Albert Steves, III, under Edmund Campbell.

The three Steves brothers, the first of the name to attend Washington and Lee, were known as "the three Bismarcks," and the older residents of Lexington still remember them this way.

The canal was built in sections and reached Lexington in 1852. It took eighteen hours to make the trip from Lynchburg, with three trips weekly for passengers. The boat was drawn by three horses, which were changed every twelve miles. The old canal rendered splendid service for many years, but went into disuse with the coming of the railroad into town in 1880. Ruins of the dams and locks remain today, relics of this system of transportation of a bygone day. Like everything else of importance about the place, the canal was constructed by Colonel John Jordan.

A dear lady of Lexington delighted in telling of her honeymoon trip from Lynchburg to Lexington. It was a hot summer night and they sat on the top of the boat all the way, in the moonlight. In later life she traveled extensively, yet she claimed that this was the loveliest trip of her life.

Social life on the boats was enjoyable. Ladies would sit on deck in pleasant weather, and sew and gossip. Men would occasionally jump off and walk or run alongside "to stretch their legs." For sleeping quarters, one-half of the boat was given to ladies and the other to the men. Berths were in three tiers, folded up by day and suspended by leather straps when not in use.

Bagby, in his *Canal Reminiscences,* gives this picture of the old travel system:

"And now the canal, after a fair and costly trial is to give place to the rail and I, in common with the great body of Virginians, am heartily glad of it. It has served its purpose well enough, perhaps, for its day and generation.

"The world has passed it by as it has passed by slavery. Henceforth, Virginia must prove her metal in the front of steam, electricity and possibly mightier forces still. The dream of the great canal to the Ohio, with its nine-mile tunnel, costing fifty or more millions, furnished by the General Government and revolutionizing the commerce of the United States, much as the discovery of America and the opening of the Suez Canal revolutionized the commerce of the world, must be abandoned along with other dreams."

The railroad was quite an innovation and Lexington was sure that the "speed age" had arrived.

One of the most familiar and useful landmarks of old Lexington was the town clock on the steeple of the Presbyterian Church. For many generations it marked time for the populace. However, with the coming of the "milk and honey age," with wrist watches for everyone, the faithful old clock was no longer consulted and went out of business and was finally removed from the steeple. It was an ornament, picturesque and reminiscent of old Lexington and should have been left there, even though retired from active service. Humorous remarks are often made, sometimes bordering on sarcasm, even by those who love the old town and who would admit that its shortcomings often contribute to its charm. Buz Letcher's description of the town is: "Two people sitting—rocking—a pistol shot nearby—'what's that?'—'just a pistol shot.' (Continued rocking)."

CHAPTER XXX: BIOGRAPHIC SKETCHES

LEXINGTON has given to the world many great personalities. Those who, either by birth or adoption, have belonged to this community, comprise a long list of men and women who have been leaders in their day—trail-blazers—ministers, educators, inventors, who in every line of endeavor in which they found, themselves, stood paramount among their fellow men. In war and in peace, in the arts, in the sciences, and in religious thought, this community has never lacked leadership from its earliest days to the present time, which suggests Athens during her era from the Battle of Marathon to the time of Macedonian rule, when she produced so many great men of genius.

The McDowell family, the first white people to settle on the great Borden Tract, is doubtless the most distinguished family in Lexington history. In local, state, and national affairs it has always been prominent. The progenitor, Ephriam McDowell, was not a young man when he came to America, yet he lived many years in Rockbridge County and left his mark. As he and his descendants are so interwoven in the history of Lexington and of Washington and Lee, the following extracts from the historical papers of the college are given:

"When the morning broke over the singular national system, known as the Clans of Scotland, there emerges from its mists a bold individual named Dugall. By and by he wins his way to the leadership of a warlike clan, which, as the centuries pile up, attains historical prominence, and his name, after a number of orthographical gymnastics, whether Gaelic, Celtic or Norwegian, nobody can tell, appears as Macdougal. In early times, this tribe owned an estate so large and rich as that it became the entire portion of one son who, after awhile grew into such strength and fame, as to create a new clan, called the Macdougals of Lorn. It was not easy in the rude condition of human society then existing for a dainty morsel of land to remain long under one ownership; especially was it difficult under the moral code that 'might makes right,' inherited by those clans from their pirate ancestors and, for a wide stretch of years, kept in vigorous exercise. We wonder, as we see the little kingdom twined around by poetry and romance, at the secret power that kept it firm within the grasp of the original owner during all those mighty convulsions and changes in the minds and affairs of men, which had transformed the wild Highland clansmen into the earnest-minded Presbyterian followers of John Knox. Whatever it was, however, it was beguiled into surrender by Sir Colin Campbell, who, about the middle of the sixteenth century, bore away in loving triumph, as his wife, the fair Macdougal heiress, with all her ancestral titles and demesnes. Forever since her blood and her wealth have gone to enrich the cormorant clan of McCallum More. But if her title yet remains the highest decoration in the Dukedom of Argyle, we look upon it without regret for, in free America, where every man is a sovereign and, in our gallant Virginia, where every woman is a queen, coronets and crowns do not wear the insignia of the greatness that we have lost, but that of the evils from which heroic fathers have delivered us. This idyl, like a bit of point lace carefully wrapped in linen and lavender, from the boudoir of poor Josephine, has no value beyond that of furnishing from the confused rubbish of a boisterous past a scrap of an ornament for a modern story.

"From the best authority, the correctness of the lineage of the Mc-Dowells in the United States, here traced, is assumed, though the changes in the name have been so bewildering as to make it difficult to keep up with them.

"The family was devoted to civil and religious liberty and was prominent in the struggle that led to the expulsion of the Stuarts and the rise of the Commonwealth. When McDonnell of Antrim approached the walls of Londonderry, Ephriam McDowell, then sixteen, was one of the young Presbyterian lads who fled to the defense of the heroic town and assisted in closing the gates against the intruding Irish. Two years later he is with the victorious army of William the Third at Boyne."

Little is known of Ephriam McDowell from this time until, past the age of sixty, we find him seeking a home in Virginia. Even at this age, he was wide awake to the interests of Rockbridge and was highly regarded for his intelligence, usefulness, and probity, wielding a singular and beneficent influence among the intrepid and independent spirits with whom he was surrounded.

He died in 1775, at the age of 104 years, retaining all his faculties until the end. He survived both of his sons. His son, John, was a surveyor of note and laid off the Borden Tract. He died in a battle with the Iroquois Indians and is buried in the family plot in the Colonial cemetery near Fairfield, where his father is also buried. On his gravestone is this inscription:

Hier Lyes The Body of
John Mack Dowell
Decd December 1743

Samuel McDowell took part in the Revolution and commanded a militia at Guilford Courthouse. He later became a lawyer and judge in Kentucky and was much honored. His daughter, Magdaline, married Andrew Reid, of Mulberry Hill. His son, Ephriam, who received his M.D. degree from Edinburgh, became a great surgeon and one of the famous men of his generation. He was known as the father of abdominal surgery.

James, a cousin of Ephriam, born at Cherry Grove, near Lexington, was graduated from Princeton, from which he also received his LL.D. In 1843 he became governor of the Commonwealth of Virginia.

"A nobler gentleman, a more upright man, a truer patriot never graced his native State. He was distinguished for his native talents and intellectual attainments and for the virtue and amenities which adorned his personal character."

His Lexington home, Col Alto, was the center of charm and hospitality, where he and his wife and daughters entertained in the grandest manner of the time. His daughters, having mingled in the best society of Washington and Richmond during their father's public career in the two capitals, constituted a real addition to the already fine society of Lexington. Governor and Mrs. McDowell and other members of the family sleep in the Lexington cemetery.

One of the most interesting personalities of early Rockbridge was Mary Elizabeth McDowell, who became the wife of James Greenlee and was thereafter known as Mary Greenlee—and very well known, too. She was the first white woman to come into this section. Most of her recorded life is as a widow and she proved capable of caring for her own interests. For many years she kept an inn and was known far and wide for her keen mind and ready wit and more than once was accused of witchcraft.

At the age of ninety-five she was called upon for a deposition in connection with a lawsuit and was asked her age. "Why do you ask my age? Do you think I am in my dotage?" she replied. Longevity characterized her family. It seemed easy for them to round out the century mark. Her grandson, John Greenlee, the last of the family, died in Lexington in 1915, having lived his ninety-nine years in "blissful bachelorhood." He was a delightful, gentle gentleman and a walking encyclopedia of Rockbridge history. Not until his last years would he ever tell his age. When asked this question, he would smile and say, "O, I'm this side of forty."

Mary Greenlee was also known for her bravery. On one occasion a child was stolen by the Indians. She went to the father and offered to rescue the child if the father would supply horse, saddle, and bridle. The condition was that if she brought back the child, she was to keep the horse, saddle, and bridle. She followed the Indians to Mammoth Cave in Kentucky and brought the child safely back. On another occasion, an old schoolmaster came along and offered to write her epitaph in exchange for a gallon of brandy. She agreed. He wrote:

> Mary Greenlee died of late
> And went straight to Heaven's Gate.

He demanded the brandy before finishing. She demurred, but finally gave it. Then he added:

> But an angel met her with a club
> And knocked her back to Beelzebub.

He ran and she after him, with a stick.

Andrew Reid, of Mulberry Hill, was the first clerk of Rockbridge

County. He married a daughter of Samuel McDowell and had a large family.

Dr. W. H. Ruffner has left this intimate glimpse of this good man: "Andrew Reid was a strong man intellectually and physically. I remember him well, as he sat on the front porch of his Mulberry Hill mansion, which in those days was embowered in vines and trees, and within was a beautiful picture of shining brasses, well-waxed passage and floors and that air of order and neatness, combined with ease and comfort, which seemed to welcome, rather than embarrass the visitor. Miss Magdaline was the housekeeper and Miss Nancy the reader. On a couch, in an inner room, reclined the aged mother, nee Magdaline McDowell, daughter of Samuel McDowell and Mary McClung, now totally blind and near the end of her useful and honored life. Mr. Reid's favorite seat in summer was on the vine-covered porch of the family mansion. Here he sat in his armchair, or rested prone on a bench, at one end of which was a pillow of folio volumes, a leather-bound illuminated edition of Hume's England. The old gentleman was a great favorite of us boys. He was so companionable and allowed us to climb the cherry trees and to thrash down the mulberries without restraint. There are not many homes nowadays like old Mulberry Hill."

Like most of Lexington's great, he sleeps in the Presbyterian cemetery.

Samuel McDowell Reid, son of Andrew Reid, succeeded his father as clerk of Rockbridge County. He was one of the founders of the Franklin Society, and for more than fifty years was a trustee of Washington College and of the Ann Smith Academy. He organized the Rockbridge County Fair, which in early days supplied much that was educational, social, and entertaining to the town and county people. He was also instrumental in opening North River to Lexington. Two of his daughters grew to maturity, one becoming the wife of Professor James J. White, and the other the wife of Colonel J. DeH. Ross, of Sunnyside.

In 1760, the five Taylor brothers came to Rockbridge from County Armagh, Ireland, and invested in lands and slaves. Later one of the brothers married a sister of John Paul Jones and this is claimed as the reason for the family's aversion, later, to the American institution of slavery, when they freed their slaves, giving to each freeman fifty dollars.

William, born in 1821, near Hog Back Mountain, a few miles from Lexington, concerns us here. He was a giant in size and strength. He attended school in Lexington and early in life embraced the Methodist faith and became an evangelist. He was a fine speaker and had a rare gift of song. When presenting him to the Conference, the Presiding Elder said: "Here is a young man that the sun never finds in bed." He later went to California to do mission work in San Francisco, a miserable and corrupt place of shacks and tents. His powerful physique, his tact and his gift of song, together with his fine speaking voice made him eminently qualified for the work. After several years there, he traveled throughout the United States, preaching with power, and later toured Great Britain, the Continent, South America, Malaysia, Australia, China, Ceylon, and India. In 1884 he was made Bishop of Africa.

It was claimed that no Christian minister of his day had preached so widely. He died in California in 1902 at the age of eighty-one, and is buried there. In his *Life and Memoirs* he said: "A Presbyterian divine claimed that two curses had come to Rockbridge, the blue thistle and the Methodists."

Archibald Alexander, born in a log hut near Lexington in 1772, was destined to go far in fame and influence. Early in life he decided to enter the Presbyterian ministry and attended Liberty Hall Academy. For a while he was president of Hampden-Sydney College, and later had a short pastorate in Philadelphia. He was instrumental in establishing Princeton Theological Seminary and was its first professor. He died at Princeton in 1851, in the seventy-ninth year of his age.

A forceful and fluent speaker, a brilliant mind, a prolific writer, a delightful companion, and a true friend, were some of the tributes paid him. He was probably the greatest influence of his day in moulding the religious thought of America. His great success in life was due largely to his blissful domestic environment. Regarding his marriage to the daughter of the eminent Reverend Waddel, the *Life of Alexander* says:

"It may be safely said that no man ever enjoyed a more blessed connection. If the uncommon beauty and artless grace of this lady were strong attractions in the days of youth, there were higher qualities which made the union inexpressibly felicitous during almost half a century. For domestic wisdom, self-sacrificing affection, humble piety, industry, inexhaustible stores of vivacious conversation, hospitality to his friends, sympathy with his cares and love to their children, she was such a gift as God bestows only on the most favored. While during a large part of middle life he was subject to a variety of maladies, she was preserved in unbroken health. When his spirits flagged, she was prompt and skillful to cheer and comfort, and as his days were filled with spiritual and literary toils, she relieved him of all domestic affairs. Without the show of any conjugal blandishments, there was, through life, a perfect coincidence of views and a respectful affection which may be recommended as a model. It pleased God to spare to him this faithful ministry of revering love to the very last and, when the earthly tie was broken, to make the separation short."

The year 1789 was remarkable in the history of the Southern churches, for that widespread religious movement known as the Great Awakening. Few were more familiar with or prominent in this enterprise than Archibald Alexander. The following extracts from the *Life of Alexander* will be helpful to an understanding of the deep spirituality and wide influence of this honored son of old Lexington. As will be seen, his serious attitude toward life began early and lasted to the end of his days:

"Alexander was a young man when news reached the quiet village of Lexington, that a great revival was in progress 'on the other side of the Ridge.' Immediately the Reverend William Graham decided to visit the scene and proposed that young Alexander accompany him. Such journeys were, of course, by horseback, and amid beautiful mountain scenery, through hospitable country, were exciting. On this journey, Mr. Graham was unusually open and communicative on philosophical matters, especially upon the subject of Justification by Faith and Regeneration.

"The month was August and they were exposed to the rays of the Virginia sun, without the shelter of an umbrella since such a convenience had not yet come into use. Arriving at their destination, they were entertained at the home of Samuel Morris, a name sacred in the annals of American Presbyterianism. As they approached through the fields, they saw the old gentleman walking homeward, as if, like Isaac, he had been meditating. Samuel Morris was about eighty years of age, but with the appearance of robust youth. He gave Mr. Graham a detailed account of Presbyterianism in Hanover.

"It was on this excursion that Mr. Graham took young Alexander to call on the celebrated Patrick Henry.

"There had never been a revival in the Valley, as few of the Scottish Presbyterians, there resident, had any faith in such 'sudden awakenings.' They believed that these religious commotions would pass away like the morning cloud.

"Mr. Graham, a clear and cogent reasoner, with no superior among his contemporaries, and whose preëminence was recognized by all, was invited to preach at this great meeting 'beyond the Ridge.' En route to the scene of the revival, they met a large crowd of young people, on horseback, moving slowly and singing hymns. They had traveled more than sixty miles to attend the Sacrament, and were full of zeal and affection. As soon as they espied Mr. Graham, they stopped and gave him a hearty greeting.

"Arriving at Liberty, they met a crowd of young people, who had made the trip by horseback, from Rockbridge, to attend the Sacrament. It was a time of great emotion and none were more stirred than these young Rockbridge people.

"Finally, after many days of preaching, searchings of heart and communion, they all started for Lexington, singing hymns all along the way. Near the top of the Ridge, they halted at a spring to partake of a viaticum, which some of the company had been provident enough to take along. The minister exhorted the young people to persevere in the Cause of Christ after they arrived at Lexington and this they did. There was something of youthful simplicity in the confidence with which the company expected an immediate manifestation of awakening grace on their arrival in Lexington.

"Mr. Graham addressed a large assemblage and told of all he had seen and heard in Prince Edward and Bedford. On another occasion he addressed a crowd in a large hall, which had been used as a dance hall, and many went weeping from the house. A young man was called on to pray; this struck everyone as strange; for many years no young people in Lexington has been known to be serious or to confess to religion.

"Alexander, being dissatisfied with his state of mind and sensible of the corruption of his heart, resolved to enter upon a new course. He resolved to give up all reading except the Bible and to devote himself solely to prayer, fasting and the Scriptures, until he should arrive at greater hope. His life was spent in religious company, but the conversation sometimes degenerated into levity, which was succeeded by compunction. Concerning his serious searchings of heart, he said: 'I was distressed and discouraged and convinced that I had placed too much dependence on mere means and on my own efforts. I therefore determined to give myself incessantly to prayer until I found mercy, or perished in the pursuit. This resolution was formed on a Sunday evening and, the next morning, I took my Bible and walked several miles to the dense woods of Brushy Hills, which was wholly uncultivated. Finding a place that pleased me, at the foot of a projecting rock, in a dark valley, I began with earnestness, the course I had prescribed for myself. I prayed and read the Bible, prayed and read, prayed and read until my strength was exhausted, for I had taken no nourishment that day; the more I strove, the harder my heart became, and the more barren my mind. Finally, however, there came to my mind such a view of my crucified Saviour, as is without a parallel in my experience. The whole plan of grace appeared as clear as day and I felt truly a joy, which was unspeakable and full of glory.'"

Shortly after this, he made a profession of his faith and, like most of those in the Valley who professed their faith, maintained his constancy.

Alexander struggled for an education. In his day, books were rare and money scarce. Single volumes passed from house to house, as great treasures. His ambition was to go to Princeton, to study under the eminent Witherspoon. His plans were made and the day set for his departure. He appealed to Reverend Graham for a letter to President Witherspoon, but, to his surprise, found that Graham disapproved and advised that he take his degree in Lexington.

About this time, he was seized with a fever. The physician who was called in came to the bedside drunk. The patient lay in a delirium, speechless, and the family was called in to see him die, but it was God's purpose to spare him for usefulness. For weeks, he was lifted about as an infant and his constitution received a shock from which he never recovered. In the spring of 1790, he went to the Sweet Springs, where he was much benefitted.

The Sweet Springs was already a place of frequent resort. He noted this about the place: "A company of gamblers never intermitted their games day or night, Sunday or working day, during the whole time that I was there. They would sometimes come out to the fountain, adding a horrid symphony of oaths and imprecations to these gatherings. They strove to outdo one another in the rapidity and novelty of their profane expressions. Besides other invalids, there were broken-down debauchees, who were endeavoring to prop up a shattered and polluted constitution."

His health was improving and he would have stayed several weeks longer, but finding a man from Augusta returning with a "led horse," he prevailed upon him to let him accompany him to Rockbridge. "We sat out rather late and soon lost our way, by taking a path which took us off the main road. We found ourselves on the banks of the Jackson River. For a time our position was both perilous and painful, as the ravines were very deep. After wandering for some time, we spied a light and, with difficulty, reached the cabin in the lowgrounds. We found two lone women, with several children, who were sleeping in the room, of course, the only room in the cabin; there was a reluctance to comply with our request for lodging, the reason of which transpired in due time. They gave us some supper, which was very good. Presently the man of the house arrived in a state of intoxication. He was noisy and outrageous and ordered us to leave; we expostulated and finally he agreed that we might stay and he soon fell asleep. His wife spread a bed for us on the floor. We rose early on a bright Sabbath morning. The man of the house rose early also, he was much mortified at the inhospitality of the previous night and tried in every way to make amends."

With improved health and unbounded ambition, from now on Alexander forges ahead. His thoughts were absorbed in theological questions for, in Lexington, there were many young men of marked education, with whom he carried on daily discussions. Taking nothing for granted without proof, they debated all the points in controversy between Calvinists and Arminians. No effort was too great on the part of the theologians of old to try to "set right" anyone whom they considered a teacher of false doctrines. In 1760, a minister in the Valley of Virginia heard of a minister in New England, who had some novel opinions in theology, so he took horse and traveled there to converse with him and to convince him of his error. After discussing the disputed question for many days, he returned to the Valley, himself converted to the new and novel opinions.

These incidents are mentioned to show the effect of early religious experiences upon the life and work of Alexander. His influence upon his generation was enormous, as it has been upon succeeding generations, through voluminous writings which he left, and which remain unsurpassed in theological soundness and depth.

Doubtless the most distinguished couple ever to have lived in Lexington was Colonel J. T. L. Preston and his talented wife, Margaret, daughter of Dr. George Junkin, president of Washington College. Colonel Preston was born at Blandome, his father's home in Lexington. He became a prominent lawyer and a great orator, and for more than forty years was known as the "town speaker" and Lexington's Demosthenes. He was active in establishing the Virginia Military Institute, in which he taught for many years.

Mrs. Preston, no less distinguished than her famous husband, was the Poet Laureate of the South. Her songs and lyrics cheered the Southern people in their darkest hours. "Beechenbrook, a Rhyme of the War," a vivid picture of the time, is her best known poem.

Among her intimate and congenial friends were Whittier, Ingelow, Longfellow, John Burroughs, and Elizabeth Barrett. To the latter, this friendship meant much, for it cheered the shut-in days, before the coming of Robert Browning with love, romance, and sunny Italy.

Great sorrows came to Mrs. Preston in early life—the loss of her mother, her sister, Eleanor, wife of Major Thomas J. Jackson; and others of her home circle—which had a marked influence on her writings. Her life, in Lexington, however, must have been a happy one. She was the center of the social and intellectual life of the community and was adored by her husband and family. Typical of the adoration of her husband for her is this, from one of his letters written from the field of battle:

"I know what I am best suited for; it is to make your happiness in securing mine. I claim not to be equal to many men in military talents. I find and acknowledge many superiors in business, in oratory, in scholarship and in many other things, but that man who knows better than I do how to appreciate and return the love of a noble woman, I never expect to see."

During Mrs. Preston's last days in Lexington, she was an invalid, and much brightness came to her through the daily calls of her hosts of friends and admirers. The Hills, Pendletons, Lees, Dabneys, McDowells, Letchers, Moores, Barclays, Nelsons, Bacons, Stuarts, Jordans, Whites, and many others were constant in their attentions.

Both Colonel and Mrs. Preston are buried in the Presbyterian cemetery, and shading this sacred spot stands one, if not the only one left, of the great forest oaks that a century or so ago grew in profusion there. This stately tree has been included in *Historic Trees of Virginia* and titled the Margaret J. Preston Oak.

Shortly after Mrs. Preston's death, Professor James A. Harrison, of the University of Virginia, wrote an appreciation of her, from which the following extracts are taken:

"The old Valley of Virginia is a delightful spot to be born in and to live in. It is one of the picture places of the old Commonwealth and whoever has had the good fortune to have followed with childish or with aging eyes its mountain trails and its shimmering waters is already half a poet, of infinite mood and memory, if not of actual metre and stanza.

"As the great vale sweeps down to Harper's Ferry from the green heights of the Alleghenies, full of their memories of the Knights of the Golden Horseshoe and the Revolutionary times, it leaves behind many a cliff and gorge and lateral fissure in its sides, wherein nestle unique little towns and hamlets that hover about a spire, or a manse, or cling lichenlike to the mountain slopes. Here a rushing mill-wheel crushes a mountain torrent into millions of sparkling jewels, mingling the beautiful with the prosaic utilitarian grinding of wheat. Yonder an old-fashioned tavern and smithy remind the traveler of the times when Lord Fairfax and surveyor Washington used to stage it in 'chariots,' with easy relay distances of ten to twelve miles, up and down the Valley, in the time of the Indian wars; and away on the mountain side one descries some plantation house of lordly name and lineage.

"Everywhere through this charmed region of great elevations and verdure-clad peaks and mountain ranges one meets with towns of good old English names: Winchester, Woodstock, Staunton; some of them strung together on the silver cord of the Shenandoah and all of them filled with Old Virginia homes and hospitalities that have become proverbial for good cheer and heartiest welcome.

'In the greenest of these valleys
By good angels tenanted,'

lies the little town of Lexington. For generations the sturdy Scotch-Irish population, full of Macs and clan names found in Scottish history, have lived and labored in this picturesque region. Here they found the beautiful upland reminiscent of green Erin and bonnie Scotland. Everywhere they established their farms and their homes, built kirk and manse, erected mill and hostelry, bringing along the parson and the schoolmaster, bell and book, till soon the whole Valley rang with the hum of hammer and anvil, church bell and hymn, spelling book and Thursday meetin'. As early as 1784, Lexington began to flutter educational wings. One of the learned Grahams established an academy near by and later there came into being the Virginia Military Institute. These two institutions would mark any place with distinction. Many men of prominence were added to its population and a gracious hospitality pervaded the place. The old Franklin Debating Society and the fine library drew men together to read, discuss current questions, and hear lectures from eminent specialists; and the College Debating Societies had their discussions, their magazines and their celebrations through the year to garnish and embroider the dull edges of collegiate life.

"Then the commencements! prolonged between the Institute Hill and the College Campus, sometimes for a clear six weeks. Balls, field sports, boat races, addresses, camp scenes, dress parades, parties, receptions, entertainments of all sorts, an unceasing inflow of strangers and outflow of diplomaed and graduated, or 'flunked and flustered' students and cadets. The little town has gone through this annual whirl since 1784.

"Such were the surroundings in which Margaret Junkin Preston passed the happiest years of her life, from 1848 to 1892. More delightful conditions for a sensitive literary nature like hers could not have been found, a nature delighting in fine landscape scenes, impressionable to a degree to all the varying moods and whimsies of a mountain environment and thrilling with Eolian music at the touch of beauty."

Their daughter, Elizabeth Preston Allen, was also a gifted writer, having edited for many years the *Children's Friend*, a widely used Sunday School paper of the Presbyterian Church. She also contributed generously to secular and religious papers. She was the wife of Colonel William Allen, a professor in the college and author of *Jackson's Valley Campaigns* and of *The Army of Northern Virginia*, two authentic and valuable books on Southern history.

George Junkin, born 1790 and educated at Jefferson College, devoted a lifetime to educational and religious endeavor. He organized the first Sunday Schools and temperance societies in central Pennsylvania and founded Lafayette College at Easton, and presided over Miami University in Ohio prior to coming to Lexington, in 1848, as president of Washington College. Here he stayed until Virginia seceded. Being a staunch Unionist, he returned to Pennsylvania. At the outbreak of the war, the Washington College students raised a Confederate flag on the main building of the college and Dr. Junkin took it down and burned it, whereupon the students, backed by the faculty, put up another one and set a watch to keep it there. This, together with Virginia's seceding, was too much for him and he left Lexington immediately. It is said that when he crossed the Mason and Dixon line, he got out of his carriage and washed the rebel-dust from his horses' feet! His attitude was not shared by his entire family, as several of them remained on the Southern side. It is hard for us of a later day to appreciate the hard and bitter separations that existed between families and communities of that time. There was no middle ground. Men had to decide and act. Dr. Junkin's life in Lexington was, however, a happy one, and his influence was great as was that of his family.

A description of their coming to Lexington and something of their life in the community is taken from *Life and Letters of Margaret J. Preston* (a daughter of Dr. Junkin):

"About the middle of the nineteenth century, Dr. Junkin and family, after a roundabout journey by steamboat from Baltimore to Fredericksburg and by rail to Gordonsville and thence by stagecoach, reached the village of Lexington, where they were to play a large part in the life of the community.

"My first impression of Lexington was of arriving at midnight in a December snowstorm, after a twelve-hour ride from Staunton in an old-fashioned stagecoach. The ups and downs made as much impression on our bodies as on our minds. We were received with the greatest kindness by the Lexington people and soon made many friends. Their kindness in our sorrow, so soon to follow, I shall never forget. I do not know a people anywhere so kind and sympathetic. We soon felt at home and got into the Lexington way of living and were very happy. For those of us who made it our home, it was the scene of our greatest happiness and our greatest sorrows, and as nothing so tests the real friendship and worth of friends as emergencies, we proved that of the Lexington people.

"We all took delightful rambles, rather to the surprise of the Lexington people, who were not so energetic as we were. Our walks were often to the cliffs or to Cave Spring and we always stopped by the ruins of old Liberty Hall for a rest and to admire the scenery."

The people with whom the Junkins cast their lot were descendants of that bold stream of immigrants which rolled down the Valley of Virginia from Pennsylvania and on into North Carolina, South Carolina, and Georgia; those pioneers who had been fitted by their God-fearing love of liberty and enduring of hardships and overcoming of difficulties to found a race and establish a government. Their descendants were and still are a quiet, undemonstrative people; more careful of truth than of pretty politeness of speech; dignified rather than graceful; earnestly religious, but not very tolerant of any other than the simple form of Presbyterian worship and church government; intensely proud of their Scotch-Irish ancestors; good lovers, good haters; unfaltering in courage, immovable in their convictions; rather dull as pleasure seekers, but with active and alert minds, addressing themselves to the upholding of their country and the public welfare, and to the education of their children.

Religion, education and political honesty! What triumvirate could have been more exactly suited to George Junkin—preacher, teacher, and reformer?

The Junkins had moved about considerably before coming to Lexington, but here they found the most peaceful and congenial home they had ever known. Dr. Junkin did not find as many students at the college as he had expected, but he found the morale of the students high and the discipline good and genuine harmony between the faculty and the trustees. The Junkins were received in Lexington with something more akin to enthusiasm than these sonsie Scotch-Irish often exhibited, and the eldest daughter was especially admired and sought after. True to the old Southern custom, which was a mingling of familiarity and respect, this eldest daughter was soon known as "Miss Maggie." She was not pretty, but she was charming and attractive and possessed a brilliant mind, making her a rare conversationalist, which compensated for any lack of beauty of face. Miss Rebecca Glasgow, then a young lady of Lexington society, who became one of Miss Maggie's best friends, recalled how much admiration was expressed by the young gentlemen of the town for this young stranger.

A letter from Miss Maggie, dated September 9, 1852, to a friend in the North, shows how happy she was in her quiet Lexington home:

"You have been pitying me this summer, haven't you? Tied down, as you know I have been, in my quiet country home, while you have had the pleasure of Newport, Sharon and Saratoga and many other places of fashionable resort. Well, if such has been the case, I have only to say that your commiseration is very superfluous, for I question if your migratory life has had as many of the elements of happiness centering in it as has my stationary one.

"Why did you not accept our invitation to come down and breathe the sweet, pure air of our Virginia mountains, instead of whirling off to those everlasting springs where life seems, to my rustic taste, the most artificial thing in the world? You should have risen while the birds were at their first overture, for you cannot imagine what a peal of vocalization ushers in our day! Such as all the Parodis and Linds and Albonis in the world could not equal. Uncle Felix should have had our horses saddled for us at half past five o'clock and what a gallop we should have had over the misty hills and down into the little green shaded glens, under overhanging branches, all sparkling with silvery dew. And what views! 'Beautiful, exceeding!' They should have appealed to your admiring gaze with such power as to haunt you like a passion, seen under the brightness and breezy freshness of 'one of those Heavenly days that cannot die.'

"And then, as the ascending sun rose higher over the mountains and the full orchestra of bird-music began to settle into a subdued murmur that seemed fading away into the forest, and the canter of several miles through the bracing atmosphere whetted our appetites, we should turn our horses' heads and scamper away homeward. Then you should have changed your riding gear for the simplest morning dress, and with glowing cheeks and brightened eyes and a sense of invigoration that nothing short of such a gallop can impart, you should have sat down to an old-fashioned Virginia breakfast.

"As to the occupation for the forenoon, here is the Knickerbocker, Harper's and the Eclectic and a package of new books. After dinner you might have a nice siesta, with grasshoppers and katydids to sing your lullaby. The little rockaway should have been at the door at six, if you chose a drive, or we might walk to the cliffs to watch the sun go down behind the mountains, and saunter home just in time to have our coffee handed us in free and easy Virginia style, in the library.

"Mingled pleasantly with our rambles and rides, we have an occasional taste of society that is extremely agreeable. Dining the other day at the home of a friend, I found that not less than four of the party had been abroad and so we had racy descriptions of men and things in other lands and spicy anecdotes of celebrities whom we all knew 'upon paper.' While the servants were carrying around *les entremets,* a gentleman beside me described the kind of breakfast he used to take with the Count de Survilliers, when he resided in the country, and I learned what I did not know before, that *la salade* was as indispensable at a French *déjeuner* as coffee."

Quoting from another place in Mrs. Preston's Diary, we learn something of the charm of life as she found it in Lexington during the shut-in days of winter:

"As the season of your city parties and gaieties draws near, we, who live in the shadows of the Virginia mountains, are compelled to find our enjoyment at our firesides. Not that sociality, which is the atmosphere in which Southern people live, move and have their being, is by any means done away with by the approach of winter; that would indeed be out of the question, for visiting with them amounts to something like a passion.

"If we wished for some designation that would embrace a prevailing characteristic, such as we use when we speak of the 'Fox-hunting English,' the 'Smoking Germans,' or the 'Opium Eating Chinese,' no better could be found than the 'Visiting Virginians.' Dining people and being dined is one of the weightiest businesses of their lives. But a great barrier exists to such enjoyment in the winter, which is answer to the caricature, which you may remember Dickens gives in his American Notes, of a ride from Washington to Alexandria. We do not set any claims to public spirit in the matter of internal improvement and are shamefully content to let all the glory that appertains to them belong to the go-ahead, active Yankee. We have, however, such long delightful autumns that winter does not set in before Christmas, but after that—shades of Macadam! What mud we have!"

Dr. Junkin never returned to Lexington after the war. He died May 20, 1868, in Philadelphia, where he was buried. About fifty years later his descendants removed his remains to Lexington, to the family plot in the Presbyterian cemetery, where he sleeps near those who in life were so near and dear to him.

Sam Houston, the rugged pioneer and liberator of Texas, was born March 2, 1793, eight miles from Lexington, and was considered by many, the greatest character to come out of Rockbridge County. His name and fame is inseparably linked with Texas history. After the death of his father and while still a small boy, he went to Tennessee, where he spent many years.

Upon leaving Lexington, an uncle said: "I have no hope for Sam. He is so wild." Sam replied: "Uncle, some day I will came back through here on my way to Congress." And so he did.

At the age of twenty-three he took up the study of law and was elected to Congress for two terms. He was a born leader of men and rose rapidly to prominence and public favor, and in 1827 was elected governor of Tennessee. It is said that on the night of his wedding, he found his bride weeping bitterly. She told him that she did not love him, but loved another, and that her parents had forced her to marry him, because he was the governor of the State. He left immediately for distant parts beyond the Mississippi, where he lived with and for the Indians, constantly fighting for a square deal for them.

At the age of forty, he began his conspicuous career in Texas' history. Being put in charge of the Texan forces against Mexico, on April 21, 1836, he defeated Santa Anna and won the great battle of San Jacinto, thus establishing the independence of the Republic of Texas, of which he was the first and only President. When Texas joined the Union, he became its senator and later its governor. He was removed from office in 1861 because he would not swear allegiance to the Southern Confederacy.

He lived simply and quietly at his home in Huntsville, Texas, until his death in 1863.

Houston was of imposing appearance, over six feet tall. It is said that on public occasions he wore rings on every finger, including the thumbs. He cared not at all for money. His father served as a rifleman under General Morgan in the Revolution.

Colonel John Jordan came to Lexington in 1802, from Halifax County. His mansion, known as Jordan's Point (now Stono), he built in 1818. This remains one of the handsomest homes of Lexington and commands a wide sweep of magnificent scenery. Colonel Jordan's interests were varied, including iron smelting and grist mills, blacksmith shops, weaving woolen and cotton cloth, contractor and builder. As contractor he built nearly everything of importance that was built in the town for more than fifty years, including the Washington building at the College and the Ann Smith Academy. He constructed the Bateau Canal at Balcony Falls and built many of the best roads of that day. One monument to his memory is the Jordan Trail over the Blue Ridge.

Iron-making was bred in the bone, his father having made cannon balls for the American Army during the Revolution. Colonel Jordan introduced colonial architecture into Lexington and to him is due most of the credit for the handsome old homes which constitute much of the atmosphere of the old town. Some of the earliest houses were built of stone, but few have survived. The Castle, on Randolph Street, is the oldest of this type.

Colonel Jordan was of commanding appearance and very handsome. He was kind, honorable and charitable. His household was of the Baptist faith and his large family composed about half of that congregation in the local church.

He was a very close friend of General Francis H. Smith and they spent many hours together on the balcony at Jordan's Point.

Mrs. Jordan was a beautiful blonde, six feet tall. She maintained quite an establishment, superintending all the weaving, spinning, dyeing, sewing, laundry, dairy, orchards and gardens. In addition to this, she reared a family of twelve sons and two daughters, all growing to maturity and all very handsome. The family played a large part in the early development of this entire section and wielded much influence.

Colonel and Mrs. Jordan are buried in the Presbyterian cemetery.

Goodness and greatness in a man is often hereditary and certainly this might be true in the case of William McCutcheon Morrison. Born near Lexington, in 1867, one of eight children, of a long line of godly ancestors, he was at birth dedicated by his parents to the ministry. They thought that no greater honor could come to them and to him than a dedication to this highest of all callings—greater than any earthly potentate, prince or ambassador.

In after years it was claimed that one of the reasons for his marked success in Africa was due to the fact that he had been reared in Lexington, where the understanding of and feeling for the colored people was so good. Young Morrison showed no inclination toward the ministry, however, until after his college career, the practice of law being his one aim and ambition. And what a magnificent barrister he would have been! His marvelous physique, his superb and forceful voice and his logical reasoning powers were evidenced especially in his trial at Brussels, when tried by the Belgian Government for his denunciation of the atrocities against the natives in the Belgian Congo, of which accusation he was cleared. This trial provoked Mark Twain to write his widely read "King Leopard's Soliloquy."

There is a destiny, however, that shapes our ends and a study of this life shows that his destiny was marked. After graduation from Washington and Lee, with high honors, among them the orator's medal, he taught in Arkansas. It was there that the call to the ministry came to him and, like Paul, he could not turn a deaf ear, and for the first time in his life considered it seriously. We soon find him at the Presbyterian Seminary in Louisville and while there the definite call to Africa came to him. He left his home in Lexington on November 5, 1896, for the Belgian Congo, where he became one of the great missionaries of modern times.

The best insight into the life and character of this great man and of his absolute consecration is found in his diary. Note the petitions and how they were fulfilled in his daily life:

"This day, I leave home and mother, brothers and sisters and many hallowed memories of home and native land and go far hence in obedience to the command of my Master, 'go ye into all the world and preach the Gospel to every creature,' This desire came to me through the peculiar dispensation of God's providence about eighteen months ago. I have every reason to believe that it was in direct answer to the prayers of some children in Louisville. As I enter upon this great work my prayer is: 'O, God, I beseech Thee to give me an abundant outpouring of Thy Holy Spirit, making my own life an open gospel, an epistle known and read of all men. I pray for Thy richest blessings to rest upon those to whom I shall preach the unsearchable riches of Christ. Open their darkened understanding. May Thy truth have free course and may many be brought into the fold of Christ, through the Gospel that I may be instrumental in preaching. O, God, pour out Thy Spirit upon darkest Africa and may the long night be broken and may the brightness of the sun of Righteousness illuminate that benighted land. Give me O God, strength of body, vigor of mind and above all, purity of heart. Help me to bear the burdens and keep me ever humble and enable me to love all men. Give unto me wisdom and discretion. Thou hast promised that to those who ask wisdom Thou wilt give liberally. Verify this promise unto me. Keep me during the perils of the voyage, deliver me from dangers seen and unseen, and may I arrive at my destination, sound in body and in every way fitted for the preaching of the Gospel. O, Lord, help me to overcome the sins of my life, the besetting sins, may I be able to mortify the deeds of the flesh and to grow more and more in all the Christian graces. O, for a purer, holier, nobler, loftier, more Christ-like life! Bless in an especial manner, my precious mother, comfort her heart and give her the consolation of the Gospel and may she experience a rich outpouring of Thy Spirit in her life. I pray for the church universal; open Thy truth to all; help me to search the Scriptures with an understanding heart. I ask these things, not for my own, but solely for Christ's sake, whose atoning blood has washed away my stain and renders possible my approach unto the Throne of Grace. Amen.' "

Upon his arrival in Africa he found less than fifty converts, but he lived to see more than 17,000. He traveled widely, especially throughout the continent of Africa. He was the first to reduce the Baluba language to written form and to write a grammar and a dictionary of that language—a monumental task!

Most of his work in the dark continent was done single-handed. After spending several years there, he came to America on furlough and before returning he married Miss Bertha Stebbins, of Natchez, Mississippi, who returned with him, but who lived a very short time after arriving in the Congo. She was the first white woman in some parts of that country and the native women were very much attracted to her; especially were they interested in her long straight hair. She was constantly asked to display it and to tell what it was, and was surrounded from morning till night by the curious. She spent her time ministering to the ills of the body and the heart of these poor natives. The beauty and sincerity of her Christian character made a deep and lasting impression upon the people and it is said that "the perfume of her life yet lingers along the path she trod," and the natives still speak in endearing terms of "Mama Mutoto." The manner in which the natives received the Gospel was an inspiration to her; their faith was so simple, so childlike, so joyous.

On March 14, 1918, Dr. Morrison's wonderful life and service came to an end, but his influence upon that land he loved so well and upon the whole missionary enterprise, lives on. Like Livingstone he measured the natives by the best that was in them and not by the worst.

> Life's duty done, as sinks the clay
> Light from its load the spirit flies;
> While Heaven and earth combine to say,
> How blest the righteous when he dies.

"The best part of a good man's life, is his little, nameless, unremembered acts of kindness and of love." This surely applied to Morrison, whose life was filled with acts of kindness and of love.

> Servant of God, well done!
> Rest from Thy loved employ;
> The battle fought, the vict'ry won,
> Enter Thy Master's joy.
>
> The voice at midnight came;
> He started up to hear:
> A mortal arrow pierced his frame;
> He fell, but felt no fear.
>
> The pains of death are past;
> Labor and sorrow cease;
> And life's long warfare closed at last,
> His soul is found in peace.
>
> Soldier of Christ! Well done!
> Praise be thy new employ;
> And while eternal ages run,
> Rest in thy Saviour's joy.

Lexington's contributions to the mission field, both home and foreign, have been large. The Prices, Pattersons, Myers', the Womeldorfs, Junkins, Bradleys, Vinsons, Grahams, Bells, Shields, Morrisons, and many others who have been and are lights in dark places, represent old Lexington and the Gospel in the far corners of the world.

Dr. William Henry Ruffner, born in Lexington in 1824 and graduated from Washington College in 1842, became one of the foremost citizens of Virginia and one of the greatest educators of his day. He was trained for the Presbyterian ministry, but had only one short pastorate, the old Pine Street Presbyterian Church in Philadelphia. He preferred educational work and scientific study and research and to this he devoted his long and influential life.

He was titled the "Father of Virginia's Free School System" and was the State's first superintendent of public instruction. He founded the Virginia Polytechnic Institute and the State Teachers College at Farmville. Of the latter he served as president for three years. In 1887, after an exceedingly busy life, he retired to his estate, Tri-brook, near Lexington, devoting his last years to research and writing. He passed away in 1908 and was buried in the Presbyterian cemetery in Lexington.

It is claimed that the first game of lawn tennis ever played in the South was played at Tri-brook, in the days of the Ruffners. Relatives from Philadelphia introduced the game there, shortly after it had been introduced in the North from England. The new game created quite a sensation in Lexington.

Tri-brook is now the home of the Tri-brook Golf and Country Club. Peaceful meadows, rolling hills and glorious mountain scenery in all directions—a more beautiful and inspiring setting for a golf course could not be found. The country about is reminiscent of Bonnie Scotland.

He was a son of Dr. Henry Ruffner (president of Washington College), who was also a pioneer of Presbyterianism in and about Charleston, West Virginia, a notoriously irreligious place of that day. Distinguished alike as author, preacher and instructor, he added graces of mind and charm of manner to his splendid personal appearance, which endeared him to all. He was the peer of the most eminent ministers of his day and enjoyed a national reputation.

Few men, if any, have been more loved and honored in Lexington and Rockbridge County and throughout Virginia, than John Randolph Tucker and his son, Henry St. George Tucker. The very name is a synonym for the finest in character and public service.

John Randolph Tucker, born in Winchester in 1823 and educated at the University of Virginia, came to Lexington in 1870 as professor of law in Washington College. Though a resident only a few months during the régime of General Lee, they, nevertheless, became warm friends, and the charm and atmosphere which made Lexington such a congenial home for the great general was enhanced by the presence of the Tuckers.

Mr. Tucker was one of the ablest men ever to have lived in Lexington and enjoyed unusual popularity, as evidenced by the fact that he was elected six consecutive terms to the Congress of the United States. He was an orator of convincing power and was considered one of the most forceful personalities in the South. In his later years, he was known as a "gentle-man of the old school." Very handsome, and exceedingly versatile, he would have graced any vocation. It was said of him that when he spoke in church in his persuasive, magnetic way, faultlessly groomed in his Sunday morning attire, that he should have been a preacher. Again, when he chose to be humorous and entertaining (being a master story-teller), it was said that he should have been an actor. Yet, in the school, as the superb teacher and expounder of the law that he was, everyone agreed that he was "right where he belonged."

He possessed an almost inspired knowledge of the Bible and taught a great Bible class in the Presbyterian Church. Tucker Hall, the home of the Washington and Lee School of Law, was built by friends and admirers to his memory. This building was totally destroyed by fire in December, 1934.

He spent the evening of life at Blandome, his Lexington home. He is buried in Winchester.

Henry St. George Tucker, born in 1853 in Lexington, and educated at Washington and Lee University, was a distinguished son of a distinguished father, and like his father, honored Lexington with his residence. He gave many years to the teaching of law at Washington and Lee, and for a while was acting president of the college. It is interesting to note that he was a student at the college when Valentine's statue of General Lee was brought to Lexington from Richmond. An old newspaper reports that "when we reached the final leg of the trip to Lexington, we were met by the Wash-ington and Lee boat-crew, which acted as escort. The captain of the crew was Henry St. George Tucker."

Like his father he served the old Tenth District in Congress for many years. He was a recognized authority on international law and on woman suffrage by constitutional amendment, and wrote widely-read books on these subjects.

His stately home, Col Alto, was the mecca for thousands of his friends from every station in life. He loved his fellowmen and this love was heartily reciprocated. No man of his generation had a stronger hold upon the affection and admiration of the people of Virginia. His cordiality and hospitality were proverbial and will ever remain in the grateful memory of his friends. He is buried in the Presbyterian cemetery.

Born in 1812 and educated at West Point Military Academy, General Francis H. Smith was known as the father and founder of the Virginia Military Institute where, for fifty years, he was superintendent. He was affectionately known to the cadets as "Old Specks." A unique custom of his was that, with each diploma given a graduate, he also gave a Bible. His contribution to Lexington and to the institute, which he helped create

Natural Bridge
(Note man standing in creek bed at right)

Lexington Presbyterian Church

Lee-Jackson House, Washington and Lee University campus

Virginia Military Institute cadets on parade (Note damaged building)

General Lee on Traveller, late 1860's

The Lee Chapel, Washington and Lee University campus

and maintain, has been great. He died at Fag-end, his Lexington home, in 1890 and is buried in the Presbyterian cemetery. Here, also, sleep his two successors, General Scott Shipp, the gallant commander of the Virginia Military Institute cadets at New Market and General Edward West Nichols, who gave fifty years service to the institute.

Both the "Old Specks" and the Bible custom have been memorialized in the bronze statue to General Smith on the parade ground, which represents him with "specks" on and with a Bible in one hand and a diploma in the other.

Born in Lexington in 1813 and educated at Washington College, John Letcher was one of the really great men of Virginia. In 1851, he was elected to the House of Representatives where he rendered a fine service and won the sobriquet of "Honest John." He was also known as the "Watchdog of the Treasury."

In 1859 he was elected governor of Virginia and has ever been known as Virginia's War Governor and a great statesman. After the war he returned to his home in Lexington, where he practiced law, and for a while edited the local newspaper, the *Valley Star,* thus giving to the public the benefit of his wide knowledge of state and national affairs.

He was a man of the finest spirit who, when the war was over, was ready and willing to forgive and forget and to be about the task of rebuilding. Surely he had much to forgive and to forget.

Typical of the bigness of the man, is this utterance of his to the Lexington people after the war: "The War has ended, we are again a united people. Let the passions, the prejudices, and the revengeful feelings which have existed between the sections and which were intensified by the war, be consigned in solemn silence to a common grave, there to sleep forever. The past is gone and should be forgotten, the present is upon us."

A handsome shaft marks his resting place in the Presbyterian cemetery.

Born in 1809, near Lexington, Cyrus Hall McCormick inherited an ingenious trend from his father. When a small boy, Cyrus invented a hillside plow, "the very best that had been made," wrote a neighbor. Of all the inventive geniuses that have gone from this community, the name of McCormick is preëminent. His name and fame are known around the world. In Europe, Asia, Australia, South America, in the great wheatfields of North America, wherever great crops are to be gathered, there will be found this Rockbridge invention, bearing the name McCormick.

The first machine was tried on the farm of John Ruff, and because the field was on a hillside the new invention did not work well and the indignant Mr. Ruff ordered that it be taken off his premises at once, as it was ruining his crop. This was in 1831 and great crowds had gathered to see (many to sneer and criticize) the new invention to help the farmers. According to Honorable J. W. Houghawout, long mayor of Lexington,

Colonel William Taylor, with more vision and sympathy than Mr. Ruff, invited Mr. McCormick to try it on his farm, which he did; it worked, and great cheers were heard from the crowds. The first time that a local paper considered the invention worthy of notice was September 14, 1833, when the *Union* noted the fact that an ingenious and respectable county man had invented a machine that would really cut grain.

McCormick's father, who had tried to perfect a reaper said, "I am proud that my son could do what I failed to do."

In the *Staunton Spectator,* July 18, 1839, the inventor announced that in a few days he would demonstrate his machine on the farm of Joseph Smith (now known as Folly). In connection with this announcement he explained that in consequence of other engagements and the failure of crops, he had done nothing with the reaper for some years. Now, however, he had made improvements in it, and during the present harvest he had cut seventy-five acres of wheat and rye and considered its performance exceptional. He claimed that the machine was not complicated and would not easily get out of order, and that it would cost fifty dollars.

In 1841, two machines were sold, and in 1844 orders were received for seven machines and were designated "Virginia Reapers." Some of these were to go West. They had to be taken by wagons over the mountains to Scottsville, by canal to Richmond, down the James to Norfolk, by water to New Orleans, and up the Mississippi to various points. The first ones to go to the far west had to go by water around Cape Horn. The inventor made a trip west and found that while in Virginia, the reaper was a luxury, in the great fields of the west, it was a necessity and concluded, after much investigation, that the village of Chicago would be a strategic point for him, so in 1848, he settled there and the reaper and the great city of Chicago have grown up together.

Referring to the sensation caused at the London exhibition in 1854, Seward said: "The reaper of 1834, as improved in 1854, achieved for the inventor a triumph which all felt was not more personal than national. It was so regarded. No general or consul, drawn through the streets of Rome, by order of the Senate, ever conferred upon mankind more than he who thus vindicated the genius of our country."

Later, McCormick received the Cross of the Legion of Honor at the hand of the Emperor Louis Napoleon, and a similar decoration from the Emperor of Austria. He was elected a member of the French Academy of Science as having done more for the cause of agriculture than any other living man.

In 1859 it was claimed that he had contributed an annual income to America of fifty millions of dollars and enabled the food supply to keep pace with the population.

He was a generous benefactor of Washington and Lee and a trustee of the institution and his memory is cherished and perpetuated by a bronze statue on the campus.

James E. A. Gibbs, born near Lexington in 1829, easily rates among the great inventors of America, having invented the chain stitch sewing machine. As a mere boy he found himself with only the clothes on his back and his mother's blessing with which to start life. He had, however, inherited an inventive genius from his father. Success and failure followed each other for many years, but after determined perseverance, success seemed assured. In 1857, he visited Philadelphia where he met James Wilcox, in whom he found a business associate and a lifelong friend. The two entered into an agreement and the Wilcox-Gibbs chain stitch sewing machine was perfected and put on the market in 1859. When Sumter was fired upon, Gibbs immediately joined the Confederacy and toured the country in the cause of secession. His machines were used to make uniforms for the Southern army and his shops were kept busy repairing guns and pistols. After the war he found himself in financial difficulties and he made his way north to his partner, Wilcox. There, to his delight, he found ten thousand dollars to his credit which placed him, for the first time in his life, on "easy street."

His school days had been few, but he had an inborn love for intellectual improvement, and later in life he built up a very fine and complete library, which he used well. He traveled extensively throughout the United States and around the world. Though a man of decided views, he was tolerant of the opinions of others. He loved young people and was loved by them and he loved amusements, despite his Presbyterian proclivities!

He spent the evening of his life quietly at his estate, Raphine (from the Greek *raphis*, meaning a needle), a few miles from Lexington. A village grew up around his estate, and bears the name Raphine.

Upon the passing of General Robert E. Lee, his son, General G. W. Custis Lee, succeeded his father as president of Washington and Lee University. He was graduated from West Point in 1854. At the outbreak of the War Between the States, he was a captain of engineers in the United States Army. He became an aide-de-camp in the Confederate Army, with the rank of colonel, and before the end of the war, rose to the rank of major general.

He taught at Virginia Military Institute prior to his connection with Washington and Lee, of which he served as president until 1897, when he retired to his estate, Ravensworth, in Fairfax County. He died in 1913 at the age of eighty and is buried in the Lee Chapel.

William Nelson Pendleton, soldier, minister, and teacher, was General Lee's chief-of-staff. After the surrender he returned to his home in Lexington and resumed the rectorship of Grace Episcopal Church. He was a West Point graduate and had a fine record as a soldier as well as a minister.

His home, The Pines, was, and remains, an intellectual and social center in the community. For many years General Pendleton, assisted by his brilliant daughters, conducted a private classical school.

His daughter, Susan Pendleton Lee, wrote histories of Virginia and the United States, which were widely used in the Southern schools for many years.

It is said that General Pendleton would not pray for the President of the United States, and on one occasion made some reference in his sermon which was unpleasant to some United States officers present. After the service they arrested him and put him on parole and the church was closed for several months.

General Pendleton was a very handsome man and strikingly resembled General Lee.

W. A. Wallace, known to history as "Big-foot Wallace," was born near Lexington in 1816. While working quietly on his farm, word reached him that the Mexicans had killed his brother. He left everything and started immediately on a mission of revenge. He joined the Texas forces and became a lieutenant. He lived near San Antonio until his death in 1899.

Judge John Brockenbrough, born in 1806 in Hanover County, and educated at the University of Virginia, came as a young man to Lexington, where he spent his long and honored life. He was an eminent lawyer as well as a United States Judge for the Western District of Virginia. He represented Virginia in the futile Peace Conference which sought to avert the calamity of war. In 1849, he established his law school at Lexington, which was successful from the start. With the coming of General Lee and the reopening of Washington College, his school became a part of the college, with himself as the head of the department.

He was, therefore, the founder of the great Washington and Lee School of Law, from which have gone so many men to distinction on the bench, at the bar, and in the legislative halls of Congress, as well as in many other useful pursuits.

Judge Brockenbrough also served in the Confederate Congress. He was an intellectual giant and wielded great influence. He died in 1877 and is buried in the Presbyterian cemetery.

Commodore Matthew Fontaine Maury, born in Spotsylvania County in 1806, was one of the great men of science of the nineteenth century. At a very early age he circumnavigated the globe, after which he was associated with the National Observatory in Washington and was largely responsible for the development of the Weather Bureau as we know it today. Because of his maritime knowledge, his ability to sound the depths, and his wise instruction regarding the laying of the Atlantic cable, he won the title of "Pathfinder of the Seas." He disclosed to the world the secrets of trade winds and ocean currents. He was offered a knighthood by Great Britain which he declined. Many honors and medals were awarded him by his own and by foreign countries.

He discovered the plant, or weed, from which iodine is derived, and wrote a standard book on physical geography which has been widely used in the schools throughout the country. He aided the Confederacy by his coast defense instructions, and after the fall of the Confederate government he went to Mexico and joined Maximilian's cabinet, later going to England to receive his LL.D. degree from Cambridge University. In 1868 he returned to Lexington, where he spent the remainder of his life as professor of meteorology at the Virginia Military Institute. He was one of the most notable men ever to have lived in Lexington, and probably sacrificed more than any other man for the cause of the South, excepting General Lee.

His hospitable home on the parade ground was a mecca for his hosts of friends and admirers. One who knew the family well, said: "He was a perfect host, full of gay 'bonhomie,' radiantly happy to once again enjoy domestic quiet, surrounded by his family and friends."

His wife was a woman of rare charm and a great addition to Lexington society.

Though not the heroic figure in the world's eye that Lee and Jackson were, he had achieved wide fame and when coaxed to show his honors, his ex-Confederate coat would fairly blaze with Royal decorations. But, like General Lee, he lived among his friends with simplicity and neighborliness. His love for and interest in the solar bodies remained almost a passion to the last. During his final illness, when too weak to sit up, he would ask to be placed near the window, in the evening, where he could commune with the stars. "He loved the stars too fondly to be fearful of the night." At the age of sixty-seven, he passed quietly away, in 1873, at his Lexington home and, because of his love for Goshen Pass, he had requested that his remains be carried through the Pass when the rhododendron was in bloom. He died in midwinter, and his body was kept in a vault at the institute until spring, when the Pass was in its May day splendor. Accompanied by the Virginia Military Institute cadets, it was then carried through this Pass on the way to its last resting place in beautiful Hollywood, Richmond.

It is true that "nae man can tether time nor tide," but Maury discovered ways of understanding and using these mighty elements. His fame belongs to the seven seas.

John Mercer Brooke was Maury's most able assistant in compiling Wind and Current charts and Sailing Directions. While on duty at the Naval Observatory he invented a deep-sea sounding apparatus, to which the world owes the means of finding what is at the bottom of the ocean, and by the use of which the Atlantic Plateau was explored and the feasibility of the Atlantic cable demonstrated. He commanded the *Fenimore Cooper* in survey of routes between the Sandwich Islands, Japan and China.

He entered the Confederate service in 1861 and was made chief of the Confederate Bureau of Ordnance and Hydrography. He invented the Brooke gun and designed plans for an ironclad vessel with submerged ends, which plan was used in converting the U. S. *Merrimac* into the ironclad ram *Virginia.* The famous battle between this ship and the *Monitor,* March 9, 1862, in Hampton Roads harbor, revolutionized the naval architecture of the world.

After the surrender, upon the reorganization of the Virginia Military Institute, he accepted the chair of physics, where, after a long and useful life, he passed away, full of honor and of years.

He was born in Tampa, Florida in 1826, and was a member of the first graduating class at West Point. He sleeps among Lexington's great in the Presbyterian cemetery.

Following these sketches the author desires to name some of those whom he remembers with affection and gratitude, who added richness to the social, intellectual, political, and spiritual life of Lexington since the turn of the century and who have passed on to their reward. It is not given to all to be listed on the scroll of fame, but these men labored for this community, which they greatly loved and their contribution should not be forgotten. This list is necessarily incomplete, as it is solely from memory. It includes:

John Alexander
Colonel J. DeH. Ross
Major Francis H. Smith
Henry H. Myers
Professor A. L. Nelson
John L. Campbell
Colonel William T. Poague
Samuel R. Moore
Honorable William T. Shields
Dr. Harry D. Campbell
J. William Moore
Dr. G. B. Strickler
Judge Houston Letcher
Dr. James A. Quarles
Dr. James R. Howerton
Dr. J. Hammond Campbell
Dr. W. LeC. Stevens
Captain Samuel B. Walker
Randolph Blain
Dr. Daniel A. Penick
J. Harvey Moore
Robert R. Witt

Edward A. Moore
Dr. J. W. Kern
— A. T. Barclay
Captain J. Preston Moore
A. Nelson Myers
J. Ed. Deaver
Dr. Chas. Davidson
Frank Brockenbrough
William A. Glasgow
Dr. Reid White
Dr. Robert Glasgow
Dr. B. W. Switzer
E. L. Graham
Judge A. P. Staples
Judge Martin P. Burks
Dr. Henry A. White
William R. Kennedy
John Sheridan
Thomas S. White
Frank T. Glasgow
Jas. Hamilton
Dr. B. B. Glover

G. A. Jones
John Whitmore
William Wright
O. B. Dunlap
Dr. C. G. Dold
L. B. Turnbull, Jr.
General Scott Shipp
General Edward West Nichols
Honorable William L. Wilson
Dr. William T. Lyle
Dr. D. B. Easter
W. C. Stuart
Judge W. P. Houston
A. W. Harman
S. T. Moreland
Dr. Frank Davis
Captain J. W. Gilmore
Joe Gilmore
Colonel Forsyth
Robert L. Owen
Charles A. Graves
S. O. Campbell
Joseph R. Long
W. W. Dunlap
Colonel Francis T. A. Junkin
General William A. Anderson
Major Finley W. Houston
Colonel C. A. Watts
William S. Hopkins
General John Mallory
George Womeldorf
G. W. Effinger
J. A. Jackson
"Squire" Houghawout
R. S. Anderson
J. Gassman
E. R. Funkhouser
W. A. Davidson
S. W. Donald
Dr. Wm. S. White
Joel Ruffner
Thos. H. Deaver

A. L. Koontz
Jos. Holmes
Jos. G. Ridgely
Reverend Root
W. B. Harrison
W. B. Hutton
Jack Withrow
Jonathan Herring
J. T. McCrum
B. H. Gorrell
W. Harry Agnor
William Ross
L. R. Miller
Captain Jas. Gillock
Fred White
D. E. Strain
Charles Effinger
M. Miley
D. C. Humphreys
Wm. G. McDowell
Dr. R. J. McBryde
Chas. R. Deaver
Harry Waddell
Wm. Walz
Major Thos. M. Wade
Dr. R. Granville Campbell
Dr. John H. Latane
John W. Barclay
Dr. F. L. Riley
J. Houston Leech
George White
Captain M. B. Corse
Captain Dave Moore
Colonel Beverly Tucker
Colonel Robert Marr
J. C. Loyall
W. O. Beasley
Dr. W. Cosby Bell
J. V. Grinstead
F. P. Rhodes
E. M. Pendleton
Sandy Waddell
J. P. Welsh

Dr. G. A. Wilson
J. W. Shaner
W. R. Humphries
Thos. S. Burwell
Colonel R. B. Poague
B. Estes Vaughan
Matthew W. Paxton

Colonel T. A. Jones
J. D. Varner
J. P. Ackerly
John M. Quisenberry
John Hutton
Thomas Crigler
E. A. Quisenberry

CHAPTER XXXI: MISS ANNIE JO WHITE

ON THE lovely campus of Washington and Lee University lives a good woman, who doubtless has the largest circle of friends of any woman in the South. Affectionately known to her friends as "Annie Jo," this little lady has touched the lives of thousands of boys of the college and of its close neighbor, the Virginia Military Institute, through her long connection with the college.

Miss Annie comes of an old and honored family of Virginia; the type that has moulded life of the highest order and made of the Old South such a fine place in which to live, creating those undying traditions of which every Southerner is proud. Miss Annie, however, does not need reflected glory from other generations, for her own good work and striking personality are sufficient reasons for the wealth of attention given her. Wherever she goes she is the recipient of much entertainment, and receives a royal welcome by the alumni, scattered throughout the world.

Endowed with a keen mind, which has been highly cultivated by travel, reading, and fine contacts, she is a conversationalist par excellence. Thoroughly at home with the classics, she is equally versed in the books and authors of today, and it would be difficult to name one that would be unfamiliar to her. After a splendid service in the teaching profession, the board of trustees elected her librarian of the college, a position she held for many years with efficiency. Though a busy librarian, she found time to lend a guiding hand to the social activities of the college and the town. In doing this, she endeared herself to thousands of the boys and their girls, many of whom have kept in touch with her through the years. Seldom was an entertainment of any kind given without her supervision and direction. Her interest in the boys' pleasure caused her to inaugurate the Fancy Dress Ball, which has been an annual event for the past twenty-eight years, and is rated by many the most elaborate social function in the college life of the South.

Such attractions as David Garrick, *The Rivals, Esmeralda,* Gilbert and Sullivan's *Pinafore,* and many other performances were given by local talent under her guidance for the benefit of college athletics. Whenever money was needed for sweaters, a new boat or other necessities, the boys would invariably turn to Miss Annie for assistance and she would, with great effort and much hard work "find a way."

When that great statesman, William L. Wilson, Postmaster-General under Cleveland, became president of Washington and Lee, he found Miss Annie such an indispensable asset that he titled her his "Lady Vice President."

Miss Annie's interests and activities have not been confined to school life. She has been equally interested in community affairs and in the larger concerns of the Commonwealth and of the Nation. No movement for social or civic improvement ever fails to enlist her whole-hearted support. She was one of the organizers of the district nurse work in Lexington, which was such a blessing to the poor and needy. She was one of that undaunted group of women, who, several years ago, purchased the home of Stonewall Jackson from Mrs. Jackson and converted it into the Jackson Memorial Hospital. This was a big undertaking, and none other than a group of Miss Annie's type could have succeeded. Her interest in this institution has never waned and she is still a power among those who direct it.

The Lee Chapel, where so many important functions are held, has always received much care and attention from Miss Annie. For years she supervised all the decorating for Finals and other public affairs.

In literary circles, the United Daughters of the Confederacy and the Daughters of the American Revolution she maintains a lively interest. Through years of such varied activities she has touched the lives of all classes and conditions, giving variety to her circle of friends.

When Lee Week was inaugurated at the White Sulphur Springs, the management invited Miss Annie and Mrs. W. LeC. Stevens to be their honor guests. They both added interest to the week by relating their memories of General Lee and his family in Lexington. Mrs. Stevens, a daughter of the Honorable John Letcher, Virginia's war governor, has the proud distinction of being General Lee's only godchild. The Lees and the Letchers were close neighbors and intimate friends during the Lees' residence in Lexington.

So few people today remember General Lee that it is remarkable to find one who does, and is at the same time so alive to all current affairs as is Miss Annie. While most people cling to their generation and its ideas and standards, she is interested in and appropriates all that is worthwhile in each succeeding generation, and this makes her, to a marked degree, a contemporary of several generations and accounts for the intimate friendships which she has with the boys and girls of today. They recognize in her an understanding friend.

In her home on the college campus about a dozen of the boys live, and scores of others are daily visitors. Many of them owe their success, both in college and in after life, to her wise counsel. She never fails to remind them of their golden opportunity and to spur them on to do their best. Few women have lived such a full and useful life, and it is only natural that her circle of friends is wide and ever widening.

It is not amiss to add that, while Lexington has been proud to claim Miss Annie as its own and ranking "first citizen," she has also been honored to have had Lexington as her home, for where else could she have found so congenial a place in which to spend her wonderful life?

CHAPTER XXXII: MR. McELWEE WRITES OF BASEBALL

OF interest to lovers of college sports is the following on the first curve ball in college athletics, written by William M. McElwee: "My earliest knowledge of the game was during the Presidency of General Robert E. Lee. The game was in its infancy and many teams were organized. This was the only sport on the campus at that time. As a lad I never missed a game between the students and the cadets, always played on the Virginia Military Institute parade ground. I had my hero then, as the boys have their Babe Ruth now. The structure of the game is unchanged, the grounds, the diamond, the number of players, the position of the players, innings, fair and foul balls, strikes and balls. The rules governing the game, changeable as they are from year to year, have possibly made the game more scientific, but the interest in the game has continued through the years. The squeeze play and the bunt were not used then, in fact there was no occasion for such plays, as the scores were always large and one run on either side had little effect on the score. The pitcher held the pivotal position just as he does today, but he was handicapped by a rule that he could not raise his arm above his thigh in pitching the ball. Later on, the rules allowed him to raise his arm horizontal with his shoulders.

"The catchers had no protection of mask, pads, or gloves, but with bare hands caught under the bat, only upon the third strike or when a man was on base. A foul ball caught on the first bounce put the batter out and the catchers purposely played back for the foul ball.

"There was no charge for admission to games and the players furnished their own outfits, while the balls and bats were obtained by taking up a collection.

"There was little or no change in the game or the rules of the game for the first ten or fifteen years. As I grew into young manhood, our family moved to Kentucky. There I first met George A. Sykes and then with two other members of our famous team of 1878, we played ball together before coming to Washington and Lee. Composing our team were five boys from Kentucky, two from Lexington, Virginia, one from Lynchburg and one from Galveston, Texas. We had a well balanced team of seasoned players, who could run, bat and field with the best of them, and our pitcher was the first to use the curve ball in college athletics. He was a great pitcher and won the game for us at Charlottesville in 1878, almost by himself. He was simply unbeatable that day and his curves kept them all wildly guessing, striking out 16 and not a batter getting further than second base.

"Our trip was by stage-coach through Goshen Pass to Goshen, where we boarded the train for Charlottesville. Word had been circulated that we had a 'curve pitcher' and there was much interest and speculation as to the outcome of the game."

Mr. Sykes recently passed away, and last year a handsome portrait of him was presented to the Washington and Lee Alumni Hall, where it will always be a reminder of the great and eventful days of 1877, '78, and '79.

CHAPTER XXXIII: NEW ALSACE

DURING the latter years of the nineteenth century, there came from Alsace-Lorraine, the Weiss family: father, mother, and son. Of all the wide, wide world, they chose the east slope of Brushy Hills, overlooking Lexington, and here these thrifty, artistic people built a charming chalet and developed vineyards of Concord grapes equal to those of the Old World; they also created gardens, both quaint and formal. This, their new home in America, they named New Alsace, and older Lexingtonians have very happy memories of the Weiss hospitality—grapes, wines, and flowers. In their gardens the snowballs and cinnamon roses bloomed, the sweetbrier and honeysuckle clambered over the fences, and old-fashioned flowers filled every nook and corner with fragrance and color. Fine hickories and oaks shaded the greensward that led to the gate. The house stood on a lovely slope, open to all the winds that blew, with marvelous mountain scenery for miles around and little Lexington nestling in the center of it all.

These wonderful people built themselves into this place and gave it rare charm and interest, and for many, many years it was a popular rendezvous for Lexington people. Mr. Weiss claimed that here they had successfully reproduced a bit of the old country, amid scenery suggestive of the Alps. It has been claimed that the first night club in America was at New Alsace.

Early in the twentieth century this quaint, picturesque place was sold, and for some unforgivable reason was torn away and a modern town house built upon its foundation. Instead of the old oaken bucket at the well, the open fire places, the oil lamp and candles, rag rugs, and a one-horse shay, we find running water all through the house, steam heat, electric lights, Persian rugs, spirited horses, and high-powered automobiles. The modern house today looks deserted, and one recalls with a feeling of sadness the original home, its fascinating gardens, and above all, its charming host and hostess who created it.

Life may have been a bit primitive, but under their rooftree dwelt peace and contentment. Truly big-hearted people they were. They loved and were loved by everyone. They had a way of training ivy up on the house to represent crosses, anchors and hearts—a feat requiring skill and artistry.

Here at New Alsace, far from their native soil, they sleep on this lovely hillside they loved so well.

CHAPTER XXXIV: COLORED PERSONALITIES

MANY striking colored personalities, unique and interesting, some with a keen sense of humor and the wit of a Neapolitan, have lived in Lexington and have helped to "atmosphere" the place. Mostly religious, superstitious, imitative, they took on the best from their fine contacts. There were many cases in Lexington where former slaves remained with their "white folks" throughout their lives. The finest feeling has always existed between the races and doubtless there is no community in the whole country where understanding and harmony is more evident.

Several years ago Representative H. St. G. Tucker met Booker T. Washington on a train and engaged him in conversation. He told Washington that he was from Lexington, Virginia, but no mention was made of Lee or Jackson. After talking awhile, Washington asked: "What kind of people do I have in Lexington, Mr. Tucker?" "The very best—law-abiding, home-owning, and highly respected," was the reply. After a pause, Washington said: "I am not surprised; no people could live in the fine atmosphere of Lee and Jackson and not be the best."

No picture of Lexington would be worthy the name without some mention of a few outstanding and well-known colored characters, honored and loved by everyone. They have contributed much to the community life.

Jefferson Shields, "Uncle Jeff," ebony in color, with his snow-white beard, twinkling eye, high silk hat, and Prince Albert coat, was a sight as familiar on the street as the postoffice, and known to literally thousands of college men, many of whom continued, years after leaving college, to send him "spending money."

He claimed the proud distinction of having been Stonewall Jackson's bodyguard during the war, and this honor he did not fail to commercialize, for it assured him a comfortable income to the end of his earthly pilgrimage.

A visitor to this community several years ago claimed that he had found so many ex-servants of Generals Lee and Stonewall Jackson that he had concluded that these two gentlemen must have had as many servants as Solomon had wives.

"Uncle Jeff" attended all Confederate reunions in many parts of the South, where he was always the recipient of much attention, about which he talked freely. Especially was he "puffed up" after a visit to Memphis, where he claimed to have slept in Mr. John Speed's parlor. After each reunion he had a fresh supply of medals and when he would proudly open his coat to display them he looked like the Kaiser on parade.

James Jackson, "Deacon," as he was affectionately known, had been General Lee's barber and told interesting stories of his services to "de Gen'l." At one time, four generations of Jacksons worked together in the

"Deacon's" barber shop, which was a popular place with the townspeople and the college students. The place is still operated by his descendants. Its slogan is "It was good enough for General Lee, it is good enough for you."

A story has come down of John Bowyer, the village sexton and the right hand of the minister. A better and more reliable sexton than "Uncle John" never lived. He was more warmly attached to the white people than to his own race. He swore by every word that the minister said or did, in the pulpit or out, and considered his every word as gospel truth.

The church bell was rung on time, the fires lighted and the church aired, and every service punctually set in order. Burial arrangements were carefully attended to, nothing overlooked. When death at last claimed the old sexton as its own, it was truthfully said of him that a more faithful servitor in little things was never laid in mother earth.

The *County News* of January 23, 1885, noted: "Siamese, a little negro boy, who has been running the streets in rags, was taken to Larricks', by Student Carlisle, and dressed out in a splendid suit, from tip to toe, since which he has been strutting around with cigarette and canette in regular style." Siamese and his twin sister were literally reared by the students and cadets. He became an "institution" and knew, and was known by, practically every student and cadet. Thousands remember him, astride his horse, with cowbell in hand, racing up and down Main Street, yelling at the top of his voice:

> "O yes! O yes! there will be a football game
> on Wash-Lee (or V.M.I.) grounds at
> three-thirty. 'Mission fifty cents.
> Ladies free!"

Siamese was a real college town product. He would have been a misfit anywhere else. With him as town crier, handbills and bulletin boards were unnecessary. His cry, like the fire bell, never failed to cause everyone to stop, look and listen!

His old black mother was known as "Pick-head Milly" because she was completely devoid of hair and wore a "home-made" wig. Upon the occasion of her baptism in the river, she became uproariously happy and unmanageable. Her wig washed off and went downstream, causing several bystanders to swim after it.

Negro baptisms in the river were great Sunday afternoon occasions in the early days of Lexington. Hundreds of students, cadets, and townspeople were always in attendance.

Many years ago it was a Lexington custom to announce funerals by having a negro man walk slowly about the town, carrying an announcement, written on fine white paper, mounted on black crepe and reading:

Mr. John Doe
died at nine o'clock
funeral at
Presbyterian Church
Wednesday, 5 o'clock
All invited.

The sacred duty was performed for years by Jim Rose.

One of the college servants, whose duty it was to ring the bell for classes, on one occasion got "too much to drink" and failed in his duty. When called before the president and reprimanded, he smilingly said: "Well, you know, Boss, all us Virginia gentlemen takes on a little too much sometimes."

In the early years of the twentieth century, Jim Humbles, a famous negro chef, conducted a popular restaurant on Washington Street. It was a rendezvous for the students and cadets who could mobilize the two-bits, the tariff for a table d'hote dinner, or on big occasions, a banquet that often came as high as fifty cents per plate.

The list of these faithful servants of other days, who were bound by the strongest ties to their "white folks," could be lengthened indefinitely. They were loved and respected and are greatly missed.

Phil Nunn, better known as "Dixie," is one of the few surviving negro characters on the Lexington streets. Towering more than six feet, wearing his "own make" carpet-shoes, with wooden soles, his clothes, being of a nondescript ensemble, set him apart as unique. He belongs to a past age, and yet, when asked his age, he tips his hat and smilingly says, "about twenty, Sir."

He has a queer custom. As he walks about the streets, he tips his hat to every automobile, telephone post, and person he passes, as well as to every house in which he has ever been employed.

He is very versatile in his services, from house-cleaning and "tending" children to moving iron safes. He is kind, simple, and gentle, yet he hardly knows his own strength.

CHAPTER XXXV: THE TURN OF THE CENTURY

ROCKED in the cradle of the American Revolution, developed through years of pioneering; through Civil War and Reconstruction, being in the very wake of its havoc and those experiences that try men's souls; through the sentimental Victorian era and the Gay Nineties; through the World War, with its terrible aftermath, Lexington has weathered the storms and has played her part nobly. Never has it been found wanting, where courage, devotion to duty, and defense of high ideals were called for. Built upon a firm foundation by the Scotch-Irish, with whom principle was the first and last consideration, and who faced danger unafraid, this community could hardly be otherwise. Though a peace-loving people, nevertheless they have always been present in the defensive struggle of their country, for man could not take from them, unopposed, their God-given rights. During the Revolution, the Liberty Hall students won fame on the field of Guilford and elsewhere for the cause of American Independence. Young yeomen of the Valley counties, including Rockbridge, who were accustomed to making the wild turkey's head the mark for their bullets, joined Daniel Morgan; to their skill and daring is attributed the success at Saratoga. For Morgan's distinguished service at Cowpens, Congress voted him a gold medal. He was known as a veritable thunderbolt of war. Later, when the country was torn by civil strife, there went forth in defense of home and native land the Liberty Hall Volunteers and the Rockbridge Artillery, composed of the noblest of blood and breeding, to aid the Southern cause.

Still later, when our common country was drawn into the vortex of a great world struggle, a Lexington contingent, under the patriotic leadership of Captain Greenlee Letcher, a noble son of a noble father, went overseas to fight with the Allies. This company was christened the Rockbridge Artillery, in honor of the earlier one by that name. In the quality of its leadership in every pursuit of life, this community has always been conspicuous; in religious thought and activity, in educational endeavor, in political and social standards, it has never lacked trained and able leaders. For more than a century it has been a training ground, a home town, and an educational center with the finest environment, where thousands of the nation's choicest young men have spent their formative years, and from which they have gone forth as leaders in thought and action throughout the world. Here they were prepared for life and service, for fame and fortune. History can show few that equal, none that excel this little community in its contribution to the welfare of the world. A rare, delightful home life has always characterized Lexington—a home life centering around unusual men and women whose ideals were high, whose religious principles were unquestioned and whose educational and cultural standards were preeminent. Into these homes, beginning mostly with General Lee's régime, boys came annually from far and near. General Lee preferred that the boys stay in Lexington homes for the good influence which he believed was conducive to fine Christian living and good citizenship. The cadets of the institute were also frequent visitors in these homes, and alumni of these two great schools, scattered throughout the world, carry with them affectionate and lasting memories of these old Lexington homes.

Some have claimed that the cold, formal crust of Lexington society was hard to break through, and that a caller might be offered a "cold red pippin on a cold white plate" while he shivered on a hair-covered early American sofa, built for looks and not for comfort, in a dark and musty parlor, with portraits of stern ancestors looking down rather disapprovingly upon the intruder! There was a staid and orderly appearance to these old parlors, with their dark red "churchy" carpets, their marble-top center tables, their ever-present family Bibles, recording weddings, births and deaths. Horsehair mahogany furniture and richly figured lace curtains were essentials. Open only when the local minister or other formal visitors called, it was reasonable to expect that they would present a musty and unsociable atmosphere. It was also claimed that death was preferable to unwarranted familiarity with strangers—strangers being those who were not well versed as to their ancestors. It was further claimed that only generations of native born were recognized Lexingtonians. Mr. Frank Glasgow, an outstanding and honored citizen, once said that he was still an outsider, since he had lived in Lexington only about forty years!

Many of the residents were satisfied with life as it was and did not welcome any change at all. They resented strenuously the coming of the railroad, with its noise and smoke; the canal and the stagecoach were excitement enough. They would have "Carcassonned" Lexington to keep those in, in and those out, out.

This exclusiveness was shared by some of the less prominent, as well. A seamstress, who considered herself among the élite, resented the admitting of so many "plain people" into membership in her Presbyterian Church, and insisted that a wing be built for them.

However, those who have known the truth—and most have—know that underneath this apparently strained and formal surface and these rather strictly drawn social lines, were the most wholesome, genuine and true qualities of mind and spirit and the most lasting friendships known. What grateful memories come to mind when recalling associations with these charmed circles of old Lexington!

Mr. John W. Davis, in a reminiscent mood, recalls these happy days in old Lexington, and says that he does not know which has meant the more to him, the "town or the gown."

Home life and college life were one and the same, and a feeling of ownership possessed the townspeople. They never felt detached from the school life, and this was natural, for they contributed much toward the greatness of the two institutions of learning. Into these homes the boys had free and easy entrée and most of them claimed at least one as their home. Good etiquette and fine manners contributed to the atmosphere in which these people lived and moved and had their being; these they considered more important than material things. It is quite possible, then, that occasionally the boys grew tired, perhaps a bit bored, by so much ancestry and family silver, and wished instead for more food.

With the passing of the years have passed also most of these old residents, and a new order has come about—that of fraternity house life, or dormitory and Greek restaurant life. The student-Lexington home life is only a memory.

Mr. James Veech, of Louisville, recalls his student years spent in the Tucker home circle at Blandome as the happiest years of his life. This home he pictures as of the very highest type possible. Typical of the appreciation of the alumni of other days is that of Dozier DeVane, of Washington, who, in retrospect, tells of the home life of the students in the home of Misses Mary and Sue Davidson, those regal ladies who retained much of the elegant eighties and the gay nineties in dress and manner. He counts it one of the great privileges of his life to have been a member of this circle during his college days, and feels that their memory and influence have meant more to him through life than anything else of his college days. Such testimonials could be duplicated by the thousand.

No resident of Lexington was more admired for keen intellect and understanding, for poise and executive ability, than Miss Sue Davidson. In these qualities, she was a tower of strength. More than one admirer expressed the desire to vote for her for President of the United States; she could have sat with grace upon a throne and directed the affairs of state. Decidedly Victorian, especially in queenly manner, charm, and appearance, Miss Sue and the other charming women of old Lexington created a fine and wholesome atmosphere for college students.

Until the outbreak of the World War, with its hectic and upsetting influences, Lexington retained much of its old-time complacency, with many earmarks of the latter years of the nineteenth century. Innovators seldom appeared; those who came into the village liked it and soon fell into the Lexington way of life. Religious thought, literary taste, and life in general remained mostly unchanged, despite the fact that the inhabitants kept well abreast of the happenings in the world outside. Locally, however, a self-satisfied state prevailed—"a comfortable isolation." In those days it was a common sight to see the white flag, signifying an empty jail, displayed in front of that building for weeks at a time.

But now changes came thick and fast, affecting every phase of community life. The ladies, who, with trailing skirts, tight waists, long hair and fluffy, ruffled parasols or "sun-shades," had long clung to the styles of Godey, now felt the encroachments of Vogue and Élite, with startling suggestions of shorter skirts, shorter hair, and shortness in many other things. Such would have been shocking indeed to their mothers, grand-mothers, and spinster aunts who had moved about rather mysteriously on some unseen lower extremity. Who does not remember the first "ankle-high" skirt? When an ankle was visible, every one looked; now, with practically the entire anatomy visible, nobody looks! Some few were slow to accept these innovations, and, clinging tenaciously to the styles of the late nineteenth century, were considered, by some, quite queer. One such lady, who was the object of much interest and admiration, when asked if it were not embarrassing to have people stare at her, replied that they were just so many cabbage heads to her!

There were also a faithful few who considered themselves quite matronly at thirty, and obeyed the scriptural injunction by putting on sober apparel at that questionable age. A college boy, when speaking of his sister as elderly, was asked what he meant by elderly; he replied, "O, she's nearly thirty."

It is said that with the advent of shorter skirts, a minister's wife went a bit modern, and, having ventured out with an abbreviated skirt, was promptly the recipient of more than one anonymous letter from "the good town sisters."

Those who welcomed the new styles and the new freedom, however, had a feeling of pity for their mothers, who had been bound by convention, corsets and shoes.

Likewise, the men changed from the easy-going, take-your-time, horse-and-carriage age, to the restless, uncertain, what-to-do-next spirits of today. The old stores supplied chairs and unbounded hospitality for all, which seemed the prime reason for the stores' existence. Clerks and proprietors alike were solicitous as to the comfort and entertainment of the callers, and upon seeing a lady enter, an easy chair was immediately offered and ac-cepted. One lady, when offered a chair, said, "Yes, give me a chair; I never stand if I can sit, and I never sit if I can lie."

When the stores failed to satisfy the gentlemen, there was the Never-Sweat Club, ever in session on the courthouse balcony, where conversation, time, and easy chairs were all abundant, and where neither clock nor cal-endar ever disturbed. This honored club was composed of generals, colo-nels, captains, and a few privates, all ex-Confederates and the real intelli-gentsia of the day. Their heated arguments often furnished amusement and entertainment for the college students. Prior to the World War this club was conspicuous, and was known alike to students and visitors to the village. With the passing of these learned and cultivated men, who were tested in those hard years through which the South passed, has likewise passed this unique club, and it is today only a memory. Halcyon days they were! History does not record, nor can the mind conceive, a finer, nobler type of men and women than the residents of old Lexington. Intellectually, spiritually, socially, and physically, they remain unsurpassed. They left their impress upon this community, and, regardless of the changes that will come, their influence will last to the end of time—"As good as gold, as true as steel."

For many years there was a custom in Lexington, which was claimed to be unique, of honoring both the ex-Confederate soldiers and the memory of General Lee. A dinner—and a dinner it was—was served annually, on January 19, the birthday of General Lee, in the Presbyterian Lecture Room by the ladies of the community. Here everything was done for the entertainment of those who followed Lee and Jackson. This custom was recently discontinued, with the passing of the last of these wonderful men. With their great commanders, they have answered the last roll call.

Bicycling had its day in old Lexington! Occasionally a long ride, culminating at Natural Bridge or some other far distant place, was indulged in by the most ambitious and athletic. For the most part, however, the smooth cinder walk through the campus to the Institute was the popular rendezvous for cyclers. There they would witness dress parade, and enjoy the thrilling brass band of six. Bicycles, like carriages, were owned only by the "upper crust," the plainer people caring little for such extravagance, which they conceded to the gentry.

Dress parade being the most exciting entertainment of the time, "the best people" felt a certain obligation to attend, both to see and to be seen. What an array of hacks, red plush-seated traps, victorias, and family surreys! Equestrians and equestriennes also were there—for before the advent of the motor car, this form of sport was popular in Lexington. Before the firing of the "evening gun," the coachmen would detach their horses from the carriages and lead them a safe distance away, as most of them never became accustomed to the noise. What would some of those old dobbins have thought of Big Bertha on Paris!

Many men of today can recall how, as boys, they made their pennies opening the college and institute gates for the élite to ride through. What a scramble when, with Rockefeller generosity, some pennies were tossed to the ground! Very often a penny, and just as often a smile, was the only reward to the small boy; since he believed that only the rich passed this way, this seemed tough luck, but he held his ground and hoped for better luck next time.

Family life was pleasant, complacent, and self-sufficient, and only when some local talent entertainment, a spelling bee, or a visiting stock company appeared, could the populace be induced to leave their firesides in the evening. The college boys, numbered among the inner circles of these homes, shared in the interests of the families and were apparently contented and happy; there were no fraternity houses, radios, automobiles, or movies, and no complete week-end exodus, as is the case today.

These high-class institutions brought to the village an unusual number of refined and cultured people, who found already established there, as their home for generations, the very pick of the Scotch-Irish and of the Tidewater English. Through the succeeding years this has continued, and today one finds Lexington just as different from other communities as ever; an intangible something, hard to define, but nevertheless real, constitutes this difference. Wherever two Britishers meet around the world, their point of contact is cricket; wherever two Virginia Military Institute or Washington and Lee men meet around the world, their point of contact is the Lexington people.

The old stock companies came often, offering *Ten Nights in a Barroom* or some other equally melodramatic production, and they were always well patronized, as were the local talent "benefit" plays. The spelling bee was popular and frequent, and the coming of the circus was always a great event in the town. In those days Christmas came but once a year, and was made much of; it was truly a great day, and everyone looked forward to it with pleasure, not with modern dread. Santa Claus was believed in, and parties, square dances, and taffy-pulling contests for the "young ladies and gentlemen" were largely attended.

Until recent years, Christmas Day was the one and only Christmas holiday given the cadets, and what celebrating it brought forth! Dold's, being their headquarters for eats, drinks, and fireworks, made this ancient corner the most popular place in town with the young people. Famous it was for its peanuts and "hot dogs." On this one-day holiday, the cadets' chief occupation was chasing the colored population with firecrackers. Only the most daring of the "darkskins" ventured out, for to do so invariably meant trouble. On Christmas Day, 1901, the cadets were on a rampage, and this story is told thirty-four years later, by one who was a cadet and a participant:

"The policeman tried to prevent their chasing the negroes, so the cadets tolled him into an alleyway and overpowered him, casting lots for his billy, cap and gun. Some of them got a large box from Graham's store and put him in it and nailed the lid on and left him there in the alley, while they continued their chase. They ran a negro into Sheridan's Livery Stable and up the hay ladder; one cadet followed him to the top of the ladder, where his head came in contact with a brickbat—down the ladder he tumbled, and when he came to himself, he was in the V. M. I. Hospital, where he spent several weeks."

The same week, the First Class held their banquet at the Lexington

Hotel, and they didn't get beyond the second course. By that time a rough-house had started, and they had to pay Mr. Brockenbrough $180.00 for damages to dishes and furniture. The cadets being required to remain in school, and many of the college boys having remained in Lexington through choice, the result was that throngs of visitors, parents and friends of the boys, came to Lexington for the holidays and made it a very gay place at the Christmas season. Many pleasant and lasting friendships were thus formed between the village people and the visitors. When the school year was over, and the special trains "backed in" to accommodate the hundreds of boys leaving at the same time, there would be great demonstrations at the railroad station. The stagecoach and the canal boats having gone out of business, and the motor and the plane being almost undreamed of, the old "Virginia Creeper" was the only means of getting away.

Commencement was the great event in the town. At this time homes received their annual "tidying up," and all the girls had new dresses and bonnets in which to attend the celebration of the Literary Societies. These exercises over and the boys gone, Lexington would settle down for its long summer's nap. This has been an annual experience since 1784.

The *County News* of many years ago reported the following:

"Friday night there was a Spelling Bee at the Presbyterian Lecture Room, which proved a very pleasant entertainment. It was given by some young ladies for the benefit of charity. Referees were Profs. Nelson, Harris, and Harrison, and Colonel Semmes gave out the words. Colonel Ross and Major Jolliffe led the two sides. The awards were, as usual, a dictionary and a speller to the one who held out the longest, and a primer to the one who missed first.

"There were twenty-five spellers in all, some of them very good, as Miss Lilly Sellers, W. H. Waddell, Mr. Crow, J. A. R. Varner, M. L. Bobbitt, Prof. Swartz, and others that we did not know. Quite a number of easy words were missed, such as lily, blouse, buoy, control, lyre, and brooch. One could hardly look at these words and believe that persons can be found in the Athens of Virginia who could not spell them correctly; yet, so it was.

"One gentleman of high culture went down on 'prior,' even after a second chance. Colonel Ross carried off the first honor, that is, the first earned, and Mr. Waddell held out the longest. Professor Nelson presented the primer, with a short speech which, judging from the Colonel's face, must have been very touching!"

Prior to the coming of electricity into the town, there stood on each street corner picturesque oil lamps, and it was the small boys' delight to follow the lamplighter, with his little ladder, as he would light up the streets and dispel the approaching darkness. The lights were few and far between, but as everyone, including the night watchman, was supposed to be at home by nine o'clock, at which time peace, silence, and sleep settled upon the community, lights were little needed. With the distribution of the evening mail, residents would wend their homeward way, not to venture out again until after family prayers on the morrow.

An abundance of good, faithful, and satisfied domestics was another contribution to the ease and comfort of home life of that far-off day. A genuine interest in and affection for the servants was shown, and in return the servants were loyal and grateful. "The fence was as it should be," commented an old lady, "and not as it later got to be, the bottom rail on top, and it rotten."

One woman, who had difficulty securing a good servant, said in desperation, "I hired one to save my body, but I fired her to save my soul," and added, "Paul might have struggled with the beasts of Ephesus, but he was a novice; he should have tried this cook of mine."

Another good woman, interested in social and moral welfare, became agitated over rumors, and advocated that lights be strung through the campus for the improvement of the servants' morals!

One of the most exciting and eagerly anticipated events of the whole year was the college boat races on old North River. The entire citizenry of the town was concerned with the merits and demerits of the Harry Lee and the Albert Sidney; over their colors, red and blue, and the prospect of victory, small boys fought and big boys gambled. The annual decoration of the town would begin weeks in advance of the races. Everyone, white, black, and chocolate, showed his colors; ladies carried the Harry Lee or Albert Sidney parasols, while others wore red or blue rosettes.

Old George, on top of the Main Building at the college, would receive his nightly coat of paint, and a daring feat this was, on the part of the college boys, to plant their color there! One morning the statue would appear brilliant in its coat of red, and the next morning, as if by magic, it would be as blue as indigo. This change of color scheme would occur nightly, for weeks. By the day of the races, Old George seemed to be wearing Joseph's coat of many colors; but soon thereafter he would be restored to his snow-white robe, so to remain until another commencement season rolled around.

It is claimed that these hundreds of coats of varicolored paint are responsible for the excellent state of preservation of the statue. It is a remarkable piece of sculpture in wood by a local carpenter, Mr. Kahle, and was made many years ago. It may not be a Michelangelo creation, but in the sentiment and affection of Washington and Lee men, it means more than the Winged Victory or the Venus de Milo. Some time ago, the following illuminating note regarding this piece of sculpture appeared: "From driftwood to monument . . . is the rags-to-riches story which Horatio Alger might have written about the majestic white statue atop the Main Building of Washington and Lee University . . . it happened this way; a giant hardwood log came drifting down the James River and into the view of Matthew Kahle, venerable wood-carver, and so into the history of Lexington and Virginia. That was in 1840. "Hardwood, big, very big, magnificent, just the thing for my sculpturing hobby," murmured Kahle. He pursued it into the yellow mud, on to the bank and pulled it out, hauling it to his shop, where, after whittling, chipping and sawing, gradually came the striking figure of George Washington, which Kahle swore the log had always contained.

"It was not erected on the cupola of the College until 1844. It represents Washington standing erect, one hand on his scabbard . . . in the other is his Colonial hat, as he looks serenely, approvingly, Lexingtonians point out, eastward, over the descending campus to Lee Chapel and the Shenandoah Valley. Gleaming white, perfectly preserved, taken nearly always for marble, he is lordly still, his lonely vigil unscathed by winds and rains of many years. . . .

"From wandering log to legacy of tradition on one of the oldest campuses in America. Alger might have written it, but historians of the University are recording it now."

The activities and excitement of boat-race day, like other celebrated days, would invariably terminate in a great callithump, followed by a soirée on the campus, "around some friendly kegs."

CHAPTER XXXVI: BARNUM'S CIRCUS IN LEXINGTON

CIRCUS DAY was always a gala time in old Lexington! For many weeks the gay billboards would be watched and studied by young and old, until everyone was familiar with all the offerings, real and fantastic—and what wonders! Lions, tigers, and everything!

From the earliest days, Lexington has been visited by the best shows that traveled. They offered much in education and entertainment, and were enthusiastically received. Naturally, the Scotch-Irish felt a bit guilty indulging in such utter "worldliness," but the children had to be amused!

Eighty years ago, Barnum's museum and menagerie paid Lexington one of its annual visits. This was before the coming of the railroad into town, and the circus traveled by wagon train over very bad roads.

In 1854, this rather lengthy ad appeared, for many weeks, in the local paper:

"P. T. Barnum's Grand Colossal Museum and Menagerie. . . .

"The largest travelling exhibition in the world. . . .

"Being a combination of all the most popular and unexceptional amusements of the age . . . enlarged and improved for the season of 1854.

"A team of eight elephants will draw the great car of Juggernaut.

"A baby elephant, only one year old and but 3½ feet high, will carry upon his back, around the interior of the immense pavilion, the Lilliputian Tom Thumb.

"The magnificent cortege comprises 140 horses and 100 men.

"The Pavilion of Exhibition has been enlarged until it is capable of accommodating 15,000 spectators at once. The collection of wild animals includes the most splendid specimens ever exhibited in America. Among others will be found eight beautiful lions, fresh from their native forests— a monster White, or Polar bear, of prodigious size and ferocity—a magnificent Royal tiger, the largest one ever captured alive—a pair of young lions, only six months old.

"Brazilian tigers, black and Poonah bears, hyenas, etc., etc. A drove of elephants—captured in the jungles of Central Ceylon, by June and Nutter, assisted by 260 natives, after a pursuit of three months and four days in the jungle. They were finally entrapped and secured in an Indian Kraal of enormous dimensions and prodigious strength, where they were subdued.

"P. T. Barnum, Professor of the American Museum, New York, has the honor to announce that, encouraged by the brilliant success which has attended all his various efforts for the amusement of the public he has been led to form the project of organizing a vast travelling museum of wonders —which comprises a great variety of attractions and more extraordinary novelties than any travelling exhibition in the world.

"Every feature of the mammoth establishment is of a peculiar and inter-

General Robert E. Lee
(The Victoria picture made by Miley at the Queen's request)

Virginia Military Institute, viewed from Diamond Hill
(Note shell-damage repairs)

Anne Smith Academy

Washington and Lee University, circa 1890

esting nature, and the whole is produced upon a gigantic scale of magnitude. The travelling paraphernalia of the American Museum, as it enters each town, is preceded by the gorgeous Car of Juggernaut—drawn by eight elephants superbly caparisoned, being an accurate model of that terrible engine of idolatrous sacrifice, finished and decorated in all the extravagance of the Hindoo style. Following this monster vehicle is a long procession of costly cages and carriages—the whole forming a spectacle of more than Oriental splendor.

"The exhibition will take place within a magnificent variegated pavilion composed of American flags and waterproof fabric. The real, genuine, original General Tom Thumb is attached to this exhibition and will appear in all his performances as given before the principal Crown-heads of Europe, including songs, dances, Grecian statues, and his admired personations of Napoleon and Frederick the Great. The little General is twenty-two years old and weighs fifteen pounds, and is but twenty-eight inches high.

"Also engaged—Mr. Nellis, the man without arms, who will execute his extraordinary feats of loading and firing a pistol with his toes—cutting profile likenesses—shooting at a mark with a bow and arrow—playing upon an accordion and violoncello, etc. Mr. Nellis, in these performances, exhibits a wonderful example of what indomitable energy and industry can accomplish, even when laboring under disadvantages apparently the most insurmountable.

"A complete menagerie of wild animals is also included in the American Museum, and at a convenient period during the exhibition Mr. Lengel —the Lion King—will enter the den of wild beasts and give a classical illustration of Hercules struggling with the Naemean Lions, Daniel in the Lion's Den, Samson destroying the lions, etc.

"One of the most interesting portions of the exhibition is formed by the display of a great collection of Wax Statuary, including figures of the size of life of all the Presidents of the United States and also of a number of noted characters, American and foreign, all of which are accurate likenesses and appropriately costumed. In fact, the whole establishment is a vast repository of wonderful objects of nature and art—the full particulars of which it would be impossible to give within the limits of a newspaper advertisement, and which has been brought together at an enormous expenditure of means, forming the largest and most novel travelling exhibition in this or any country.

"A fine military band will perform the most popular airs of the day as the procession enters the town and during the hours of exhibition.

"The American Museum and Menagerie will exhibit at Lexington, Va., August 12, 1854 . . . price of admission 50 cts., children under nine years and servants, 25 cts., to the whole of this establishment, including

General Tom Thumb, the entire collection of wild animals, wax statuary, Mr. Lengel's performance in the dens, the baby elephants, Mr. Nellis' performances, etc., no extra charge under any pretense whatever, let the report be what it may. Doors open from 1½ to 4 and from 7 to 9 o'clock, p.m."

The week following the performance, this editorial, appearing in the local paper, shows that the populace was not disappointed and that they "had a good time."

"Barnum's Museum and Menagerie came according to appointment on Saturday last.

"The precursors of this splendid array of penny-catchers were three sets of organ grinders, who arrived early in the morning and gave their music gratis, wherever a crowd could be found sufficient to justify an expectation that a few six-pences could be had upon the same terms. The performers in this department were six ladies, fresh from Italy, charming and beautiful, of course, and unrivalled in the art of organ-grinding and tambourine beating—next came the grand entrée, preceded by a few straggling baggage wagons and the great polar bear, which, from his puffing and blowing, seemed as if his constitution was not suited to the temperature of this climate and season. He needed shearing, but no one had sufficient confidence in his grateful appreciation of the kindness to undertake the job. The Car of Juggernaut was actually drawn by elephants, as advertised. The baby elephant proved to be a very interesting bantling, weighing some two thousand pounds and measuring some six or seven feet in height, instead of three and a half, as advertised. He had grown this much since the date of the bills, and from the avidity with which he ate the hay placed before him, we supposed his teeth were fully out and that his sucking days were over. He was, in fact, a baby elephant no longer.

"The mammoth pavilion was opened at the hour appointed, and soon was filled with a crowd variously estimated from two to three thousand, and certainly as large as any that ever assembled in this place upon a similar occasion.

"In this was exhibited all that was enumerated in the bills, except such as were reported dead, lost, strayed, or stolen since the date of the advertisement. The wax figures of all the Presidents, Bonaparte and the man who licked him at Waterloo, Queen Victoria and her numerous progeny, the temperate family, etc., were all there, but badly collapsed and distorted, we suppose, from the melting of the wax—they, like the polar bear, did seem unsuited to the temperature of this climate. They bore not the slightest resemblance to any human beings we have ever seen, and we presume were not very striking likenesses of the members of the human family whom they were intended to represent.

"The Museum of Wonders was not a collection extensive enough to occupy much of the mammoth pavilion or require a team of elephants to draw it. It consisted of an Egyptian mummy and sarcophagus— a coat of mail for man and horse, and sundry other antediluvian relics, too numerous to mention, and, as we suppose, fresh from Barnum's New York manufactory of such commodities and made according to the most approved pattern.

"The stock of monkeys and baboons in the cages was small and indifferent—those outside were more numerous.

"Tom Thumb, the greatest man, of his inches, in the world was there. He was, as we believe, the genuine article, and not the spurious imitation, as some believed. He played Bonaparte, rode the baby elephant, and repeated the smart things he had said in the present of the Crown-heads of Europe. Outside the mammoth pavilion there were celebrated dancers, unrivalled singers, a Rocky Mountain bear with two legs, a mustang pony without hair, and a great boa-constrictor, to be seen in separate tents and for separate tickets of admission.

"The show came fully up to our expectation, and we commend it to the patronage of all who have a fondness for seeing things."

CHAPTER XXXVII: LEXINGTON TODAY

THOUGH changes have come to Lexington since ante bellum days, it still has that intangible something that people love. It remains a residential and an educational center, and because of its high class institutions many delightful people come into the village life; be it literature, art, music, science, religion, or politics in which they are interested, here they are sure to find kindred spirits. There are few places in America whose inhabitants are more interested in and intelligent about so many worthwhile subjects. It is not surprising, therefore, that so many men and women from this place have gone out into the world and written their records high on the scroll of fame.

The most noticeable change is that of Main Street. Once a quiet country-town street, with rows of chairs and benches under the shade of the trees, where the village gentry could rest and enjoy leisure and comradeship, far more important to them than buying and selling, it is today a typical American small-town Main Street, with its share of glaring electric signs of Greek restaurants and garages, and is a busy link in two great national highways, Nos. 11 and 60, over which move heavy bus and tourist travel. The occasional stray pig, cow, or chicken of yesteryear would find this thoroughfare a dangerous rendezvous today!

The physical features of the town remain much the same, despite some residential growth. It still impresses the visitor as unique; a quaintness that was noticeable a hundred years ago still lingers and the Arcadian simplicity that described the Lexington life of long ago has not entirely passed away. Changes will and must come, but with its priceless traditions, the town can never become commonplace. Health, contentment, and tranquillity of mind and spirit are characteristic of the inhabitants. What prince would not envy them?

The old town is rich in places and things of historic interest. The tombs of Lee and Jackson, the two most vivid military figures of the War Between the States, are meccas for countless thousands; the matchless Washington and Lee campus of ninety acres still reflects the calm dignity of Lee, whose spirit seems to hover over all; and at the Institute, the military exactness and preciseness of Jackson is equally felt.

The school of Washington, and more especially of Lee, should stand ahead of all other schools in America in its contribution of permanent values to life. "By their fruits you shall know them" is as true of an institution as of an individual; and so of Washington and Lee it may be said: "Upon every scroll of fame since 1749 are found the names of her sons."

Lee, a lover of trees, spent much time planting and caring for those, especially the stately ash, that today grace the campus from end to end. In their friendly atmosphere lovers stroll through the heavenly moonlight and alumni return with their brides to reënact these scenes of earlier times and tell, with softened Polynesian intonations, of the "good old days." Their days in college were, of course, the most glamorous!

It has always been true that men think of their days in college as the best in the history of the institution and feel that after their departure a rather rapid decline took place. It is true that Washington and Lee and Virginia Military Institute have had glorious days, but they still have, and look forward to even more glorious times. The older alumni often doubt that the faculty members, the mighty men of intellect of their day, can ever be duplicated. They were exceedingly brilliant and scholarly men, particularly those who assisted in rehabilitating the schools after the War, but there are brilliant men today on these faculties who would have graced these noble institutions in any period in their history. What influence these men exert! They are Epistles, known and read of the students, far more than they realize. One freshman gave evidence of this truth recently, when he said to a friend that he hoped some day to develop into just such a man as Dr. Howe; he considered Dr. Howe the very embodiment of all that was best and finest. Sentiments similar to this are frequently heard from college boys in speaking of their instructors, but, unfortunately, they seldom make this known to those whom they admire. Meet any Virginia Military Institute man, anywhere in the world, and you will hear his affectionate and hearty words of appreciation of Colonel Hunter Pendleton, one of, if not the most beloved man ever connected with the Institute.

One who has watched many student bodies come and go, bears witness that a finer type of man has never been known at either school than those of today. The same quaint remark that was made of the students under General Lee's régime, might still be made: "eager and ingenuous boys, from all sections of our common country, whose zeal and devotion in search of knowledge, and whose gentility of deportment, have won the commendation of both the community and the college authorities."

The alumni of these schools keep fresh and pleasant memories of their Lexington days, and preserve and strengthen the ties of friendship there formed. They maintain a keen interest in the welfare of their Alma Mater, to whom they acknowledge a debt of gratitude never to be forgotten, and when the need arises, they have never been found wanting. This has always been true. When the Trustees decided, in 1865, to reopen the College, they had to borrow ten thousand dollars on their private credit, with which to buy apparatus and to recondition the buildings to put them in a "habitable condition."

John Drinkwater, after a visit to America, pronounced the Washington and Lee campus, which he saw under a blanket of snow, both by moonlight and in the daytime, one of the loveliest spots in the world.

The spectacular infantry, artillery, and cavalry drills at Virginia Military

Institute, the corps on dress parade, as the sun sets in all its glory behind old House Mountain, the evening gun, the national anthem, and the lowering of the flags are impressive scenes long to be remembered. It is hard to believe, when witnessing this great corps of cadets that in November, 1839 a small company of seventeen cadets answered the first roll call at Virginia Military Institute. Since that far-off day, thousands of men have gone forth from this noble institution into every walk of life.

An inspection of the fine Gothic halls of the Institute, some of Davis' best work, the splendid library and museum, and the Memorial Garden should not be overlooked.

Amble about the old town and note the hospitable doorways of The Rectory, The Pines, the Barclays', Dr. White's, The Manse, Stono, Hale Houston's, Col Alto; and the public ones at the College, the Lee Chapel, the Fire House, the old Kahle House, the Sheriff's House in the courtyard, and the quaint, picturesque Lawyers' Row, in the Court Square.

The lovely columned houses on the campus, built in 1843, for beauty are still unsurpassed. It was said that when these four houses were completed, and the four families moved in, it was a harmonious group of friends, and that there was at once a decided improvement in the social life on College Hill. For nearly a century these houses have made pleasant and charming homes for pleasant and charming people, who have shed and continue to shed a refining influence upon the community life.

A connoisseur of the fine and artistic claims that the mantels of Lexington homes and in this section of the State, excel in beauty those of Tidewater houses, and that nearly all of them were creations of an early resident, Letcher. The delicate and intricate balustrades of many of the old houses are works of art.

Other places of interest to visitors should be the only home ever owned by Stonewall Jackson, now the Memorial Hospital; the Castle, with its terraced pleasance, doubtless the oldest structure in the town, suggesting a bit of old Italy (this was the home of the Castilians of a bygone age); the Lee Home, on the College campus, in which General Lee lived and died; and the home of Traveller, near by.

In the Presbyterian cemetery, note the "Macs" and other clan names of old Scotland. Here sleep many who won fame through military leadership, the moulding of religious thought, the establishing of high educational standards, and contributions to scientific research and discovery. Here one must realize what a large contribution this little community has made to the welfare and advancement of the world. Truly a cosmopolitan "City of the Dead," for here are stones and monuments to natives of Ireland, Scotland, England, Germany, China, and other far places, who sleep in peace in this lovely spot. Few places, indeed, bear stronger testimony to

real greatness. How proudly Lexington has guarded and will guard the
ashes of those who have lived so nobly within her borders!

Here one finds stones to faithful servants, resting close by their masters.
One, Samuel Hayes, has this fine epitaph on the simple stone that marks
his resting place, at the foot of his master's grave:

> In loving remembrance for faithful services, this stone is erected by
> the desire of his master. He was loved, honored, and respected by
> three generations.

Another, Amy Hill, who departed this life in 1839, aged eighty years,
and whose grave is marked by a modest sandstone slab of simple design,
has, for nearly a century, slept among her "white folks." It was said of her
that she was kind, thrifty, and industrious, and had a strong affection for
her white friends which was generously reciprocated. She weighed over
three hundred pounds.

Davy Buck, long the sexton of the Presbyterian Church, which stood
in the cemetery, rests in the north corner. His grave, a simple, periwinkle-
covered mound, is otherwise unmarked.

Near the entrance gate is found this interesting stone:

> David McKinley, died 1854.
> Aged about seventy years.
> "My trust is in God"
> Erected by Peter Fleming,
> His former slave.

The shaft marking the soldiers' plot bears this lovely inscription:

> Let us gather sweet flowers and garland the
> simple stone
> That marks the spot where some one lies
> In a strange land unknown.

As interesting as the annual return of the swallows to Lexington is the
return of the blackbirds. Records show that for more than a century,
literally thousands of blackbirds have arrived each year to spend their
nights hovering about the Lexington cemetery; annually they come, as
surely and regularly as the seasons. They have proven themselves a nuisance, and every effort has been made to induce them to change their migratory habitat, all in vain. Bells, installed in the tops of the trees, powerful
streams of water thrown on them by the Fire Company, shooting at them,
and other means have been employed, but no permanent riddance has resulted; still they come, and doubtless will continue to come.

Lovers of the fine in art should visit Miley's Studio to see the photographic studies of Lee, Jackson, Tucker, Davis, Nichols, Paton and the
famous "photographs in color," made by a process or formula developed
by Miley, and for which he received national recognition. The etchings

of Hoyt and Junkin, and the paintings of Hamilton, Stuart, Riegel, and Northern would interest art lovers.

This community has never lacked writers of the first rank. Some few of them have written delightfully of the village life, but mostly they wrote upon wider fields. Among them were Joseph G. Baldwin, W. A. Caruthers, John Lyle Campbell, John Finley, Adam Rankin, James G. Ballagh, Archibald Alexander, Bishop Taylor, John Leyburn, Jesse Fremont, Margaret Junkin Preston, George Wauchope, Matthew Fontaine Maury, Alex Paxton, Elizabeth Preston Allen, William Allen, Francis H. Smith, Susan Pendleton Lee, Edward West Nichols, Edward A. Moore, Franklin L. Riley, Mrs. John H. Moore, John H. Latane, H. St. G. Tucker, James A. Quarles, Henry A. White, D. B. Easter, James R. Howerton, Francis P. Gaines, and O. W. Riegel. The list might go on *ad infinitum*.

The *Helix nemoralis* furnishes an interesting study for many, as they are rare in this country. They were first brought here in 1883 by Mrs. John H. Moore, from one of her European trips. It is still unknown whether she brought them purposely or by accident. At any rate, they found the residual limestone soil of Lexington a favorable environment. Some years ago, Dr. Howe examined over fifteen hundred specimens and reported three hundred and eighty-five varieties, among them various and beautiful patterns in yellow, pink, orange, and red casts. For many years they were not found beyond the confines of the campus and adjacent properties, but are now found throughout the town.

Almost every street and home in Lexington is associated in story and legend with the glorious past and even the streets and sidewalks seem holy ground, when it is remembered that Lee, Jackson, Maury, Brooke, Preston, and others walked these same ways. Places of historic interest are to be found in every section of the town, reminders of a great past.

In the vicinity of Lexington are many fine old manor houses, which through the years have been famous for their unbounded hospitality. Among them are: Thorn Hill, the home of Colonel Bowyer, which some have thought Page immortalized as the home of Marse Chan; Stone Castle, famous for having entertained Andrew Jackson en route from Nashville to the White House; Mulberry Hill, the home of the Reids; The Oaks, the seat of the Camerons; Clifton, the home of the Johnstons; Tuscan Villa and Green Forest, homes of the Glasgows; Spring Meadows, the home of Colonel Lady; Fancy Hill, many years ago one of the most famous taverns between Baltimore and far-off Tennessee; Virginia Manor, the home of General Fitzhugh Lee and later of George Stevens, president of the Chesapeake and Ohio Railroad; and Church Hill, the home of the Thompsons, built on the site of, and partly upon the same foundation of, the birthplace of Sam Houston. On the cellar door-frame is still visible the mark left by Sam, when thirteen years old; standing, with his back to the door, he leveled his gun over his head and shot a bullet into the frame of the door, thus designating his height. According to this story, he lacked one inch of being six feet. Hinges and locks of the old house are still doing service on the present house, as is a fine mantel from the original Houston home.

The Farrar home, with its enchanting gardens of color and fragrance; Fruit Hill, Hickory Hill, and Herring Hall, homes of the Grigsbys; all bear testimony to the glamorous days of old, and each has its own history and tales of romance, not to mention the "ghosts that walk by night."

A state of aristocratic decay possesses some, but in most cases these lovely old homes are occupied by appreciative owners, are in a fine state of preservation, and appear to be as equal to the long years of the future as they have been to the long years of the past. Belfield, the home of the Gilliams, though new, has all the charm and atmosphere of an ancient English estate. In its enchanting box gardens, under ancient trees, one might naturally expect to meet Queen Mary, so beautifully does the house and garden typify Merrie England.

Along with beauty, permanence, and comfort, fine scenery was a prerequisite in building a home; therefore all the old places around Lexington enjoy glorious vistas of mountains, and rolling hills and meadows. These which we admire and delight in today, have been equally enjoyed by those who have gone befor. Nature, always generous and often lavish in her gifts of beauty, has been exceedingly kind to the Lexington countryside. It is not surprising that the great soul of Lee was stirred by Rockbridge landscape, with beauty and interest abundant in every season of the year.

In the aesthetic, Lexington claims preëminence; in the culinary art, the claim of transcendence is justified. Man does not live by bread alone, but he does enjoy good food, and if there is any place on earth where queens are found in the kitchen, it is in Lexington, where this art has been developed into a science, and may be listed among the master arts. Mr. Tucker claimed that every Presbyterian girl could sing and cook, and no one has ever doubted it.

A glance backward reveals the fact that foods are more easily obtainable today than they were in old Lexington. Then, there were no markets. Meats were brought into town, by the country people, early, very early, in the morning, and sold in front of the courthouse; the early shoppers got the choice pieces. The only vegetables were home-grown. Few places offer finer accommodations for the entertainment of guests than the homes of Lexington, permeated, as they are, with old-fashioned hospitality—the comfort and welfare of the visitor being foremost in the mind of the hostess. The famed Dutch Inn, picturesque and homey, from which one is ever loath to depart; the modern Robert E. Lee Hotel, and the Mayflower, together with numerous overnight tourist homes, offer rest and refreshment to travelers who come this way. The Natural Bridge Hotel, Herring Hall, the Little Inn, and Forest Tavern are all within a twenty minutes drive.

Several years ago, a guest at the Virginia Hot Springs made a visit to Lexington, coming with some friends on horseback. His presence was unnoticed, and not until some years later, when he passed away, leaving his entire fortune to Washington and Lee, did anyone know that one of the University's greatest benefactors had visited it. From boyhood, this good man had adored the memory of General Lee, who had been his ideal, and he had long cherished the desire to honor his name. Upon this, his only visit to Lexington, he was tremendously impressed with the College, the town, and the countryside with its magnificent scenery. This generous benefactor, Robert Parker Doremus, died in 1913 and to help perpetuate General Lee's memory, he left his estate, which, upon the death of his widow, will come into the possession of Washington and Lee.

The Doremus Gymnasium, given by Mrs. Doremus as a memorial to her husband, is evidence of her interest in and affection for the College. The gymnasium is an indispensable asset to the college life, both physical and social. Here, every form of modern gymnasium athletics is possible. Athletics has grown in interest and variety through the years; in 1886, tennis was paramount in school and town.

In 1887, the Final Ball was held in Newcomb Hall, and in 1906, Miss Annie White gave the first Fancy Dress Ball. It was given in the old gymnasium (on the site of the present Chemistry Building), and cost $42.00, with music by the Virginia Military Institute band. Today all of the dances, including the Fancy Dress, are held in the Doremus Gymnasium—and quite an extravaganza the Fancy Dress has grown to be, costing many thousands of dollars. For this gala occasion the monstrous hall is transformed into a royal palace ballroom scene, and to the minutest detail is reproduced the elegance and glamour of Russian, Austrian, or French court life. For this great event, hundreds of America's prettiest girls are imported, from Maine to California, from the Lakes to the Gulf, and the town takes on a holiday spirit.

Close proximity to Hollins, Sweet Briar, Randolph-Macon, Stuart Hall, Southern Seminary, Mary Baldwin, and others a little more distant, does not detract from the charm of Lexington as a school town for young men!

A hundred years ago, it was said by the college authorities: "The object of every boy in college is to learn, and nothing is better calculated to defeat this object than free and easy access to the ballroom." This claim would find very few supporters today.

Tucker Memorial Hall, the home of the Washington and Lee School of Law, erected in 1900 by friends and admirers of John Randolph Tucker, was totally destroyed by fire on the night of December 16, 1934. A new and more harmonious structure, now in process of construction, will give perfect symmetry to the colonnaded facade of the College.

The two personalities most missed on the campus by the present generation are Dr. Harry D. Campbell, long the Dean of the College, and known to thousands of boys as "Old Harry," and Dr. D. B. Easter, long the Assistant Dean, and affectionately known as "Cutie." These two men, with their charm of manner and their cordial spirit, were greatly beloved by the students and the townspeople alike, and seemed as much a part of the University as the buildings themselves. When Dr. Easter passed away, a dear old woman paid him this tribute: "He was the one person I met on the street who always put cheer into my life."

Members of the first Board of Trustees included: John Hayes, John Bowyer, William Alexander, Arthur Campbell, Samuel Lyle, James McCorkle, William Christian, Alexander Campbell, William McKee, Samuel McDowell, William Graham, George Moffatt, Andrew Moore, John Montgomery, Archibald Stuart, John Trinkle, Cabel Wallace, Joseph Walker, John Wilson, and William Wilson. The men who have served on the Board through the long years have been among the most influential men of their generation—leaders in thought and action; the "refining influence" which this great school has shed upon the world is largely due to the ability and unselfish enterprise of these men.

This fine type of personnel continues in the present members of the Board: George W. St. Clair, Harrington Waddell, John W. Davis, Charles J. McDermott, James R. Caskie, George Bolling Lee, W. L. Carson, Newton D. Baker, William M. Martin, George C. Peery, Louis S. Epes, Herbert Fitzpatrick, Fowler McCormick, and Paul M. Penick, Secretary.

One may spend a few days in Lexington and succeed in pulling himself away, but should he stay through the year, and taste of the changing seasons with their many attractions, the chances are ten to one that he will fall into the Lexington way and "take root;" many have done this.

A cosmopolitan place, with a charm and a provincialism all its own, it casts its spell—now, as always, marked by intellectual attainments, a fine spirituality, a care for the moral and physical welfare, and a decided sense of beauty in homes and gardens.

From Mrs. Lacy's kindergarten to the Edmonia Smith Academy, through the primary and the Harrington Waddell High School and on through Washington and Lee University or the Virginia Military Institute, Lexington is unexcelled as a place of preparation. For more than a hundred years it has been claimed that a man who had received his training in Lexington could hold his own anywhere. This is true today, and its institutions are represented throughout the world, in every walk of life, by men who reflect honor upon their Alma Mater. The faculty members have been, and are, the peers of the great educators of America.

Doubtless the most enthusiastic visitors are the mothers of the boys. A cadet's mother, rejoicing over the protected life in barracks, said that it was such a comfort, when in her far-off Louisiana home, to know that at ten o'clock every night, her boy at Virginia Military Institute was in bed and fast asleep! A college boy's mother, visiting her son's fraternity house, said to the hostess, "These are such wonderful boys; none of them ever drink, do they?"

Washington and Lee has long been known as a college of fraternities, and, with the spirit which prevails on the campus, this is natural. The palatial homes of the fraternities, presided over by charming hostesses, are among the handsomest buildings of the College. Represented at Washington and Lee are the following: Phi Kappa Psi, Beta Theta Pi, Kappa Alpha, Alpha Tau Omega, Sigma Chi, Sigma Alpha Epsilon, Phi Gamma Delta, Kappa Sigma, Sigma Nu, Phi Delta Theta, Pi Kappa Alpha, Phi Kappa Sigma, Delta Tau Delta, Sigma Phi Epsilon, Pi Kappa Phi, Zeta Beta Tau, Phi Epsilon Pi, Lambda Chi Alpha, and Delta Upsilon.

The Kappa Alpha (Southern) fraternity, founded at Washington College during General Lee's régime, has the proud distinction of claiming General Lee as its spiritual founder. It was he who inspired and visualized in actual living the matchless ritual of the fraternity. John Temple Graves has given this toast to the matchless Lee: "Lift high your glasses here tonight, and in the liquid, spotless as his fame, let us pledge for all time 'the spiritual founder of the Kappa Alpha Order, Robert Edward Lee of Old Virginia.'"

Only those who understand our Southern people can comprehend how powerful are our traditions which hold a man steadfast to his anchorage of honor.

Rarely does one fail to return to Lexington. One visit calls for another, which suggests the farewell of the Florentine shopkeeper, as he smilingly says: "Addio—Ma lei verra di nuovo a Firenze—tutti ritornano." ("You will come again to Florence; everyone does.")

May Lexington retain for all time much of that spirit of the Old South of song and story!

INDEX